MARKETING HEALTHCARE SERVICES TO EMPLOYERS

MARKETING HEALTHCARE SERVICES TO EMPLOYERS

Strategies and Tactics

FRANK H. LEONE, MBA, MPH

This book is dedicated to all healthcare professionals—past, present, and future—for addressing and improving the health and well-being of others.

Sea Hill Press Inc.
Santa Barbara, California
www.seahillpress.com

Published 2012
ISBN 978-1-937720-06-3
Printed in the United States of America

Contents

Preface

Epiphany is defined as "a sudden, intuitive perception of or insight into the reality or essential meaning of something, usually initiated by some simple, homely, or commonplace occurrence or experience."

I assume there are spiritual, personal, professional, and many other types of epiphanies. Some of us may have many such epiphanies, others none at all. In my case I have had a single professional epiphany.

My simple, commonplace occurrence occurred deep within the stacks of the UCLA Health Sciences Library one day in May 1981. In those days MPH students were asked to read large stacks of relevant journal articles in order to get a handle on their course work. The article before me that day caught my eye in that it was written by Dr. Marianne Brown, who at the time happened to be the wife of my advisor in the MPH program at UCLA.

The topic of her article was "occupational health," two words I had never before heard in the same sentence. In less than a month I was about to get my MPH degree to couple with an MBA in Marketing that I had earned nine years earlier. Like many public health students, I dreamed of going out there to help enhance the health of our population. During the mere five minutes it took me to read Dr. Brown's article, I had my professional epiphany: the workplace will become the prime venue for addressing the health of large populations. I instantly knew where I wanted to be.

Flash forward thirty-one years—as I type these words and reflect.

My professional journey began a few months after that day in the library. The *New York Times* advertised an opening for a Director of the Occupational Health Service at the University of Massachusetts Medical Center in faraway Worcester. I got the job and worked with the program's founder, Dr. Barry Levy. Barry and I were contemporaries and kindred spirits, and I learned three important lessons from Barry:

1. The workplace is a unique and exceptional setting to address the healthcare needs of large population segments.
2. Employers and workers often have markedly different views. Balance and compromise is the key to success.
3. Never underestimate the power of commitment. A single person really can make a difference.

These past thirty-one years have been a blur in many ways. I have never wavered, not for a second, from the vision that I had that day in the UCLA library: the workplace will be the focal point of the healthcare delivery system of the twenty-first century.

I speak often and have frequently told my audience how blessed we are to be involved in healthcare. Daily irritants and frustrations aside, we are out there working to make a real difference in people's lives.

I learned long ago that I best leave the clinical side of medicine to the extraordinary practitioners who are well trained in this area. I retreated to sharing my vision of the "employer healthcare portal" and advising people how to best get their product to that market.

The spirit of this book goes well beyond the classic definition of occupational health to encompass any healthcare service that may be sold to employers for their workforce. The principles in the book apply equally well to such services as urgent care, wellness, women's health, and sports medicine, to name a few. It is my wish that readers can develop their own vision of providing healthcare services to employers and learn how to market such services in a practical, cost-effective, and ethical manner.

Shortly before he passed away in 1994 at the age of ninety-three, my beloved father sent me a card inscribed with the following:

> *"The doctor of the future will give no medicine but will interest his patients in the care of the human frame, in diet, and in the cause and prevention of disease."*
>
> — Thomas Alva Edison

He included a hand-written note on the card: "Frank, I thought you could use this phrase when speaking at gatherings." Hopefully this book will grant him his wish.

Many believe that we are in a transformative era in healthcare, one that rejects the enduring medical model and gives more than lip service to the notions of holistic medicine and prevention. This book is intended to shape this vision and provide readers with practical advice for getting their healthcare services to the employer market.

Most authors express their gratitude to others with an appreciation list—I am no different. At the risk of omitting names that should be on the list, I offer my gratitude and affection to:

- My wife, Diane, who has been at my side for thirty-five years and counting.
- Our son, Ryan, whose name on the company masthead has been a good luck charm.
- Karen O'Hara, my RYAN Associates sidekick for almost twenty-two years.
- Donna Lee Gardner and Roy Gerber, my RYAN Associates teammates since the 1990s.
- My sales and marketing training program co-faculty over the years: Ken Mack, Carolyn Merriman, and Jack Harms.
- Dr. Barry Levy, who got me started in occupational health and whose oft-stated mantra, "One person can make a difference," brings tears to my eyes.
- UCLA professor Marianne Brown, whose circa 1980 article on occupational health provided me with my first exposure to this extraordinary field.
- Dr. Bill Newkirk, Sandy Young, Dr. Jay Hammerstein, Don Barger, David Dann, Diane Wildermuth, Ray Breswick, Kendall Fults, and many others who were with us right from the start (our first national conference in 1987) and continue their leadership roles in occupational health to this very day.
- Howard Anderson, that once-in-a-lifetime inspirational academic mentor, who gave me the confidence I needed to succeed.
- Stacey, Jenny, Tonya, Megan, Rachel, Angeli, Janelle, Kristin, Leyla, Melissa, Jennifer, Judy, Elizabeth, Maria, Mindy, Sonya, Elaine, Leah, Cheryl, Mike, Sam, Kim, and many others who

made daily office life not only highly productive but also a heck of a lot of fun.

- The ever-cheerful Greg Sharp and the Sea Hill Press team for providing me with the opportunity to publish this book.
- My father, Frank Sr., and mother, Dorothy, for fifty years of love, kindness, and encouragement.

I hope that this book finds a broad readership and is helpful to all who explore its contents. I am pleased to hear from anyone at fleone@naohp.com.

Frank H. Leone
Santa Barbara, CA
May 2012

Chapter 1:

The New Horizon

— Marketing Healthcare Services to Employers

My colleague Roy Gerber often refers to a memorable quip from notorious bank robber Willie Sutton, who when asked why he robbed banks noted, "because that's where the money is."

The same might be said about healthcare organizations and employers, "because that's where the people are." If you are reading this paragraph on a weekday between 8:00 a.m. and 5:00 p.m., chances are that the majority of citizens in your market are working somewhere.

Changes in Healthcare

Consider four aspects of our country's evolution during these transformative times:

1. **The economy** — The economy of the twenty-first century likely will continue to be weaker than the economy of the late twentieth century. Employers seem to realize that their company's prosperity during lean times is closely related to the health and

vigor of their workforce. In such a climate, employers are more likely to look for innovative, proactive solutions from their provider partners than they had in the past.

2. **Telecommunications revolution** — Communication methods seem to be changing by the day as hand-held devices, the World Wide Web, email, and social networking permeate our daily lives. Suddenly there are new ways to inform, educate, screen, and counsel. The practice of proactive, holistic healthcare, always advisable but seldom effective, suddenly seems different and within reach.

3. **Rush to the community** — Once upon a not too distant time, hospitals were places where people went when they were sick. During the past two decades that has changed; healthcare organizations spread their wings by offering greater access to walk-in clinics, outpatient surgical centers, women's health pavilions, home healthcare, telemedicine, and of course, workplace-based health services.

   The decentralization of healthcare delivery is likely to continue as technologies become more dramatic and costs become more critical. In time, hospitals are likely to become the resource of the last resort for the most chronically ill with many other services exported to convenient community venues. Given its inherent population base, the workplace is poised to play a pronounced role in this evolution.

4. **Population medicine** — Over the last century and beyond, healthcare was largely practiced qualitatively: let an adverse condition occur and fix that condition. Most would view this approach as neither cost effective nor humane. An approach toward a proactive rather than reactive system has always made sense, but movement toward that ideal has been stymied by a lack of urgency, vested economic interests, and powerful interest groups.

   The times are changing. Twenty-first century economic realities beg for change. The vast baby boomer generation is reaching retirement age and beginning to view healthcare in a different light. Enter the era of population medicine where healthcare organizations are encouraged to address the health status of large population clusters and are rewarded for making a quantifiable difference in the health status of these populations. Once again, the workplace is the ideal setting for the emerging emphasis on population medicine.

Employer-directed healthcare services are considerably more than another set of product lines or another clinic. Rather, the employer portal should be viewed as a broad platform for a healthcare organization to pull together and market multiple services to employers and their employees.

Wellness services, health risk appraisals, health coaching, biometric testing, travel medicine, women's health, disease management, and executive health are a few examples of service lines that can and should be folded together under a single sales and marketing initiative. These integrated services should be seen as a unique business opportunity to vertically expand service relationships with employers (and their employees), attain far greater community visibility, and generate new ancillary services and referrals for your system.

The bundling of employer-directed services often begins with an occupational health program. A stand-alone, single-clinic, occupational health program typically faces a marginal profit margin due to tightening state fee schedules, reductions in workplace injury rates, higher unemployment rates, the outsourcing of many jobs overseas, and the continued transition from a manufacturing to a service-based economy.

The value of an occupational health program increases dramatically when an organization factors in specialist referrals, ancillary revenue, rehabilitation and other downstream revenue, and enhanced community visibility. The program's return becomes even more valuable when a healthcare organization increases the visibility and market penetration of multiple other service lines that can be channeled to their populations through a single point of employer contact.

THE INTERNAL RATIONALE

Why should a healthcare organization commit to packaged services in the first place?

REASON 1: Bundled services are a critical adjunct to your institutional mission statement.

I noted a common thread when I looked up the mission statements of five health systems with which I am familiar:

> *"Together we make a difference through our commitment to excellence in healthcare."*
>
> *"To enhance the health of the communities and customers we serve."*
>
> *"To meet the evolving healthcare needs of our citizens and provide access to high-quality medical care."*
>
> *"Easy access to the finest medical care available."*
>
> *"To improve the health of our patients and community through innovation and excellence in care."*

Serving the community and addressing the totality of its constituents' healthcare needs are recurrent themes. Since workers and employers are a significant part of a community, services earmarked for employers and their workforce should be a key component of the mission. Failing to reach out to employers runs counter to the pervasive "community" theme.

Many services are well positioned to address the totality of a community's healthcare needs (the public health model). Occupational health inherently addresses the full patient care continuum, from prevention to acute care to rehabilitation. The astute organization should look to occupational health, wellness services, and other prevention-oriented service lines as point programs in tying your institutional priorities together.

REASON 2: The employer portal is a catalyst to integrate service lines within the organization.

Most healthcare organizations isolate services such as wellness, executive health, and rehabilitation into independent silos with little more than lip service given to the need to tightly integrate such services with one another.

This is where a coordinated employer portal fulfills a critical function: to serve as a catalyst to bring such services (and others surely to emerge) into a relatively seamless system with the intent of serving the needs of the community at large.

REASON 3: Healthcare services present a platform to introduce new services.

As healthcare delivery becomes more externalized (moves myriad services outside of clinic and hospital walls and into the community), most organizations are likely to see their role continue to evolve from an inpatient care provider to a community health services provider. The definition of community health ("the study and betterment of the health characteristics of biological communities") highlights the benefits of community-wide initiatives designed to enhance collective health status.

During my tenure at the helm of RYAN Associates, I have noted that an increasing variety of services are incorporated under the occupational health banner. What began as work injury management has expanded to a variety of screening examinations, rehabilitation services, and other activities.

More recently, free-standing clinics that blend occupational health and immediate or urgent care services have become more common. Wellness and health promotion, travel medicine, and executive health are other examples of services that have become integrated into the occupational-health product line.

An organization must view employer-directed healthcare services as a platform upon which many other services can be built. It makes sense: many services are already synergistic, and there are considerable economies of scale to be gained by bringing them under the same umbrella.

We can expect healthcare organizations to package community-related services in the coming years. In most instances, occupational health and related services, a customer-driven business, would seem to be an optimal foundation for a virtually limitless array of community-oriented services.

REASON 4: Occupational health offers a symbol of a newly emerging healthcare delivery paradigm.

The employer opportunity emulates the emerging healthcare delivery paradigm. Occupational health offers a network—both from within (prevention, wellness and safety training, primary care, specialist care, rehabilitation) and beyond (employers, workers, payers). The emerging delivery paradigm features tightly constructed networks complemented by timely communication systems that are overtaking traditional, but increasingly obsolete, medical delivery models.

The healthcare organization that works through employers, develops a strong series of healthcare services for employers, and uses modern communication tools to deliver its services is going to be well positioned to expand into the healthcare world of the next decade and beyond.

REASON 5: Occupational health is a stand-alone product line.

Occupational health is a critically needed and growing discipline. As long as there are workplaces and workers, there will be work-related conditions to be addressed and unique opportunities to reach out to large clusters of individuals for screening and education programs.

When managed effectively, a core occupational health clinic should be profitable in its own right. When the other opportunities enumerated above are factored in, occupational health becomes even more valuable.

THE EXTERNAL RATIONALE

The rationale for an employer to use the services of an external healthcare organization is compelling. Few employers have their in-house health and safety functions totally in order; they are spending money they do not need to spend—a potentially fatal problem.

That is where occupational health, wellness programs, and other services become relevant. The best way to thwart unnecessary expenses is to work with an external occupational health provider capable of making a difference.

Be the best by managing conditions most effectively, getting workers back to work more quickly, identifying and acting on environmental contaminants appropriately, and blending in multiple other relevant services under a single delivery mechanism.

Understand and embrace the long-term relevance of employer-directed healthcare services to their parent organization and articulate value when meeting with current and prospective clients.

Chapter 2:

Strategies for Marketing to Employers

When I refer to marketing, I refer to strategies and tactics that may be used to introduce, en masse, what you have to offer potential users. Marketing is vastly different from sales, which pertain to addressing an individual or small group directly.

To be successful, marketers must reach as many potential users of their services as possible, reinforce the name of their organizations in their public eye, and ingrain why their services are the preferred option. Marketing is the strategy and the route that one takes to achieve these goals.

Healthcare Marketing Principles

Ten principles seem to govern the art of healthcare services marketing:

PRINCIPLE 1: Brevity.

Marketers vie for a prospect's attention in an information-saturated world. How much spare time do you have at your disposal these days? Virtually everyone feels overwhelmed and tends to be protective of their time. The first tip to the aspiring marketer is avoid conceptual clutter. Keep your message simple, short, and focused. Then make that message even simpler. Remember, every extra word takes a proportionate amount of attention away from the words that describe your core message.

> **Action step:** *Review a professional email or letter that you recently sent to a client or prospect. Eliminate unessential verbiage, including paragraphs, sentences, and words. Then shorten it even more. You are on your way to mastering the art of brevity.*

PRINCIPLE 2: Timeliness.

Develop a brief and simple message as your starting point. Present the message at a time when there is comparatively minimal competition for a prospect's attention. If you send a piece of snail mail on a Friday, the recipient is likely to receive it on Monday along with all of their other mail received on the heaviest mail day of the week. Send the mail when it is more likely to arrive on a Tuesday or Wednesday.

Likewise, if you send an email message at virtually any time, it will likely sit with scores of other promotional messages that are usually ignored. Schedule email messages to hit during the workday when your email will be isolated from other emails.

> **Action step:** *Develop a written strategy for sending correspondence and emails and placing phone calls that will reach recipients at a time and day most likely to get their attention.*

PRINCIPLE 3: Innovation.

A golden rule of marketing is to use tactics that are different than the mode du jour. Choosing a promising marketing tactic is akin to buying a stock low and selling high. Resist the temptation to react to yesterday's good news.

Unseasoned marketers find it difficult to avoid jumping on the what's-hot-is-hot bandwagon. They often presume that if a marketing tactic worked before, or currently works for another organization, it will work for you. Given the marked absence of marketing innovation in today's healthcare environment, the easy way out is to do the same ol', same ol'.

Action step: *Write down three marketing tactics that your organization or service has never tried before. Ask two other members of your team to do the same. Combine all nine tactics, discuss them, and pick the most intriguing three for potential cultivation and rollout in the near future.*

PRINCIPLE 4: Differentiation.

Be different from your competitors. Define what makes you different: what does your organization or service offer that arguably makes it the best option in the market?

Many would-be marketers have a difficult time identifying what makes them different. There is a temptation to focus on unsubstantiated platitudes (e.g., "We offer the best customer service") when articulating a point of differentiation. Justify your most compelling competitive advantage in quantitative terms. If you are marketing the most experienced program in your community, say so:

"We have treated more than 30,000 work-related conditions since 1995 and are more likely to correctly diagnose and manage a work-related injury, thereby saving your company time and money."

Such a statement is accurate, quantifiable, and sets your organization apart from the others.

In lieu of platitudes, quantify. Whenever possible, tie your argument into your organization's ability to save employers money in the long run.

Examples of such differentiation include:

- **More experience** = superior diagnosis and patient management = saves employer money
- **More locations** = less lost work time = saves employer money
- **Excellent care-management software** = more appropriately and expeditiously managed cases = saves employer money

> **Action step:** *What is your service's primary competitive advantage or point of differentiation? Is it experience, training, locations, patient and customer satisfaction, breadth of relevant services, or something else? How will you* ***quantify*** *your primary competitive advantage? Write it out and see how well it plays with your colleagues.*

PRINCIPLE 5: Agility.

Marketing is best defined as an art, not a science. Many tend to view marketing more as a science by expecting and using one-size-fits-all marketing strategies and tactics. If marketing is largely about being different, the astute marketer must be agile and willing to devise strategies that reflect unique circumstances.

Variables that should be addressed when devising strategies include:

- **Size of your market** — Use different strategies for major metropolitan areas, midsize communities, and small and rural markets.
- **Position in the market** — Is your organization the market leader, the market challenger, or a new-market entry? Each scenario is likely to suggest a different approach to marketing.
- **Industrial mix of the market** — Demonstrably different markets are likely to require different strategies; for example, Erie, Pennsylvania, (manufacturing); Bakersfield, California, (agriculture); and Las Vegas, Nevada, (gaming/hospitality).
- **The nature of your team** — In football there are passing teams and running teams. Each team adapts to the personality and strengths of their personnel. Assess and reassess these and perhaps other variables, and then design marketing strategies around the realities of your particular set of circumstances.

> **Action step:** *Identify where your organization fits along a continuum representing each of the categories listed above. In some cases it will be in the middle, in other cases at one extreme or the other. What unique strategies, if any, will you devise in response to these positions?*

PRINCIPLE 6: Selectivity.

A time-honored Hollywood adage is that "all publicity is good." Even bad boy and bad girl actors seemingly enhance their careers whenever they get their names in the news. The same idea applies to marketing: all marketing tactics are good, but some are better than others.

While pursuing my MBA in marketing, I took a course entitled Creative Problem Solving. We were taught to approach most challenges by sitting down and coming up with a list of potential solutions. Many ideas were silly, but even the silliest solutions provided a kernel for a more interesting approach. The concept was to think, create a laundry list of possible solutions, and whittle the list down to one or two strategies.

How do you determine which tactics take priority? If they are all good ideas to some degree, how do you rank one above another? It comes down to return on investment. Primo tactics provide you with the greatest opportunity for financial return for the lowest investment in human and financial capital. Judge the merit of a strategy by a reasonable estimate of both its human impact and cost.

> **Action step:** *Review the three new marketing tactics that you came up with. Once you factor in human and financial costs, how do they stack up against each other?*

PRINCIPLE 7: Planning.

I ask registrants at our sales training programs if they have a formal sales and marketing plan, and if they do, whether they feel that it is a good plan and if they actively follow it. Most participants tell me that they have a plan, only a few believe that the plan is "good," and rarely does anyone state that they actually follow a plan.

Sales and marketing plans break down because they are lengthy and verbose, too general, uninspired, or forgettable. A written plan is the foundation of any business endeavor; it is the master document intended to keep you moving forward and on track.

Mission: A marketing plan should begin by stating your mission and how that mission relates to the larger mission of the parent organization.

Goal: A financial goal (e.g., to grow profit by 10 percent during the coming year) should follow. Do not mix apples with oranges when stating your financial goal. Increasing injury management revenue by 12 percent and discretionary services revenue by 15 percent represent two potentially competing goals and are more specific than necessary: keep it simple by basing your goal on only one parameter—gross revenue.

Strengths and challenges: Your next step involves an examination of a service's inherent strengths and challenges. Describe your competitive market as a foundation for developing and setting priorities for your marketing plan.

Place marketing tactics and discrete steps to execute each tactic on a master calendar, update it as needed, and follow your plan meticulously.

> **Action step:** *Ensure that relevant team members have an opportunity to review a draft marketing plan and offer their input and buy-in before it is considered final.*

PRINCIPLE 8: Universality.

Marketing is a numbers game. Conduct twice as many sales calls and you may well get twice as much business. Touch twice as many employers with a marketing tactic and your clinics are likely to get twice as much walk-in business. More up front usually means more at the end.

It makes sense to build a large and up-to-date prospect universe. Maintenance is as important as building your prospect universe in the first place; in an era in which perhaps 20 percent of the labor force turns over every year, yesterday's pristine mailing list is today's inaccurate one.

> **Action step:** *Set aside time at least once a year for an hourly employee or volunteer to call virtually every company on your prospect mailing list in order to ensure that the prospect is still actively employed and the information in your database is accurate. If the contact person is no longer at the company, get the name of the replacement.*

PRINCIPLE 9: Differentiation.

Exactly why are your services the best option for most employers in your market? If you are unable to provide a concise and supportable answer to this question, the success of your marketing effort is in doubt.

Five criteria support the viability of a competitive advantage statement. The statement must be:

- Short (one or two sentences) and to the point
- Legitimate
- Able to meet a clear consumer desire or need
- Quantifiable
- Unique

> **Action step:** *Answer the question, "Why should our company use your services?" Write a response and measure it against the five criteria listed above.*

PRINCIPLE 10: Strategy.

Great marketing is great marketing, no matter from what product, service, or political campaign one draws inspiration. Not surprisingly, healthcare marketing as a whole would seldom be mistaken for great marketing. Keep an eye on what marketers are doing in other industries or areas. A political campaign is a good starting place because it features the basic tenets of effective marketing and communication: remain on message, keep the message simple, and keep repeating the message.

> **Action step:** *Set aside a week to focus on and scrutinize every radio and television ad, print ad, and billboard visual that comes to your attention. What caught your interest? What turned you off? What did you like the most about any of these ads? Which do you think was the most effective? What lessons can you take away from the greater marketing universe that you can apply to your world of healthcare marketing?*

Marketing Discipline

Someone once asked me what single trait sets a stellar sales professional apart from a less than stellar one. After quickly thumbing through the usual suspects—"product knowledge," "commitment," "integrity," "personality," and "tenacity," to name a few—I landed on "discipline."

What are the key marketing disciplines for healthcare sales professionals?

PRINCIPLE 1: Discipline begins with a marketing plan.

A marketing plan is only a document. It is incumbent on marketing professionals to breathe life into the plan. Execute the plan in a resolute manner:

1. **Make a commitment** — Commit to following the date-specific action steps contained in the plan.
2. **Establish mini steps** — Develop a series of small steps (e.g., create a six-month tip inventory) for every action step (e.g., a monthly tip email blast).
3. **Set mini targets** — Schedule mini-tactic targets to occur evenly over each week throughout the year. Make Monday "Marketing Tactic Day" and *never* miss executing that week's mini-tactic. It is far easier to spend thirty minutes every

Monday executing that week's tactic than to stop the train for an entire day to execute a tactic (*if* you even get to that day).

4. **Set a deadline** — Develop your next marketing plan by a scheduled date (e.g., December 15) with a full array of mini-tasks. Learn from your current year experience and avoid waiting too long to initiate this process.

PRINCIPLE 2: Discipline involves time management.

Time management is the backbone of effective sales. No one manages every minute of time effectively. Time management and discipline go hand in hand. Consider these steps:

1. **Use time sheets** — Monitor your time allocation with a series of honest weekly time sheets. Do not drift away from this commitment. Maintain time sheets through both good times and bad. Look for shortfalls on your part and minimize or eliminate these shortfalls.
2. **Do what works** — What works best may not necessarily be what you enjoy doing. I worked with a client who had two sales professionals. I asked each to make five before-hours or after-hours phone calls a day with the intention of leaving "we stand ready to help you" scripted voice-mail messages. Mustering the discipline to carve out ten minutes a day for such calls, our dynamic duo was poised to leave 2,500 voice-mail messages during the coming year, assuming a fifty-week work year. That tactic represents a deep market penetration from only ten minutes a day.

   Making such calls is not as sexy as a face-to-face meeting, but in the aggregate, may be more fruitful. While many factors influence a decision to use your services, watch for evidence of links between calls made and subsequent business activity.
3. **Just say no** — Many sales professionals report to managers who view them as utility players (people who are perpetually available to address ad hoc non-sales-related activities). Guard your precious time like a hawk.

PRINCIPLE 3: Discipline is a numbers game.

Use discipline when you play the numbers game. Set quotas and commit to them without missing a beat. Some examples follow:

1. **Write introductory letters** — Keep your pipeline full to overflowing by sending a set quota of introductory letters per week. If the pipeline starts to run dry, you will invariably spend a great deal of unproductive time trying to catch up.
2. **Make sales-oriented phone calls** — This number varies by day but is fairly consistent over the course of a week. To keep your appointment dance card full, you must be disciplined about making introductory calls—the Achilles heel for many sales professionals.
3. **Make live sales calls** — There is no excuse for not making three or four sales calls a day. Take a midpoint, eighteen in-person calls per week. Given a fifty-week work year, that is nine hundred live sales calls per year. Manage your face-to-face time well; cluster your travel, verify directions, and keep your meetings brief and on point.
4. **Send email messages** — End your workday by sending an email note to virtually everyone you dealt with that day to review and document your interactions. Also send emails to those whom you will deal with the following day to confirm the time and place for your planned encounter, the expected length of the meeting, and your objectives. Include your cell phone number in the event of a change of plans. Cluster your final hour by answering incoming emails and copying internal staff extensively and as appropriate.
5. **Schedule clinic tours** — Schedule at least three clinic tours each week, ideally on the same day/hours of the week. Carefully planned clinic tours are an integral part of every clinic's marketing plan.

Discipline is the lifeblood of marketing success. If you want to produce big numbers, focus on what is best for your sales output every hour of every day.

Exhibit 2-1. A Disciplined Plan for the Coming Year

DAILY

1. Complete ten telephone sales calls (both introductory and follow-up).
2. Complete three or four in-person sales calls.
3. Carve out an email hour including reviews, reminders of the next day's meetings, email responses, and internal briefings.
4. Fine tune your time-management plan for the following day.
5. Document activities on your weekly time sheet.
6. Leave five after-hours voice-mail messages for clients and/or prospects.

WEEKLY

1. Execute the marketing tactic listed for that week.
2. Review the previous week's time sheet; compare to year-to-date time allocation and adjust as necessary.
3. Send out at least ten introductory letters.
4. Complete at least three clinic tours.

ANNUALLY

Develop the following year's marketing plan by December 15.

Your Marketing Plan

Putting a marketing plan on paper allows you to state where you want to go and exactly how you plan to get there.

The "where we are going" segment documents the rationale of your business opportunity, determines how you plan to respond to that opportunity, and defines your anticipated financial and altruistic rewards. The "how we get there" segment is your sales and marketing plan, either as an inherent component of the business plan or a separate document.

THE RATIONALE

With everything else going on, you may ask yourself why bother writing a marketing plan? In many respects a marketing plan is analogous to a blueprint for your house: a step by step plan to get you where you need to be.

Reasons to write a marketing plan include:

- **Strategic thinking** — Your plan encourages strategic thinking by members of your team. It is valuable, if not essential, to periodically step away from the fray and re-examine what you are doing and why and how you are doing it.
- **Team consensus** — Your plan encourages a consensus that all parties are close to getting on the same page.
- **Daily blueprint** — Your plan gives you a daily blueprint. The back end of a marketing plan is a date-specific action calendar to propel your initiative from point A to point Z. Without such a step-by-step blueprint, your service initiative may be little more than a deer roaming in the wilderness.
- **A path to success** — You plan serves to connect the dots, leading you from where you want to be to actually getting there.

NOW WHAT?

Marketing professionals vary plan format markedly, yet every plan maintains the same basics: what do we want to do, why are we doing it, and how are we going to get there?

When working on your marketing plan, consider these important points:

1. **Embrace brevity** — Brevity is good . . . very good. Remember that a plan is for the real business world, not a project for "Future Entrepreneurs of America." The marketing plan should be easy to read and pragmatic (less glitter and more meat).

2. **Do not reiterate the obvious** — Lists of strengths, weaknesses, opportunities, and threats (the old SWOT analysis) are conventional and cute, but by themselves are of minimal value. Associate strengths and weaknesses with a competitive advantage or a specific marketing tactic.
3. **Link "what" and "why"** — Create clear, meaningful linkages between what you offer and why you offer it. Construct your plan to advise all readers exactly *why* you are offering a certain service or recommending a specific marketing tactic.
4. **Avoid being stuck on a formula** — I have reviewed hundreds of marketing plans and frequently note that the plans seem to follow rigid textbook formulas. Being overly mechanical and reliant on stale methods will result in documents that are as dry as they come.
5. **Use your plan** — Establish a process in which your plan becomes central to your daily marketing operations. Make the plan a dynamic, changeable document. Realities change; the sooner you regroup in reaction to these changes, the better.

WRITING THE PLAN

It will be easier to focus on the key points of your marketing plan if you identify and support the why-what-how continuum. Tie the why, what, and how in together:

- **The why** — The "why" defines why you do what you do. Marketing dogma advises us to consider the three Cs of marketing when defining strategy: the company (your services), the consumer (your employer clients and their workforce), and the competitors.

  Does your service have the wherewithal to offer what you suggest? Is there a measurable market need for these services? Do other entities fall short in meeting this need? If the answer to all three is affirmative and if pro forma projections support the ROI viability of moving forward, then, as they say, "you've got a plan."

- **The what** — Once your plan has identified a viable market opportunity, define your services and the manner in which you will provide these services to the market.

Once again, tie the what-why-how continuum together:

> *"We will introduce a line of travel medicine services because our white-collar market uses these services disproportionately more than the general population, no formal program is available in the marketplace, and one of our physicians has special expertise in this area."*

- **The how** — Taken alone, this is your marketing plan; taken as part of the overall plan, it ties the how with the why and the what.

FOLLOWING THE RULES

Although flexibility in writing a plan abounds, four fundamental rules apply:

1. **Identify quantifiable goals** — In most cases, these goals are based on gross revenue (e.g., 10 percent growth in gross revenue during the fiscal year or $500,000 in gross revenue per quarter).
2. **Segment your market where appropriate** — Common strategic segments include proximity to your clinics, industry type, or employer size. Because marketing tactics may vary within each of these potential segments, one or more marketing tactic subplans may be needed.
3. **List many potential tactics** — Virtually any marketing tactic is valuable in its own right, but some are more valuable than others given their inherent cost (in human and actual capital) and potential return. List and then rank order each marketing tactic in terms of perceived ROI.
4. **Set up an action calendar** — Translate every idea, tactic, and enhancement into a date-specific action calendar. This is the heart and soul of any plan—a day-by-day blueprint and pathway that propels your journey from point A to point Z.

A well-constructed plan can be the engine that spurs you forward. But most plans are too wordy, too predictable, and too easily ignored and then forgotten. Write a good plan from the outset and use it routinely.

EXHIBIT 2-2. WRITING AN EFFECTIVE BUSINESS PLAN

1.	Always think why, where, and how.
2.	Short is good; shorter is better.
3.	Obvious is obvious: don't restate it.
4.	View every decision in ROI terms.
5.	Adjust quickly to changing realities.
6.	Select tactics that provide the greatest return for the least capital.
7.	Apply different tactics to different market segments.
8.	Reduce your plan to a date-specific action calendar.
9.	Use your plan to unite your staff.
10.	Proactively USE your plan.

MARKETING INNOVATION

In an episode of the popular television series *Mad Men*, super ad man Don Draper opined to his up-and-coming colleagues, "marketing is all about innovation."

He is right.

But the best-laid plans often sink into the abyss of the same ol', same ol'. Why take a chance, one might ask, by not adopting techniques that seem to be working for others? After all, if marketing is about distinguishing your services from your competitors, why not rely on the tried and true to punctuate the difference?

This reasoning is flawed: marketing is all about going against the tide, not rolling with it.

AN ANALOGY

Playing the stock market offers a compelling analogy between marketing and investing. How often do people ignore the "buy low/sell high" axiom? Investors often buy a "hot" stock only to find out that it was at or near its peak and will go down from there. But those who choose to assume some risk by investing in an emerging stock frequently ride it to the winner's circle.

The same mind-set applies to marketing. Pay attention to trends, regardless of the industry, and modify them in accordance to your situation rather than merely replicating marketing tactics that seem to work for others. Those who emulate current best practices are unlikely to distinguish themselves from the pack. Those who emulate others may subsequently fall further behind while competitors move forward with marketing innovations.

Old healthcare marketing habits die hard. Hospitals, health systems, and other large healthcare organizations are often steeped in yesterday's practices, resistant to change, and averse to risk. Many healthcare marketing professionals continue to mount the horse that brought them there, embracing what worked before rather than rolling the dice on what might work even better in the future.

MODERN MARKETING

I am struck by a continued overreliance on 1980s healthcare marketing tactics such as print ads, radio and television spots, billboards, and worst of all, oversized wads of collateral material that invariably throw benefits to the wind in the name of providing a comprehensive list of services. Relying on catch-up ball to get to a twenty-first century mind-set, many healthcare marketers are beginning to focus on high-touch tactics such as the use of social media, networking, email, and text messaging.

About ten years ago, email blasts (such as RYAN Associates' longstanding "Tip of the Week") were the innovation. Now they are common—even tired. Yet many in healthcare still view them as a breakthrough marketing technique.

To move toward a more modern marketing mind-set:

1. **Look beyond healthcare** — If you want hints on the latest marketing innovations, look beyond the innovation-resistant world of healthcare. Whether you are examining a product, service, or cause, ask yourself what is really getting through to you and if it is being marketed in a manner that you have not seen before. When you find such examples, examine them and determine whether they might apply to your marketing needs.

2. **Follow politics** — Once you get beyond the sleaze and distortions that permeate modern political campaigns, there are considerable marketing lessons to be learned. Watch how campaigns develop and reinforce their message (through simplicity, repetition, and staying on message) pace their outreach, and mix their modalities.
3. **Diversify your marketing tactic portfolio** — Replacing your entire portfolio of marketing tactics with innovative ones may be going too far. In general, de-emphasize and then phase out current practices over time while incrementally adding new approaches. If you haven't already, adapt to social media and other networking mechanisms. Use them proportionately compared to techniques such as printed materials and email blasts.
4. **Let others do the work for you** — Encourage email recipients to forward your email to others within or beyond their organizations and to personal friends. If your distribution list is 1,500 and 10 percent of that group forwards your message to ten individuals, you have doubled your outreach and touched many people you otherwise would not have touched.
5. **Brainstorm** — Innovations are often spawned by "silly" ideas. Sit down with a colleague and jointly list every conceivable marketing tactic, no matter how seemingly off the wall, and you will undoubtedly emerge with several great ideas.
6. **Swing for the fences** — Become the Babe Ruth of healthcare marketing. Go for the home run, and do not worry too much about the occasional strike out.

If marketing is about innovation, then innovation is about a willingness to periodically fail as you search for a few real winners. Many of the greatest success stories in history involve people who failed many times and learned from their mistakes before getting it exceptionally right. Resistance to innovation is a ticket to mediocrity for both your organization and yourself.

TREND-SPOTTING

I have been playing a game with friends for many years: We each have a hypothetical $1 million that we can invest in residential real estate anywhere in the United States. Whoever's investment is worth the most ten years later is the winner.

I have heard many answers and all sorts of rationale. But the recurring theme is that players who react to yesterday's news are not likely to prevail. It is the player who can best predict where the *next* residential real estate boom is going to be who will win the contest.

So it is with marketing. Marketing initiatives are often uninspired repeats of what has worked in the past or is working elsewhere. Healthcare, in general, is an example of an industry that has not kept pace with marketing innovations.

Yet marketing, by definition, is all about getting the attention of prospective customers: be fresh, innovative, and different.

GENERATING FRESH MARKETING IDEAS

Constantly generate fresh marketing ideas. The battle for the attention of the consumer is merciless; you have to set yourself apart. How does one come up with new ideas if they are hopelessly ensconced at the lower end of the creativity scale?

Other suggestions:

1. **Observe other industries** — There are many big shots getting big bucks to come up with big ideas. Every now and then they actually do come up with a good one. Central to the job of a budding marketer is to pay close attention to marketing innovations across all industries and to borrow promising new concepts.
2. **Ask your constituents** — Who better to advise you than the people who will be on the receiving end of your marketing tactic? Every market mind-set is different. Informally, formally, or routinely asking clients and prospects what creative marketing approach might make sense to them never hurts.
3. **Two new ideas a year** — The best way to ensure innovation is to force you to try something new. Require two new marketing initiatives in each year's marketing plan. Make sure that the new initiatives are neither too expensive nor time consuming.
4. **Keep abreast of technology** — Innovations in communications technology drive many new marketing ideas. First, there was bulk mail and voice mail; then car phones and fax machines;

then cell phones and email; and today, websites, electronic newsletters, and web advertising. Even more dramatic innovation in communications technology is just down the road. It behooves the marketer to keep an eye on this ball and react quickly when new technology becomes available.

SET THE STAGE

Have you ever watched an artful pitcher set up a batter for his strikeout pitch or a quarterback deploy the run to position the passing game? How about a chess player thinking at least three moves ahead? Or a skilled attorney preparing for the heart of his cross examination? In every case, the initial activity was but a planned prelude to a later, more dramatic activity. This is true in marketing.

Assume that you are moving into a larger, spiffier clinic. You may be tempted to rush out and invite one and all to an open house to "show off" your new facility.

The one-shot approach, however, may not be the best way to capitalize on your new look. Instead, build momentum leading up to a clinic or women's health center opening by publicizing the opening date through emails, voice mails, or signs in the old clinic.

Alternatively, you can publicize the opening with a contest:

> *"We are opening our new urgent care clinic on October 1. What can we do at the new clinic to make life easier for you and your employees? The person with the best idea will win a ____ (courtesy of——), and anyone submitting an idea we use will win a ____ (courtesy of——)."*

This establishes linkage. You are making clients/prospects *think* about your new clinic, an essential first step in getting them to come to your planned open house. You get some potentially good new ideas—and you are doing all of this at little or no cost. Local merchants could donate prizes in return for the publicity (e.g., "Dinner for two at Chuck's Steak House—Altoona's finest venue for sumptuous dining").

Creativity is an important part of the process. To varying degrees, the development of nearly every communication requires the performance of creative tasks. Say you are designing a new brochure:

it requires creative planning and art direction, design, writing, production, and distribution skills.

Ensure that your marketing plan is forward thinking and not merely reactive to the norms of the day. This takes discipline, creativity, and brainstorming. Innovation is invariably fun, and having fun seems to be correlated with effective marketing.

THE PROSPECT UNIVERSE

Marketing is largely a numbers game. Conduct twice as many in-person sales calls and you have a chance to double your sales. Send out twice as many email messages and you double your penetration. If you make twice as many phone calls, you give your name and the name of your organization to twice as many people. The list goes on . . .

I invariably begin most marketing presentations with this axiom: A successful marketing plan is contingent on ensuring that *all potential users* of your services know who you are, what services you offer, and what sets you apart from other options available in the community. Name identification and an understanding of your competitive advantage by current and prospective customers are essential ingredients for success.

MANAGING YOUR UNIVERSE

Building and maintaining a prospect universe involves:

1. **Taking a proactive approach** — Most organizations grant lip service to employer universe management, if they address it at all; an update here, an update there, and some new contacts and companies make it onto your list. Such incremental expansion and refinement invariably keeps you perpetually short of the "all potential users" goal. Universe management must be a central focus of your marketing plan.
2. **Acquiring available lists** — Begin with the acquisition of broad-based employer lists. The Chamber of Commerce (or multiple Chambers in many markets) is a good starting point. Caution is advised: be aware that Chamber lists often contain many smaller companies, including single consultants, and include contacts

less relevant to healthcare organizations than human resource and health/safety professionals.

Depending on the market, other lists are useful supplements. Many markets have local chapters of the Society for Human Resource Management, American Society of Safety Engineers, National Association of Women Business Owners, and other local industry-specific associations that can provide membership lists. Other potential resources include your state's Department of Labor as well as purchased databases, such as those available from Dun & Bradstreet and similar national vendors.

3. **Networking internally** — Depending on the size and nature of your parent organization, you are likely to find excellent leads right in your own backyard. Members of your Board of Directors, foundation, and senior administrators are likely to know decision makers at local companies. Send them an email inquiry asking them to refer you to employers with whom they have relationships. Rank-and-file staff, spouses, neighbors, and friends also collectively represent a valuable source of information. Remember, marketing is a numbers game.

4. **Watching for new businesses** — Even in trying economic times, companies move into new markets and expand in existing ones. Be the first to approach new businesses either before or immediately after they settle in.

5. **Hopping on the social networking bandwagon** — Social networking is an effective way to ferret out new companies and contacts. As of 2012, LinkedIn, a business-oriented social networking site, consists of more than 160 million registered users.

   Once you register at www.linkedin.com, you can begin to build your network (clients, coworkers, contacts made at various functions). If you have one hundred connections, and each of those connections has fifty connections, you potentially have access to thousands of professionals at hundreds of companies, many of whom are likely to be prospects.

6. **Honing in on information you really need** — Your prospect base is more than a list of companies; it is your core database. But there is as much danger in storing irrelevant data as there is in not having enough. Core information for each company

usually includes one or more contact names, company address, phone/fax numbers, email addresses, and company-specific protocols. More extraneous information is not likely to be worth the effort to track down.

7. **Following the bouncing ball** — Given a typical annual employee turnover rate of 20 percent or more at many companies, it is likely that some of your contacts will be working elsewhere within a year. The elsewhere in question may well be a company that is not on your radar or one where your previous contact is no longer employed. It makes sense whenever possible to obtain "back-up" personal email addresses for as many contacts as possible so that you may reach them even if they are no longer employed with their original company.
8. **Keeping the list clean** — Ensure accuracy from the start and do periodic maintenance on your universe. Send contacts in your database an annual email inviting them to update their information. Call the ones that do not respond to obtain updates. This usually can be done by a minimum-wage employee, student intern, or volunteer. Your return on investment in having a pristine contact database is invariably positive.

A clean, comprehensive contact database does not build itself. It is invariably a product of a thorough, ongoing, and consistent effort. Contact list maintenance must be a central focus of your marketing plan.

Marketing vs. Sales

Let's start with a pop quiz:

1. Marketing makes up ______ of our sales/marketing budget:

    a. less than 25%
    b. between 25 and 75%
    c. more than 75%

2. Compared to sales, marketing takes ______ of our sales/marketing staff's time:

a. less than 25%
b. between 25 and 75%
c. more than 75%

3. In my opinion marketing is:

a. less important than sales
b. equally as important as sales
c. more important than sales

Honor roll status is in store for you if your answers are "a," "a," and "c."

MARKETING CONSIDERATIONS

Reconsider the definitions of marketing and sales:

- **Marketing** is everything an organization does to get its service to the mass marketplace. This includes advertising, brochures, mailings, email blasts, websites, and so on.
- **Sales** is person-to-person contacts, whether they are completed by telephone or in person.

The relative value of marketing can be characterized by three considerations:

CONSIDERATION 1: Low cost.

Marketing usually consumes little of your overall sales and marketing budget, unless you do no sales whatsoever. We are in the midst of a low-cost/high-tech marketing era in which many marketing tactics can be executed at little cost. Hence, even an aggressive marketing tactic is likely to consume a small percentage of your sales and marketing budget.

CONSIDERATION 2: Little time.

Not only is marketing notably inexpensive nowadays, most tactics also take a comparatively small amount of time to execute. Thus, we have the best of both worlds: low cost with comparatively little time expended.

CONSIDERATION 3: Disproportionate input.

Marketing is the engine that drives your sales initiative, not vice versa. Depending on the size and industrial mix of your market, your position in the marketplace, and your product portfolio, effective marketing is likely to bring greater new volume than sales.

Many companies are never approached by a healthcare service sales professional (who, after all, can be in only one place at a time). Companies often find their way to a clinic or program primarily because of name identification.

A small number of encounters from a large pool of smaller employers can easily trump a larger number of encounters from a considerably smaller number of clients.

NAME IDENTIFICATION AS AN ENTREE

It is usually easier to break the ice with a prospect that is acquainted with your organization than with one who is not. Sometimes such an acquaintance reflects a brand identification that has accumulated through months or years of articulating and repeating a simple message.

Buyers are more comfortable with a familiar name and are more likely to let a brand-identified sales professional in the door and take them seriously.

INCORPORATE PHYSICIAN MARKETING

Many clinics take one of their physicians to a live sales meeting every week or so. Such physician involvement can be helpful of course, but is it really the best use of a physician's time?

I counsel many of our clients to minimize a physician's time participating in routine sales calls while shifting their time to pre-sales telephone calls to prospects. If a physician calls up to five companies every week the day before an initial sales call, it would allow the sales professional the opportunity to hit the ground running.

Most calls take only a few minutes and are prefaced by something such as:

> *"Hello, this is Dr. David Webb calling from Community Urgent Care. It is my understanding that one of our sales professionals, Donna Rust, is scheduled to meet with you tomorrow at 3:00 p.m. I would like take a few minutes to learn about the health challenges your company is facing before you meet with Donna—so she will be better prepared, and we can save you considerable time by cutting to the chase."*

MARKETING AS AN EDUCATIONAL TOOL

As work-related injuries decline in both volume and reimbursement, many organizations diversify by providing employer clients with a broader array of services. However, many "new" vertical services, such as wellness programs or sports medicine, are difficult to sell because of consumer naivety. Marketing can take the edge off such naivety by educating employer decision makers about a new product.

Wellness services provide an excellent example. Wellness services often suggest episodic and nonintegrated education with vague promises to "increase morale" or "lower absenteeism." This image is difficult to get around if a sales professional walks in a prospect's door cold.

A wellness-oriented outreach effort built on education and awareness fosters a more knowledgeable consumer base. Consumers begin to understand the basic wellness-return-on-investment paradigm, and it becomes an easier and quicker sell (remember the adage that time is money).

A monthly *Wellness Advisor* sent via email to your client and prospect base is an excellent marketing tactic. The *Wellness Advisor* would be brief and would subtly reinforce the core rationale for employers to contract for an integrated wellness initiative. The key here, like so much in marketing, is simplicity, clarity, and repetition.

Marketing tends to be the Rodney Dangerfield of healthcare: it seldom gets the respect that it deserves. Yet, in their current incarnation, leading marketing tactics are neither time-consuming nor expensive—and they invariably energize the sales effort.

Be certain that your marketing ducks are perfectly in order before getting totally absorbed in sales.

Adapting to Change

You have heard the adage, "If it ain't broke, don't fix it." That adage may be true some of the time, but usually it is not the right position to take.

There is danger in resisting change, because the system or approach in question is bound to become obsolete and eventually break down. It is better to recognize change as part of doing business and to initiate steps to prepare for and embrace that change.

A WORLD OF CHANGE

Imagine a world in which nothing changed. That is difficult to do, because change is central to the human condition. Given that change is inevitable, it makes more sense to be an innovator who is ahead of the curve than a reactor who is perpetually a step behind.

The challenge arises with the need to conceptualize change in a non-reckless, well-reasoned manner while still assuming some risk in order to stay at the forefront.

1. **Assess your current systems** — Maintain an ongoing plan to examine all of your services, operational systems, staffing relationships, and sales/marketing initiatives. Such an assessment can be done in many, often overlapping, ways. Routinely ask clients for their opinions and suggestions for change. The more straightforward you are in asking questions, the greater the likelihood you will identify meaningful change.
2. **Learn new tactics** — Commit to a little change each year rather than stability over many years followed by a major change that is usually reactive. If you try at least two new marketing tactics every year, twenty or more tactics will be introduced during the next decade.
3. **Align the culture-of-change continuum** — View potential change as a continuum: one extreme represents strict aversion to any change, and the other represents constant change and upheaval of existing practices. Most organizations are somewhere in-between.

   How do you determine where you belong on this continuum? It usually starts with a sense of the parent organization's climate for change. Some organizations are slow to innovate; at best, you can buck this trend slightly at a singular service level.

Consider longevity of a service. A younger service is more likely to still be working out some kinks and less likely to require a great deal of innovation in the short term. Conversely, a long-established service is more likely to have entrenched practices in need of renovation.

4. **Be flexible** — Change works best when processes are in place to monitor the impact of that change and to modify the plan as realities dictate. New marketing schemes might look appealing in theory but may face unforeseen complications. A program may (a) stubbornly proceed with the plan, (b) drop the plan at the first sign of disappointment, or (c) constantly tweak the plan in response to market reactions. Proceeding with the plan is the easy choice; dropping the plan is the reactive choice; and tweaking the plan is the optimal choice.
5. **Do many small things** — When you hedge your bets by introducing constant change, introduce several small changes rather than a single major change.
6. **Strive for innovation** — Innovation is prone to miscalculation and misplaced delivery. Yet, if even one new innovation shows promise, there is something to build on during the next marketing cycle.
7. **Think in threes** — The ancient Egyptians had the right idea when they built the pyramids: think three. Three seems to be a magic number when it comes to organizational delivery. (At RYAN Associates there are three primary divisions: consulting, education, and the National Association of Occupational Health Professionals.)

   Do not put all of your marketing-plan eggs in one basket. Protect against unanticipated erosion in a single area. At the individual service level, one might divide one's attention among injury management, prevention services, and consulting. In that case, the service would be insulated in the event of a fee schedule change. Likewise, a marketing initiative could include educational forums, one-on-one contact, and email contact. If one area failed to meet expectations, the other two could carry it for a year while the first area is reinvigorated or replaced.

8. **Foster synergism** — Be certain that each of the three areas feed one another. Consider what we have done: our many educational programs provide us with information for our NAOHP publications and members, which stimulates more consulting activity, which provides us with more insights to share in our educational programs. In any event, the major component of your marketing plan is seldom a stand-alone idea; every idea should be connected to another activity or feed your initiative in multiple, synergistic ways.
9. **Talk change-speak** — Embracing constant change suggests the integration of "change-speak" into your vocabulary. Make judicious use of such words as "new," "modern," and "updated" in sales and marketing discussions, literature, and one-on-one contacts. Receptivity to change and improvement needs to be projected as well as implemented.
10. **Pay attention to technology** — When I established RYAN Associates in 1985, there were few fax machines, laser printers, or color monitors. Microsoft Word, Excel, and PowerPoint were not yet in use. Nor was there much of an Internet, email and email blasts, or cell phones. Or digital cameras. Or iPhones or BlackBerry smartphones. Yet virtually all are now central to my professional life. Stay a half-step ahead of the posse by keeping abreast of advances in communications technology and using them to your advantage.

The status quo—so pervasive in healthcare management—quickly becomes counterproductive. It is far better to get beyond the status quo by asking yourself what you can do differently each year. Someone has got to take the lead: why not you? Innovation is much more fun.

The Competition

Know your competitors—you know exactly whom I mean: those snarly, clueless, unethical, unenlightened nobodies across town (or next door) that usurp market share from you for no reason.

Know who your competition is, what they do, how they are doing, and what their basic strengths and weaknesses are. Marketing initiatives frequently address the competition issue in an unenlightened or even counterproductive manner.

MUST DOS

Marketing with the competition in mind always involves three essential points:

1. **Get a handle** — Regardless of your position in the marketplace (e.g., market leader, market challenger, new entrant), it is prudent to know who your competitors are and the nature of their business.
2. **Focus on their competitive advantages** — Selectively gather information about your competitors. Price per service might be interesting, but it is prone to nuance (e.g., discounts) and subject to change. More importantly, learn what your competitors are doing well and what they are doing poorly. This information, in turn, can be used to identify their actual or potential competitive advantages.
3. **Continuously gather competitor intelligence** — Things change, and news, no matter how seemingly valuable at the time, tends to have a relatively short shelf life. Stay up to date. Competitor intelligence is best acquired anecdotally rather than systematically. A wise sales professional will ask both prospects and clients about their experience with your competition. Questions might include:

    "How did you like your experience with XYZ clinic?"

    "What do they do well?"

    "What are their shortcomings?"

    You will quickly learn what you need to know about the competition and stay abreast of their ups and downs.

Recognize the strengths and weaknesses of your competitors *before* you craft your own competitive advantage statement. With appropriate competitor intelligence, you can determine if your reputed advantage is unique, as well as judge how easily a competitor might replicate your advantage.

EXAMPLE 1

Your service initiative is one of two hospital-affiliated women's health programs in your community. Both programs are similar, although you have repeatedly picked up concerns about the competitor's lack of post-encounter communication. Use that information to craft your competitive advantage (provided you are genuinely effective in that regard). However, a platitude such as "we communicate effectively" won't do. Rather, take advantage of a competitor's Achilles heel by developing and referring to a proactive communications package.

EXAMPLE 2

Assume you represent a freestanding urgent care clinic. Marketplace intelligence suggests that your hospital-affiliated competitors receive poor marks for long waiting times and inefficient billing practices. Your competitive advantage could emphasize your ability to process both patients and information more efficiently because of your smaller size and specific focus on employers.

RYAN Associates has conducted market research with employers since 1985 and has consistently noted that employers who favor hospital-affiliated programs over freestanding ones invariably do so because of the hospital's comprehensive services and twenty-four-hour access. A typical comment is, "I prefer to work with a hospital-affiliated program because the back-up is available in case the incident is or becomes serious." On the other hand, those who favor non-hospital-affiliated freestanding clinics tend to prefer them because they are readily accessible and focused on the specific service in question.

MUST NOTS

Just as there are "must dos" in sales and marketing that address the competition, there are also several "must not dos":

1. **Be paranoid** — It is easy to demonize the competition. Think about it: do you really like your competitors? The odds are that

they are decent and honest and have as many problems or challenges as you face. In short, your competitors are most likely not as formidable a threat as they may seem. Too great a concern could easily distract you for no just reason.

2. **Criticize your competitor** — This rule not only applies to dialogue with prospects or clients but also to discourse with anyone, including your own staff. Such criticism tends to be sophomoric and foolish and distracts you from thinking and acting proactively. A strong offense is certainly the best defense.
3. **Ignore slippage** — Market share slippage is usually measurable. Few service lines, however, consistently measure trends such as lost market share, decreasing revenue, or client movement. Immediate action should be taken to stem negative tides.
4. **Overreact to competitor actions** — Rarely respond to a competitor's actions. Attempting to match a new product offering by a competitor often is not prudent. Price reductions or discounts need not be matched in most instances. Proactively listen to your customers and offer innovative products in response to consumer needs and desires.
5. **Mention a competitor by name** — Whether you are dealing with a client or a prospect, never mention a competitor by name. Any reference tends to provide a competitor with greater credibility and elevates them to a status roughly equal to yours. Omission of the competitor's name suggests more of an "out of sight, out of mind" mind-set. Use a phrase such as "tell me more about your current provider."

Know your competitors. Understand what they do well and do poorly and what your competitive advantages are vis-à-vis others in the market. Pick your battles carefully.

MARKETING IN TOUGH ECONOMIC TIMES

On the surface, spiraling unemployment and broad-based financial pressures would seem to portend nothing but trouble for most services aimed at the employer market. Yet crisis inevitably breeds opportunity if you can avoid being caught like a deer in the headlights and proactively move forward.

THE EFFECT

To state the obvious, a high unemployment rate means fewer hires and less discretionary spending by employers. With fewer active workers in the workplace, there are undoubtedly fewer work-related incidents as well, even assuming a constant injury rate. Although unemployment numbers vary greatly by state and specific markets, most markets are feeling a severe pinch. It is hard to be optimistic about a scenario that speaks to lower patient volumes across the board.

Add to this muddle the decreasing availability of employer decision makers. As a company downsizes, staff at the Human Resource officer level become increasingly squeezed by new crises and responsibilities.

THE SILVER LINING

Circling back to the crisis-breeds-opportunity axiom: "Things may not be as bad as they seem." Having been involved with employer-directed services since 1981, I speak from experience:

- The healthcare economy does not historically run parallel to the national economy. In fact, the opposite has more often seemed true. During recent national recessions, I was pleasantly surprised that well-run programs not only weathered the storm but actually thrived.
- During economic downturns, the strong tend to get stronger and the weak disappear. My company, RYAN Associates, provides an illustrative example. Demand for our consulting services has been historically high during bad economic times. Why? Because organizations are looking for ways to increase their efficiency and sustain their business. They need our counsel during perilous times and are willing to spend their finite funds in order to do the right thing.

  The same is likely true for many companies: during such times, they need to turn to well-informed outside sources to ensure they are on the right track. This suggests it is possible for market leaders to offset potentially declining volumes by acquiring new clients from less-effective competitors.

WHAT TO DO

There are numerous steps your organization can take to cope with economic downturns:

1. **Scrub your contact base** — Update your contact lists frequently. High unemployment, turnover, and consolidation all contribute to the likelihood of a changing of the guard at many client and prospect companies. This may be a good time to establish contact with a new liaison at an old company or follow up with an established ally who has changed employment. Make a given month your "clean up the employer contact database" month.
2. **Shift some of your sales time to marketing** — Any revenue growth during a recessionary period is more likely to come from new business generated by smaller companies than from an increase in business from existing companies or large non-client targets. Comparatively inexpensive, high visibility marketing tactics are likely to pay proportionately better dividends.
3. **Emphasize return on investment** — One might surmise that price is king during a down economy; exactly the opposite may be true: high quality, positive return-on-investment relationships take on added importance among buyers who cannot afford to make the wrong choice at this time. There are a lot of defensive-minded buyers whose purchasing decisions are driven more by fear than strategic thinking.
4. **Promote on-site services** — A growing number of large companies in the United States offer on-site medical services.

    This opportunity should not be lost on healthcare providers. Most organizations have the expertise to either run or contribute to the operation of such services in a manner that provides the employer with superior management at lower overall cost. Incremental losses in patient volume can be more than offset by one significant on-site services contract.
5. **Reactivate dormant relationships** — Contact a past client and attempt to persuade them to do business with you again. At the conclusion of the conversation, you could say, "It has been good talking with you. Keep in touch, and if there is anything we can do for your company, let me know." Like so much else in sales, it

boils down to a numbers game: make ten such calls and you are likely to reactivate one or more dormant accounts.

6. **Lock in client loyalty** — Do not take your clients for granted. Call each and every one once a year and ask them if there is anything more you can do to better serve them. Saving potential revenue from attrition is as good as generating that same revenue anew.
7. **Troll for big fish** — You undoubtedly know of employers in your market that you assume are off limits: they are too big, have an in-house orientation, or have an established relationship with one of your competitors. But these companies are facing economic challenges too. All of a sudden your "help them control their health and safety costs" pitch might have considerably more appeal. Nothing ventured, nothing gained.
8. **Plan ahead** — Down economies, even deep ones, do not last forever. Meanwhile, a pent-up demand for exceptional services builds. Sales and marketing professionals who are likely to see payoffs are those who focus on establishing and cultivating relationships during the first half of a year when the expectation is that financially strapped companies will be better positioned several months down the road.
9. **Be a contrarian** — Be an optimist when others are forlornly predicting economic doom. Put a greater effort into sales and marketing when others put their collective sales/marketing heads in the sand. People tend to be attracted to optimists during a storm. Be the star upon which your employer, clients, and prospects can hitch a ride.

Prospering during a down economy begins with a realistic view of the peril at hand and a relentless drive to do more, not less, in order to sell your services.

COMPLIMENTARY SERVICES

It has been more than twenty-five years, and I still remember the Poinsettia Lady. Her idea of marketing was to load her truck up with poinsettias pre-Christmas and drop one off to each of her best clients and most important prospects. At the time it sounded good—even clever. Now it seems like a big waste of time and money.

Do not forget the trinkets era, when marketing meant producing this, that, and the next thing with your organization's name on it: pens, hats, mini-flashlights, refrigerator magnets, note pads, even t-shirts; though cute and even practical, these trinkets usually cost more than a little money, took invaluable time to distribute, and quickly faded from the recipients' minds, if not their possession.

Questions arise: Should your marketing strategy include freebies? If so, what should they be? How should they be distributed? Who should receive them?

WHAT TO OFFER

Recommended complimentary goods and services fall into one of two categories: something of educational value or something that allows the recipient to experience your services.

There is considerable value in using education and information as a prime marketing tool. Such services might include episodic email blasts about new regulations or other current topics, regular email of wellness and other health and safety tips, or leveraging your website as an information resource.

The first recommended approach involves information. You could develop a monthly email subscription at a low cost—say $49 a year. If marketed aggressively, it could be a revenue source in its own right (e.g., two hundred employer subscribers a year at $49 = $9,800 in gross revenue with minimal costs).

Beside gross revenue potential, there are inherent advantages to such a product:

- It is a low-cost way to make a prospect a "mini-client." A prospect company may not be ready (yet) to move their business over to you, but it is likely to be comfortable with a $49 subscription. Your service can remain on the employer's radar screen, emphasize its mastery of myriad healthcare issues, and be better positioned to move the prospect company into the client column at a later date.

- A renewable product such as a subscription is the close that keeps on giving and giving and giving. A $49 close can easily become a $490 close over the next ten years.
- A subscription fee waiver is an excellent freebie for certain prospects. When all else seems to fail during a sales call, the sales professional can always fall back on the following offer:

> *"What I would like to do is offer you a complimentary one-year subscription to our highly regarded* Wellness Update*. I am confident that you will find it valuable, and it would allow us to keep in touch with your company."*

The free subscription is a virtual no-brainer: an incremental email subscription costs you virtually nothing (to say nothing of prospective paid renewal revenue).

The second recommended approach involves a hands-on experience. Develop a mini annual physical that can be provided gratis to decision makers from high priority prospects.

If you provide a free exam a week and take two weeks off during the year, your fifty highest-profile prospects will experience a genuine, hands-on experience in your clinic on an annual basis. For the time expended on a personal sales call, the physician could do two or three complimentary physical exams.

Further, in most cases you want your physician doing what he or she normally does best, which is being a physician, not a salesperson.

In providing low-cost or free services, you are not losing revenue but incurring costs per unit of complimentary service.

By scheduling complimentary physicals during traditionally low-volume hours in your clinic, you are offering value at virtually no cost. I would rather have a provider spend forty-five minutes on a physical than take them away from the clinic for a sales call.

WHEN AND TO WHOM?

Freebies should reside in your marketing-option portfolio until such time as you use them. Rule 1: free offerings should be made judiciously and only as needed. Rule 2: never forget rule 1.

A free subscription (or analogous low-cost product) is best

reserved for the moment it becomes evident that a close is not likely to occur. Rather than merely an old fashioned, "Thank you, perhaps some time in the future," you can now offer a one-year getting-to-know-us free subscription. The free subscription option is applicable to virtually any prospect, regardless of their priority or future volume potential.

The free physical option applies primarily to your "A" prospects. Offer this option to prospects that have not closed the door but are not quite committed, or to the highest priority prospects that seemingly have little interest. The offer is usually made toward the end of the sales call when the disposition of the call is apparent.

MAKE THE OFFER

As with so many other things in sales (or all types of communication, for that matter), it is not what you say, it is how you say it. When you offer a complimentary service, go beyond offering the service by mentioning its value as well as an honest appraisal of why you are

EXHIBIT 2-3. TWO SCRIPTS FOR PROVIDING FREEBIES

SCENARIO ONE: A prospect appears to be a "non-sale" at the end of the sales call.

> *"Now that we have met, I would like to stay in touch with you. I wish to offer you a complimentary subscription to our highly regarded "Occupational Health Update" monthly email advisory. Employers usually pay $49 a year for this publication. The free subscription will help keep your company up to date and allow us to keep in touch with one another."*

SCENARIO TWO: A prospect is near a close or is not near a close but is high priority.

> *"We would like to provide you with a complimentary physical examination in our clinic. The process of receiving the exam provides you with considerable insight into our practice. At about $250 per exam, a complimentary exam is an exceptional value and will provide you with useful information on your own health status."*

offering the free commodity. That is, quantify both the dollar and functional value (e.g., what's in it for the prospect) of the service.

Developing a plan on who to offer, when to make the offer, and how to verbalize the offer can provide you with an excellent marketing tool for converting both near and non-prospects into clients.

FUN IN SALES AND MARKETING

> *She'll have fun, fun, fun*
> *'til her daddy takes her T'bird away.*
> *Fun, fun, fun . . ."*
>
> —THE BEACH BOYS, 1964

Back in those days I also had plenty of fun, fun, fun. Still do. And therein lies a message for everyone involved in sales and marketing.

There seems to be a correlation between fun-filled marketing initiatives and the success of such efforts. A creative, upbeat approach tends to relax all parties, whether it is your coworkers, your prospects, or your clients. Although there are many times and places for serious moments, there is more to be gained than lost with a smile, a laugh, and a gleam in your eye.

THE HAVE FUN DOCTRINE

The "have fun" doctrine can work in three areas:

1. Fun as part of your marketing plan
2. Fun as part of your daily sales effort
3. Fun as a member of your core team

MARKETING

Marketing should be fun. But it often isn't. Marketing is a creative, people-oriented discipline and one that should not always be taken too seriously.

Ask every staff member to submit three new ideas for marketing your services. Summarize the ideas, meet to review and discuss them, and establish priorities. Include at least one experimental idea that you have not tried before; you will likely be surprised at the ultimate value of that idea.

Develop little contests for every goal inherent in the plan. Rewards can be monetary, but they usually are not. Non-monetary awards ("creative genius of the quarter") may appear silly and frivolous but will attract attention and instill a sense of motivation.

Recognize the importance of establishing marketing priorities based on the projected return vs. the human and financial capital required to execute the initiative. Add a pizzazz quotient to round out the equation. If a marketing tactic is boring to you, it is likely to be as boring to the audience you are trying to reach.

DAILY SALES

An old friend of mine named Jim Madden once said, "Nervous people make me nervous." One could deduce the opposite as well: "Fun people make me happy." Yet many an inherently outgoing sales professional creates a self-defeating veneer of "all business, no levity." The bottom line: be yourself; smile, laugh, and relax if that is your inherent persona. People buy more readily from people they like, and what's not to like about a "fun person"?

Remain true to yourself. If you are a serious soul in your non-professional life, you have narrow latitude for developing a new "fun" professional façade. If you are a fun-loving extrovert, do not leave that personality at the office door.

CORE TEAM

The value of sales professionals to their team does not end with their performances on the field. In healthcare, sales professionals often function as the personality and soul of the service line they represent.

You can be the eyes and ears of your organization. You can and should bring back positive and negative perceptions that may exist in the marketplace. For such information to get noticed, understood, and addressed, you should present it with flair.

As an avid, albeit under-skilled, golfer, I have learned that the easier you swing, the farther the ball goes. So it is with sales and marketing: the more fun you have, the more enthusiasm you generate in all parties.

Add a heavy dose of "fun, fun, fun" to your latest resolution list:

- **Keep things in perspective** — I can think of ten times I have taken something more seriously than was warranted for every time I failed to take something seriously enough. I am not alone.
- **Brainstorm for ideas** — Set an end goal (e.g., expanding market share in the western suburbs or generating $500,000 in new revenue). Then, encourage staff to come up with ten creative ideas to market your service. Pool and then brainstorm to polish the ideas. Use them to generate other more synthesized ideas.
- **Conduct an internal contest** — Little contests invariably breed interest, participation, and new ideas. Have mini-contests with small yet humorous rewards. It keeps staff focused and motivated.
- **Choose photos with care** — Have you ever noticed the somber expressions on people's faces from the early days of photography, circa 1860–1930? Photos should convey the image of smiling, warm individuals who are pleasant to be around.
- **Draw attention in an information-saturated world** — One of the most undervalued requisites of effective marketing is the ability to draw attention to your services in a world of finite attention spans. People are going to notice—and remember—the unique rather than the traditional. I would rather take a chance on something unproven but new rather than stick with a "proven" yet forgettable approach.

NEW MEDIA

Sales and marketing professionals should embrace adaptability—the ability to adjust to new conditions or a different environment.

Lack of adaptability is the leading cause of mediocre marketing. In a rapidly changing business world, yesterday's approach is, well, so yesterday.

Think forward and adapt to our rapidly changing environment.

Note three caveats:

1. **Embrace change** — Embrace the concept of change before you define exactly what change you want to invoke. If you are more reactive than proactive, you are, by definition, backed into the yesterday corner.
2. **Borrow ideas from other industries** — Look for ideas outside of your core services, and for that matter, outside of healthcare. Browse the Internet for the latest marketing trends, read the hottest marketing books and periodicals, and watch how others approach you. When it comes to marketing, healthcare tends to be a step behind; borrow from beyond the healthcare sphere, and you are likely to be a step ahead.
3. **Maintain balance** — Balance your portfolio and balance new marketing tactics with proven, effective traditional approaches.

NETWORKING

The with-it marketing crowd points to networking, including and going beyond social media, as the next big thing. The time seems nearly at hand when a healthcare sales professional need never send a routine introductory letter or place an introductory telephone call to a total stranger. Rather, the name of the game in sales and marketing will be to network your way to that prospect through existing contacts.

Social networking sites provide an excellent starting point. I chaired a sales panel at a recent RYAN Associates' national conference and asked audience members to raise their hands if they used LinkedIn or Facebook, first for personal reasons and second for professional purposes. Many, perhaps most, indicated personal use, and about half raised their hands for professional purposes.

This informal poll suggests that most of us are conversant with LinkedIn and Facebook, and a considerable number are beginning to use them as vehicles for professional outreach.

Similarly, RYAN Associates has begun to assess the use of social networking sites by prospective buyers of occupational health services. The following exhibit **(Exhibit 2-4)** represents responses from employers in one West Coast urban/suburban market:

Exhibit 2-4. Using Social Networking Sites

MEDIUM USED	PERSONAL	PROFESSIONAL
Facebook	66%	21%
LinkedIn	21%	28%
Twitter	11%	21%

More than 20 percent stated they use all three sites, and 75 percent of those who use LinkedIn indicated they use it for professional purposes.

USING LINKEDIN

LinkedIn is compelling because it is basically a social networking venue for professionals (whereas Facebook is more personal-use oriented and Twitter is something else altogether).

Using LinkedIn can help a sales professional in many ways:

1. Whenever you develop a good relationship with a client or prospect, establish a link with that person. If they are not involved or familiar with LinkedIn, encourage their participation: send them an invitation to get the ball rolling by linking to you. Over time you will be linked to scores, if not hundreds, of local decision makers, and you will have access to everyone who is linked to them.
2. If you are linked to one hundred local professionals and each of them is linked to an individual of interest to you, you can encourage your contact to "introduce" you to their contact. It certainly beats the old "I'd like to introduce myself" foot-in-the-door sales method.
3. LinkedIn raises testimonials to another level by offering an easy path for any of your linkages to write a short recommendation about you. Recommendations on your LinkedIn page are readily accessible to visitors.

4. You can announce just about anything to everyone with whom you are linked. Tell them about a new product, a new colleague, or a clinic open house. It is an expedient way to spread information and a welcome adjunct to email blasts and other communication modes.

FACE TIME ON FACEBOOK

Granted, Facebook is more of a personal networking site, but its sheer number of users (current estimate is 850 million worldwide) makes it attractive. You can use Facebook in various ways. Create a business page and post photos, videos, event invitations, games and contests, discussion chains, and pages for selected subgroups in your client universe.

You can connect on a more personal level with many of your professional colleagues; the more your clients consider you a "friend," the more likely they will refer you to other companies.

MOBILE DEVICE MARKETING

Mobile device marketing appears to be a game changer. The world of apps and text messages is quickly becoming a leading portal to brand awareness. In the not too distant future, smart phone applications will be available on almost any topic, thereby providing mobile device users immediate access to any specialized information they deem valuable or essential. Healthcare apps could range from a detailed medical dictionary to a summary of work-related conditions.

Although it may seem onerous to many at this time, we need to be prepared to use text messages to transmit information to constituents. The email blast craze may well give way to the text message wave a decade later. Remember, a nuisance can become a valuable tool if the information being transmitted is of value to its recipients.

Nearly everyone has a multifunctional mobile device serving as an extension of the body. Never before in marketing has it been so apparent how to reach the consumer.

Consider two basic messages:

1. Take advantage of others you know in order to facilitate upbeat and reassuring connections with new prospects.

2. Touch prospects more often, and make each touch briefer and more valuable to its recipients.

Must-do Marketing Actions

If you are preparing a marketing plan to cover the calendar year, January is the month to jump-start it. The first month of the year often comes and goes with barely a whimper, and as the year unfolds, the marketing plan slowly dies of neglect.

Here are ten must-do marketing actions:

1. **Communicate with management** — Meet with senior management to define or refine the role of sales and marketing in your program. Understand management's expectations in clear and quantifiable terms. Percent growth in gross revenue is typically the most meaningful performance parameter. Document and measure metrics for success.

   Discuss the nature of the sales professional's role, whether it is for yourself or staff whom you supervise. Are you expected to do other things in addition to direct sales? If so, what are these activities, how much time will they take away from core sales activity, and will management factor such ancillary tasks when evaluating your performance?

2. **Embrace your plan** — Be certain that your plan is reviewed and accepted by senior management and service level operatives. Build your plan around an array of marketing tactics and a detailed calendar to execute these tactics. Schedule marketing activities by anticipated hours per week and spread them evenly over all fifty-two weeks.

3. **Prepare for off days** — Certain days of the year, such as holiday weeks (e.g., the three days before Thanksgiving, Christmas week, snow days) are invariably non-starters when it comes to sales and marketing. There is a tendency for employers to retreat during certain days or weeks to wrap up projects or get a little rest before re-entering the batter's box.

   The days leading up to Thanksgiving and Christmas week are ideal times to drop in on your clients to thank them for their business and leave a little something, or to show appreciation to your coworkers and others for their support. Have a plan in place for snow days or other inclement weather days. You could use a snow day to send out scores of personalized emails to clients and prospects. Unfortunately, many sales professionals fail to take advantage of these off days.

4. **Innovate early in the year** — Innovation tends to be more lip service than reality for many healthcare organizations. At the end of the day, your risk will be moderate and your services will be able to test ideas that may result in a home run.
5. **Study your numbers** — Previous years' numbers should be available in January. Compare last year's data to data from the previous year. What growth or decline did your services generate? Look for clues. Compare new client growth to existing/former client attrition: What types of services or employer clients are in decline? What does this tell you about what, how, and to whom you want to sell?
6. **Look beyond raw numbers** — Data from the past year are a useful starting point and provide hints regarding where to go next. Has a particular service had a major increase or decrease during the year? Does that service offer a relatively higher margin than other services? Gross revenue for drug tests may have gone up, while revenue for discretionary physical exams may have gone down. On the other hand, there is more marginal revenue in discretionary exams, so these data may be misleading.
7. **Address attrition** — List the ten client companies with the most significant decline in gross revenue over the past two years. Reach out to them to determine why they are not using your services to the extent they did in the past. Look at these figures in gross dollars rather than volumes.
8. **Clean house** — Take stock of the physical condition of your clinic. Do what you can do to make facilities more visually pleasing and comfortable for patients and staff. A clean, inviting clinic is a great marketing tool.
9. **Reconsider compensation incentive packages** — Many sales professionals receive a compensation package that does not provide sufficient incentive. Revisit compensation packages (from both management and sales professional perspectives) and

develop a gross revenue oriented package that provides optimal incentive to the salesperson.

10. **Measure your time** — Assess exactly how you are spending your time. Earmark the first two weeks of the year for keeping a time sheet in fifteen-minute segments in order to see exactly how you are using your time. Chances are you will be surprised at the amount of nonproductive and/or non-direct sales time you are expending on other activities. Readjust for the rest of the year and remember the adage, "Time is money."

Capturing Attention

An overlooked tenet in marketing is that people do not care. When people do not care, they are not inclined to look or listen, and when prospects do not look or listen, your marketing dollars go to waste. People tend to not care because they have neither the time nor the attention span. Most of us find it difficult to find enough time during a given day to do what we have to do. Why allocate precious time listening to or viewing an advertisement or thoroughly working our way through some organization's marketing materials?

When was the last time you watched a television ad and remembered who the sponsor was or sat down and read a brochure word for word? Thought so.

BUYING DECISIONS

There are ways to capture a prospect's attention even in a competitive market in which prospects seem to be preoccupied with other matters. After all, people make buying decisions every day; there has to be some reason why.

A key lies in understanding what drives those decisions:

1. **Brand awareness** — This is pure name identification. The more buyers are familiar with your brand name, the more attention they will pay to your message and the better your chance of enhancing its market share.
2. **The essence of your product** — Once potential buyers know who you are, they need to know what you do. Name identification

standing on its own means little; effective marketing must tie the brand name with product awareness in the prospective buyer's mind.

3. **Your competitive advantage** — While brand awareness and product definition are likely to capture the attention of some, they are not quite enough on their own. You must also convey to the market why your product is the best available option. The foundation of an effective marketing campaign rests with creating an environment in which as many potential buyers as possible know who you are, what you offer, and why your services are the preferred option.

   Your marketing tactics are the engine that will get you there.

OVERCOMING INDIFFERENCE

There are three proven strategies for overcoming market indifference: brevity, repetition, and relevance.

1. **Brevity** — Brevity means just that—say what you need to say with the fewest words possible. Advising prospects about a broad array of services when they are limited by a tight budget is challenging. Marketers in particular have a tendency to expound on a litany of services, features, and justifications. Before adding one more point, evaluate whether it is absolutely essential. Every additional word is likely to detract from your core message.

   Whittle paragraphs down to sentences, sentences to simple phrases, and simple phrases to a single phrase. Apply the three-second rule: if the reader (or listener) cannot comprehend your core message in three seconds or fewer, it is time to go back to the drawing board. In writing, highlight key words and use plenty of white space. Need I say anything about the one thousand word value of a photo?

   Repetition — Repetition means repeatedly stating your brand name, product, and differentiating feature until it is the first service option most prospective buyers think of when the time comes. Using multiple modalities such as email, voice mail, sponsorships, alliances, letters, and selected advertising expands the value of the repetition. Keep what you are repeating simple.

The key to effective repetition is discipline. It may be tempting to try something new in order to avoid tired phrases. But when you try something new, your former message becomes obsolete and is soon forgotten. If your original message is your best shot, any subsequent message is not likely to measure up.

2. **Relevance** — Relevance means that a brief message, repeatedly transmitted to the market, must harmonize with the prospect's wants and needs. Get a handle on buzz words that seem to work for employers and tell them what is in it for them. Use these words or phrases as often as possible.

IDENTIFY PREDOMINANT VALUE

Take measure of the **predominant** value in your market, not necessarily the value that will appeal to everyone. Get beyond simple buzzwords by tying your message to your unique ability to deliver value.

A key selling point for RYAN Associates' consulting services is, "More than five hundred clients since 1985 must be right." Our subliminal message is that we possess considerable depth of experience, many others see value in our services, and new buyers usually have great confidence in us.

Similarly, if your program is well established, you can state that you have "managed more than 20,000 injuries," thereby sending a message that you are the most reliable option.

A LESSON FROM POLITICS

Political campaigns—fraught with mud slinging and falsehoods though they may be—offer insightful hints on how to market a candidate using the three measures cited above. In my community, a candidate named Hannah Beth Jackson, whom I know personally and admire, recently ran for State Senate. The race was not particularly high profile and was eclipsed by a presidential campaign. I felt this was a year in which astute application of simple marketing rules could spell victory for one candidate or the other. Ms. Jackson's opponent flooded the airwaves and mail boxes with the same simple and consistent catch phase—"Taxin' Jackson." The accusation had no merit, but simple repetition planted a seed among the electorate that grew like a weed as the election neared.

Following an arduous recount process, Taxin' Jackson lost by a razor-slim margin. Her opponent had played it right: simplicity (two words), repetition over weeks and months, and relevance. During the economic downturn of the period, what would scare voters more than the specter of new taxes? Brevity, repetition, and relevance are a simple game plan that is available to all marketers but practiced by few.

MARKET SEGMENTATION

If you have more than one child or grew up with at least one sibling, you have probably experienced segmentation. In other words, you have most likely used different tactics and strategies in dealing with each of your children, or you were treated somewhat differently than your siblings. Classic healthcare market segmentation follows the same principle. A communication technique that is effective with one audience may not work as well with another.

MARKET DIFFERENTIATION

Regardless of the type of industry, every organization launching a market outreach effort should answer this core question: Do we have different segments that suggest different sales and marketing strategies? In most cases the answer is yes. In the generic product world, typical market segments might include age, gender, or socioeconomic status. Consider a national political campaign: a candidate's core message in California is likely to be considerably different than the message they would emphasize in Georgia or Iowa.

KEY SEGMENTS

Appropriate market segments for healthcare services are limited only by one's imagination and are likely to vary by region. However, three variables are virtually universal: employer size, industry type, and distance from your core delivery locale.

EMPLOYER SIZE

The ongoing focus for most programs is to market to midsize employers. Such an emphasis tends to ignore both the largest and smallest employers in a market, ceding a great deal of volume potential to competitors. A more fruitful strategy is to market continually to all segments: large, midsize, and small. However, each of these segments requires different stimuli to be most effective:

Large employers tend to be low-probability/high-reward prospects and need to be in your prospect mix. Traditional marketing efforts are likely to fall short with this segment. I have noticed that breakthroughs with large employers are more likely to occur when physicians and/or directors are involved in the sales process. You may schedule a weekly group sales call at a set day and hour that is devoted to large employers. With such a commitment, you will cultivate approximately fifty large employers a year.

Small employers are largely overlooked in many marketing campaigns, although in the aggregate they can produce significant volumes for a healthcare organization. When it comes to marketing to smaller employers, emphasize multiple contacts through various modalities (email, voice mail, letter) that reiterate a constant message and continuously reinforce your brand.

Midsize employers remain the heart and soul of most organizations' volume and revenue; make them the primary focus of your marketing campaign. How does one define a large, midsize, or small employer prospect? It depends on the market. The definition of employer size will vary markedly from Chicago, where a large employer might be one with more than one thousand employees, to Cullman, Alabama, where a large employer might be defined as any company with more than fifty employees.

INDUSTRY TYPE

Some markets may be perfectly heterogeneous, with an employer mix that reflects American industry as a whole. Others may have prominent niches, such as Las Vegas, resort communities, or markets with a heavy agricultural or white-collar emphasis. When a unique employer segment is identified, the marketer must determine specific outreach tactics and appropriate product niches.

PROXIMITY

Different strategies and an emphasis on different products may apply to employers based at various distances from your clinic. Showcase your convenience for employers most proximate to your delivery venues. Emphasize on-site and mobile services with employers whose primary place of business is located at or beyond the periphery of your primary market area. The Chicago-Cullman continuum applies to this segment as well: a distant employer in Chicago may be defined as being more than a fifteen-minute drive away, while those in Cullman might be thirty or more miles away from the clinic.

EXHIBIT 2-5. SEGMENTING YOUR MARKET

1.	What, if anything, is unique about your market? Does a particular type of industry dominate? Do you wish to reach outlying markets? Is there an inordinately large number of big (or small) companies?
2.	Do you offer services that are especially relevant to one or more of these segments? Executive health services may be more relevant to a white-collar market segment.
3.	What marketing tactics or products might be uniquely applicable to a segment? Be certain to incorporate these tactics and products into your final marketing plan.

Market segmentation involves only a relatively small amount of forethought, yet invariably receives scant attention in many marketing plans. A marketing plan that does not include a section on market segmentation is likely to be missing one or more outreach opportunities. Consider segmentation opportunities before you finalize your marketing plan.

The following exhibit presents a hypothetical example of market segmentation using the Las Vegas market. Employer type and proximity are traditional variables that invariably involve three segments.

Industry type is frequently confined to either a single segment market (a heterogeneous market) or a two segment market (special niche and all other employers). In some cases, a given market may include three or even more industry type segments.

EXHIBIT 2-6. MARKET SEGMENTATION

SEGMENT VARIABLE	SEGMENT A	SEGMENT B	SEGMENT C
Employer type	Large (> 400)	Mid-sized	Small (< 50)
Strategy	* Group meetings * Creative services	* Traditional outreach	* Email/direct mail * Marketing by phone
Industry type	Gaming	White-Collar	All Others
Service	* Guest services * Addiction medicine	* Executive health * Travel medicine * Background checks	* Traditional outreach
Proximity	Proximate (< 5 miles)	Mid-distance	Distant (> 15 miles)
Strategy	* Stress ease of access	Traditional outreach	* On-site services * Mobile services

MARKET LEADER STRATEGIES

In marketing it sometimes becomes necessary to play the flip side. Instead of assuming the best offense is a good defense, the best defense becomes a good offense.

It is great to be on top, but when a program is "fat and happy," its marketing can lose its intensity. Your crown may be in danger of slipping before anyone realizes your leadership position is even in jeopardy.

NOTHING STAYS ON TOP

A number of years ago, I traveled to the People's Republic of China with my son, Ryan. Our most indelible impression was that this highly focused mega-country of more than a billion people appears destined to become the world's pre-eminent economic power within our lifetime. As a proud American I had assumed that the United States would always be numero uno. But during our trip a greater truth emerged for me: no entity—whether a country, a company, a product, or an individual—remains on top for an indefinite period of time.

Nevertheless, complacency has set in for many market leaders, and it is easy to see why. Most likely the market leader has either a significant lead in what was once a more competitive market, or it enjoys a near-monopoly in a smaller market.

The following are suggestions for all organizations—whether they are leaders or followers—to help them guard against complacency and secure dominance in the marketplace:

1. **Protect your base** — Market share is the market leader's most valuable asset. Implement a plan that ensures that this market share will remain intact. Too often an organization assumes that clients are satisfied and fails to learn about any dissatisfaction until the clients have moved their business elsewhere.
2. **Stay close to your customers** — Protecting your base means listening to your customers. Continually assess consumer satisfaction through multiple modalities. Examples of intelligence-gathering mechanisms include annual employer surveys, quarterly telephone blitzes, and universal (every patient, every day) patient-satisfaction surveys. Many organizations gather such data, but tend to do it poorly:
    - They fail to ask the right questions.
    - They do not follow-up on concerns or suggestions.

- They do not sustain the effort, month after month, year after year.
- They do not provide inordinate attention to employers who generate an inordinate amount of business.

3. **Expand horizontally** — Horizontal expansion usually means increasing market share by developing relationships with new companies. As market leaders become comfortable, there is inevitably less impetus for them to extend into the prospect fringes to acquire business from less proximate or smaller companies. This is the time to become greedy and continue to expand market share.
4. **Expand vertically** — The greater your market share, the more you need to think in terms of vertical expansion (new services for existing clients) and less in terms of horizontal expansion (expanding your client base). The vertical/horizontal choice is a continuum; pursue both. Tilt toward the vertical end of the spectrum as you attain greater market share or operate in a smaller, less competitive market.
5. **Market leadership is a competitive advantage** — Prudent buyers are invariably more comfortable with proven market leaders (e.g., "They must be doing something right"). Yet market leaders, both within and outside of healthcare, seldom use market leadership as a competitive advantage. There are many ways to tout your leadership in tasteful, yet clear, terms. Some examples:
   - Make your reference list exhaustive, or at least near-exhaustive. List virtually all of your employer relationships.
   - Use tag lines, such as "The leading provider of urgent care services in Crescent City."
   - Mention your dominant position in oral and written sales presentations.
   - Frequently cite your established relationships with large key companies in your market.
6. **Offer incentives** — Sales professionals should receive incentive pay in return for attaining their ultimate goal. Use clear incentives to promote gross revenue, whether it is generated through vertical or horizontal sales.

7. **Focus on competitor vulnerabilities** — Is your team ahead by two touchdowns early in the fourth quarter? If it is, do not run the ball into the line. Open up your passing attack, especially if that strategy plays into your opponent's greatest liabilities. Stick with the playbook that got you in the lead in the first place: sell on your competitive advantages vis-à-vis your prime competitors.
8. **Leverage downtime** — There is a silver lining out there for market leaders who have been dealing with an economic downturn. Market leaders are in the best position to quickly regain their strength in the next economic upswing because survival-of-the-fittest principles tend to further weaken or put more vulnerable competitors out of business. If you are a market leader, invest in product expansion and even more intense marketing in order to take advantage of your competitors' inability to respond in turn.
9. **Monitor slippage** — The first sign of market leader slippage is usually measurable. Few organizations proactively measure trends such as lost market share, decreasing revenue, or client movement. Scrutinize these parameters and take immediate action to stem negative tides.
10. **Encourage brainstorming** — Build on market leadership rather than letting it slip away. Market leadership provides many compelling competitive advantages, yet most organizations take it for granted, thereby setting themselves up to slowly but surely lose their grip on the market.

Easing up on your marketing effort as your program becomes more dominant is not an absolute; it is a matter of degree. I am hard pressed to identify a sales and marketing plan that is operating on all cylinders, and the cylinders that are running seem to lose their momentum as market share becomes more pronounced.

As the market leader, take a hard look at the nature and intensity of your marketing effort and develop a systematic approach to respond to any deficiencies that come to light.

If not taking advantage of a great mind is a notable tragedy of mankind, not taking advantage of the inherent advantages of your market leadership is a notable downside of your marketing effort.

Exhibit 2-7. Nine Steps for the Market Leader

1. Protect your base.
2. Continue to expand horizontally.
3. Begin expanding vertically.
4. Tout your market leadership.
5. Create growth-oriented incentives.
6. Focus on competitor vulnerabilities.
7. Be patient during down cycles.
8. Proactively measure slippage.
9. Continually brainstorm.

Printed Marketing Materials

Look around. Daily newspapers at the doorstep and on newsstands are heading for extinction. What about that twenty-volume set of encyclopedias that used to sit on your parents' bookshelf? How about all of those hand-written assignments at every school level? A thing of the past.

Seems like a no-brainer: out with the paper and in with the electronic medium. Yet, when it comes to many healthcare organizations, the paper trail has far from disappeared.

COLLATERALS

I have been campaigning against this for years: a big, fat packet of printed material that covers virtually everything that you do—reams and reams of paper, and brochures and fliers summarizing all sorts of services.

Such a presentation mode is counterproductive. People do not have the time to read much of anything these days. The content of that big fat folder almost certainly will never be read and more than likely quickly discarded. Packets are a waste of money and a squandered opportunity to place customized information before your clients and prospects.

The 1980s were the heyday of healthcare marketing. Healthcare organizations were throwing all sorts of money into marketing: Marketing officers and staff were being hired at a dizzying rate. Radio, television, print ads, and billboards proliferated. Then the electronic age (e.g., email, attachments and websites) took hold, and many of the old guard did not know what to do.

WHAT TO DO?

What should you do once you have stopped generating a ton of paper for recycling bins?

1. **Put your savings to good use** — Apply the savings associated with eliminating paper material to upgrade your website, enhance your incentive compensation, and pay for a spiffy open house. If you must do something on paper, make it a simple one-page flier with a general overview featuring photos, contact phone numbers, email addresses, and third-party testimonials.
2. **Create an electronic library** — Send clients or prospects exactly what they need—and nothing more.
    - Provide a customized product; customization is invariably a leading reason why employers select a provider ("WorkWell considers the nuances of your workplace!").
    - Avoid handing off a transparent generic one-size-fits-all packet of information.
    - Seize the opportunity to show clients and prospects how quickly you can react. If you email them appropriate information within a few hours after a sales call, you invariably create a halo effect of responsiveness that reflects favorably on you.
    - Customize within your electronic forms. Be selective in the information you send, customize the information to reflect the prospect's special needs, and utilize buzzwords appropriate to a particular company.
    - Easily update information at any given moment. By contrast, you cannot make such changes in written materials, which often become obsolete even before they

arrive from the printer. An electronic library renders all materials (including staff and staff bios) suitable for immediate updating.

3. **Distribute selected materials** — Develop multiple opportunities to distribute selected materials. In the bad old paper days, material had to be either mailed or hand delivered. The electronic age opens up many new opportunities:

    - **Website access** — Add many of these materials directly to your website or link readers to printable versions of various documents. Product descriptions, legal explanations, staff biographies, clinic registration materials, and seminar registrations are but a few of the materials or links that can be available on your website.
    - **Email attachments** — Load up your professional email correspondence with direct links to various information sheets and forms, as appropriate.
    - **Mass email blasts** — Do you want to introduce a new or revitalized service? How about a new staff member or new policy? An email blast with a proper link or attachment sent to your entire client/prospect database is a super-quick and cost-effective way of getting such information out.

OTHER TRANSFORMATIVE CONCEPTS

Although collateral materials are the big daddy of wasteful, ineffectual paper usage, the use of almost any paper should be minimized:

- **A paperless office** — Backing up computer files has become so sophisticated that we have little to worry about. Paperless is not perfect, but paperless perfection is getting closer all of the time. Indeed, paperwork can be scanned and electronically filed, and the paper shredded and recycled.
- **Minimize direct mail** — Send letters via email for immediate delivery. Eliminate promotional bulk mailings. Bulk mail is junk mail and is seldom read by the intended recipient.
- **Collect survey data electronically** — It is wiser and more effective to gather survey data (e.g., annual employer survey),

regardless of the purpose or length, via an email attachment or link. Usually this approach alone does not generate the response rate you would like, and a mail or telephone follow-up is required. However, it does bring in some responses, and it saves time and money on the back end.

The basic rule of the road is clear: time-strapped people have little time to read, review, and absorb. Hence, you have to hedge your bets by providing your clients and prospects with only the information that they absolutely need in a given situation. Such targeted information saves considerable expense and time and is more likely to resonate with the recipient.

Effective marketing is about getting people's attention. Once you get a prospect's attention, do not come off as self-serving; remain above the fray. The less you look like another marketer, the better your chances for acceptance.

Marketing on a Tight Budget

Heard the adage, "You've got to spend money to make money"? Of course you have, and chances are you subscribe to that notion. Not so fast.

The healthcare marketing landscape has undergone a metamorphosis during the past twenty-five years. Rewind to 1987 and you will be smack in the era of paid advertising. A budding marketing plan was as likely as not to earmark considerable funds for an ad here, an ad there, here an ad, there an ad, everywhere an ad, ad, E-I-E-I-O.

Such advertising was invariably a waste of money. Most paid advertising used a shotgun approach, whereas health services marketing typically requires a more direct approach. In a community with a working population of 200,000, only 200–300 individuals might be in a position to make purchasing decisions that could support your initiative.

Paid advertising (radio, television, print advertising, and billboards) was often wordy, vague, and generalized, and it typically reached the consumer far too few times to leave a lasting impression. Although the reasoning behind paid advertising was logical, its cost seemed disproportionate to its value.

When paid advertising fell from favor, employer seminars,

printed newsletters, health fairs, and similar activities emerged. These marketing tactics heighten exposure among targeted consumers, but they are often perceived as self-serving and may be costly in human and capital resources. Not as much is being done these days under the guise of education and health promotion (as opposed to direct sales) as budgets and available manpower continue to shrink.

That does not mean to say that some money shouldn't be expended on marketing. Minimal marketing violates a central sales and marketing principle: **optimal achievable revenue can only be attained through a careful blend of both sales and marketing.** Only so much new business can be generated in a given time period; new business must be supplemented with business that is generated through marketing techniques that do not rely on face-to-face communication. If this marketing can be executed at minimal cost, all the better.

THE BASICS

Begin your marketing strategy with a simple question: What is the goal of our marketing initiative? Your organization most likely wants to increase gross revenue. But what do you really have to do to accomplish this objective?

1. Differentiate yourself in the marketplace by addressing the most pressing consumer need in a more effective manner than any other available option.
2. Communicate that superiority in a simple, persuasive, and relentless manner.
3. Ensure that it is reaching out to as many prospective users as possible.

Let's break this down. Most employers have a need to reduce healthcare costs. There are many ways in which a well-crafted program can meet this need, including policies and procedures, highly trained personnel, finely tuned patient management practices, specialized software, and the ability to identify high-risk employees, jobs, and workstations. The secret is to communicate this ability in a succinct and oft-repeated manner.

The essence of marketing in the new millennium is to:

Simplify: Keep your message simple by not letting it get lost among the trees. Use ten words rather than one hundred. Do not describe a litany of services; hone in on the single most important benefit to the consumer.

Brand: Brand your program name by always linking it with your core message: "WorkWell's Care Management System saves employers money."

Broadcast: Broadcast your message to the largest possible audience. This concept may appear obvious on the surface, but it requires an ongoing effort to ensure that you maintain an accurate and comprehensive contact database.

Reinforce: The same message must be repeated over and over to the prospective consumer until the consumer unmistakably recognizes your name, what you offer, and your competitive advantage.

MARKETING ON A BUDGET

How does a healthcare organization achieve these objectives in an era of shoestring budgets and strident revenue objectives? How do you stay in the face of prospects in order to supplement the results of your direct sales effort?

The simple answer is to use a blend of all the communication tools at your disposal (email, websites, voice mail, personalized letters). An attainable goal might be to touch every employer contact in your database twenty times a year. If I were the decision maker at Herman Farms, and I either heard from you or were exposed to your program's name twenty times in a year, I would surely remember and more likely use your program if and when a need arose.

Twenty hits per annum marketing outreach program might include:

Tip of the month: Develop an employer contact email list (with an option for the recipient to opt out) and provide recipients with useful information (the tip). Information about your service can be tacked on. You are positioning your organization (subliminally, if not in fact) as the area's pre-eminent expert on your service line, an excellent image to have when an uncommitted employer needs assistance.

Semiannual letters: Send a concise, personalized (with a full inside address), and individually signed letter to all employer prospects twice a year. There is a monumental difference between junk mail, basic brochures and fliers, and direct correspondence. Use direct correspondence to catch someone's attention, if only briefly, to convey a simple but meaningful message.

Quarterly phone calls: I have become somewhat of a voice-mail fan, which is a good thing, because voice mail is likely to be around for a long time. Control voice mail and do not let it control you. You do not want to leave a voice-mail message if you absolutely need to speak with the prospect. But when a "thinking of you" message is being used for marketing purposes, voice mail is an excellent means to say a lot in a few short seconds. I advocate intentionally calling at a time when you are unlikely to reach your prospect directly and leaving a carefully scripted message:

> *"Hello, this is Bobbi Wildcat calling from Community Hospital's Wellness Works. I want to be sure you know how to access our services if the need arises. We are on the corner of Highland and Route 9 and are open from 7:00 a.m. to 7:00 p.m., Monday through Friday. Our specialty is working with employers to help them reduce their workplace health and safety costs. If you have any questions, please call me at 868-2200, and I'll get back to you right away."*

The secret is scripting. Polish your script and then be prepared to say it with warmth, conviction, and self-confidence.

A consistent theme runs through each of these activities: they cost virtually nothing, consume little staff time, and are brief and to the point. Taken as a single point of communication, their value is negligible; taken as an aggregate of twenty communication moments per year, their sum impact is considerable.

Marketing has become less a matter of expensive, dramatic events and more the delivery of a simple message delivered over and over again.

Take the following three golden marketing principles to the bank:

1. Develop a short, meaningful message.
2. Isolate the receipt of that message to a time and place when your message is not competing with other messages (e.g., Monday morning email, late afternoon voice mail, midweek personalized letter).
3. Repeat the message over and over again using multiple modalities (e.g., email, voice mail, personal mail).

This conceptual leap in marketing comes with an additional piece of good cheer: such techniques offer a considerable return for little cost. It is not a matter of money—it is a matter of tenacity.

Chapter 3:

Marketing Tactics

Marketing strategies, as presented in chapter two, represent the philosophy and overall plan for enacting a comprehensive marketing strategy. Marketing tactics are specific marketing techniques used to execute the strategies.

Marketing Principles

In designing and choosing among possible marketing tactics, numerous principles apply:

1. **Adapt** — Unlike marketing strategies, which tend to be relatively constant over time, marketing tactics are highly dynamic and can change rapidly. There seems to be two major reasons:

   First, tactics burn out quickly. Email blasts were the rage circa 2002, but they oversaturated the market only a few years later. What was yesterday's most innovative idea became today's annoyance.

   Second, marketing is driven to a great extent by technological advancement. Invent a fax machine, and fax blasts take over the world for a while—the same with email. The latest technological wave may be smart phone marketing, with messages that can be targeted, timely, direct, and brief.

   Remain abreast of the latest technology and constantly explore how such technology is being used by other industries to reach the masses. Embracing technology provides you with a classic opportunity for innovation.

2. **Reach out** — Remember the overwhelmed consumer mentioned in chapter two? He or she has a limited attention span and is likely to be tired of traditional marketing tactics. If this describes your target audience, high-touch marketing, in which your tactics bring you face to face with your prospect universe, is a viable solution.

   High-touch marketing enables wholesale exposure to the potential buyers of your services. It requires a marked shift in emphasis toward events, such as social networking, personal contact through on-site education, and mixer opportunities. It shifts you away from more traditional forms of marketing outreach, such as email, letters, direct mail, and print media.

3. **Know your audience** — The selection of a marketing tactic should be driven by the nature of your audience and the message it needs to hear. If your program consists primarily of core clinic services, you are reaching out to a finite number of decision makers—often one at each prospect company. Because their needs are relatively consistent, so is your message: your ability to reduce their company's health and safety costs while enhancing the health status of the workforce.

   Alternatively, if your program offers blended occupational and immediate (urgent) care services, you have added a significant piece to your prospect universe: basically any individuals responsible for their own or their family's healthcare purchasing decisions. Such purchasing decisions tend to be influenced more by such variables as price and convenience than by outcomes (which may be perceived to be roughly equal among all providers of immediate care services). A different strategy is required for this group.

4. **Segment your market** — Once again we are running away from the "one size fits all" concept. Since every market possesses unique characteristics, different marketing tactics should be used to reach out to different segments.

   Common healthcare market segments might include:

   - **Industrial type:** Some markets are dominated by certain industrial classifications, such as the gaming industry in Las Vegas. Others are markedly heterogeneous.

- **Distance:** Some markets form common concentric circles around city centers. Others have employers clustered in a unique way.
- **Size and influence:** Some markets, particularly large ones, have a deep reservoir of employers of every size. Others are dominated by one or more large, influential employers.

Whenever a market has a unique configuration, devise your marketing tactics for both the unique segment and for "everyone else." You may employ nine tactics: five intended for all prospects and four others that are applied selectively to relevant sub-markets.

5. **Consider costs** — As discussed in chapter two, all marketing tactics are not created equal. Some may offer greater return than others, and each tactic is likely to require different financial and human capital costs. Rate every marketing tactic's projected return (e.g., What is the likelihood our message will be heard, by whom, and by how many?). Estimate costs in order to project return on investment. What out-of-pocket expenses do you require to execute this tactic? How much time will it take, and who will be responsible for this time? Do not neglect opportunity cost; if your program did not execute this tactic, what would it be doing instead?
6. **Employ multiple tactics** — Execute multiple marketing tactics in almost every instance. Certain tactics may appeal more to some, whereas other tactics may appeal more to others. Some work out as well as or better than predicted; others fall short of expectations. Some still usable tactics are time honored and not ready to be retired quite yet, whereas others are more experimental and may not pass the reality test.

   Hedge your tactic bets. Five to ten different tactics during a one-year cycle seems about right. A reasonable mix might include:

- Three time-honored tactics, three recently introduced tactics, and three new experimental tactics.
- Five high-touch tactics, three electronic tactics, and two print tactics.

- Five one-size-fits-all tactics and five tactics devised for one or more special sub-segments.
- A little something for everybody. A mixture of pace to keep everyone on their toes.

A MARKETING TACTIC SAMPLER

A sampler of low-cost/high-touch healthcare marketing tactics might include:

1. **On-site education** — As part of our consulting engagements, we often ask employers how they would prefer to be introduced to a prospective provider of your services. A "call from a sales representative" often comes in dead last on a list of fourteen options, whereas the "provision of on-site educational services" tends to be the most preferred option.

   Why? Marketing must never be about self-serving gunk. Effective marketing involves giving the prospect something of value (such as information) and benefits from the halo effect of your efforts. Websites should be laden with helpful information (rather than a more typical litany of available services). Focus email blasts on transmitting useful information.

   Within this context, on-site education becomes a powerful marketing tool. It exemplifies high-touch marketing as you actually meet your constituents (especially valuable for programs that offer blended occupational health/immediate care services).

   When you offer on-site educational services:

   - Maintain an ample but not overflowing portfolio of educational offerings. If you offer a single topic, you may often offer an inappropriate lecture to the wrong audience. On the other hand, designing a new topic every time you go to a workplace is not a cost-effective use of your time. Develop about three different topics, fine tune each, and match each topic to your prospective audience.
   - Schedule one educational program a week and keep to your schedule. It is that numbers game again. A single one-hour program every week results in a penetration of 50 programs a year or 250 programs to companies over a

five-year period. What a way to build up relationships and overall community visibility.

> **Action step:** *Survey local employers and ask what educational topics they find most interesting. Pair these topics with individuals within your organization who know the topic, present it effectively, and are willing to go to the work site. When you are done with this exercise, you will have your three primary training topics.*

2. **Clinic tours** — A personalized tour of an occupational health or urgent care clinic was the second most favored option. This leads us back into the high-touch marketing arena. Once again, the notion of a numbers game is paramount. Complete three tours of your clinic every week and you have reached 150 companies a year or 450 over a three-year period.

   Do not leave the substance of a clinic tour to chance. Be certain that tour guests meet "all the right people" (e.g., medical director or other physician, billing coordinator), and that those individuals have appropriate questions developed in advance (e.g., encourage the medical director to ask a visitor, "Are there any unique circumstances about your workplace that we should know about?"). Orchestrate every minute of a clinic tour.

   > **Action step:** *Take a fellow staff member on a pilot tour of your clinic. Following the tour ask the staff member what they liked and did not like about what they saw. Use this experience as a foundation for a carefully orchestrated tour.*

3. **Clinic open houses** — An open house at your clinic tends to be a powerful marketing tool and is especially appropriate when there is something to introduce, such as a new or refurbished clinic or a new physician.

   In some respects an open house is similar to a clinic tour in that attendees are shown around and the time period is orchestrated to the greatest extent possible. Although snacks help, there needs to be a good reason for someone to come; that reason is usually some type of educational presentation. A typical open house leaves time for socializing, touring the clinic, and listening to a short (e.g., twenty-minute) presentation about a relevant healthcare topic.

Open houses should be offered as a cluster of three options. There are many who may want to attend but are unable to if the open house is offered only once. Do a pre-registration; although far from reliable, registration gives you forewarning if things are not going well, so you can make an extra effort (e.g., a telephone blitz) to enhance attendance.

> **Action step:** *Establish a series of dates and corresponding reasons to offer three open house events at your clinics.*

4. **Website marketing** — When it comes to healthcare websites, the norm is usually far from the ideal. When a specific service is based within a larger institution, such as a hospital or health system, many service lines seem fortunate to have even a link from the organization's main website.

   When you do get to the program page, you usually find little more than a litany of services. The service "website" is barely worth the cyberspace it is written on.

   Create dedicated service websites that go beyond merely listing services. Your website should offer valuable information, be dynamic, use photos and videos to cultivate images, give visitors something to do (such as answering a quiz), and be professionally designed.

   Do everything possible to get visitors to visit your website: Exchange links with other organizations. Add a link to every staff member's signature line. Include links back to the website from virtually any email that you send to virtually anybody on virtually any topic.

   > **Action step:** *Take a look at your website: Is it freestanding? Are there ample photos, quotes, and white space? Does it appear self-serving in any manner? Are there action steps? Is there a way to capture information about each visitor?*

5. **Social networking** — As mentioned, employers in many recent RYAN Associates surveys indicated that their least favored method of being introduced to a healthcare service is a sales call from the organization's sales representative. Although often necessary, establishing initial contact with people you have not previously met can be time-consuming and challenging.

   Explore methods to better facilitate such introductions. Whenever possible, find one degree of separation and go for it. You can meet prospects by asking colleagues, board members, personal friends, and even satisfied clients for a reference or an introduction.

   The best and most progressive method of generating direct referrals comes from social networking, and in particular, LinkedIn. A vast and rapidly growing number of professionals are now members of LinkedIn; such individuals invariably include a healthcare organization's target employer prospects. Once you link to a satisfied current customer or a professional colleague, you have access to *that* contact base, many of whom represent excellent contacts at priority prospect companies. An introduction made through such contacts not only can get you through the door, but also can provide you with a higher degree of credibility once you do get through that door.

   > **Action step:** *Join LinkedIn if you have not already done so. Once you are a member, send linkage invitations to every favorable employer contact you know as well as other professional friends and associates. If you are already a member, scroll through everyone's links and send invitations as appropriate.*

6. **Cause-related marketing partnerships** — If the worst way of getting a marketing target's attention is to tout your services in a self-serving fashion, the best way may be associating your service's name with a good cause and a well-regarded organization. You usually can find a fit fairly easily.

   Consider working with high-profile not-for-profits in your area. The American Cancer Society, the American Heart Association, and the American Lung Association come to mind. They all do fund-raising and offer other events within and for the community. Strike an alliance. By combining their outreach capabilities with your employer contacts, you can double down on the event's visibility. The halo effect that you are likely to achieve by being affiliated with both an esteemed organization and a noble cause can only be good for your service and organization. This is high-touch marketing 101.

> **Action step:** *Call three high-profile, not-for-profit healthcare organizations in your area and ask them if there is anything you can do to help them maximize their outreach to local employers. If they have events coming up, the answer will likely be yes.*

Websites

The emergence of the World Wide Web is to the new millennium what the automobile was to the twentieth century.

There are positive implications (e.g., the "one world/one people" concept and hastening of real-time communication). In another way, potential outreach can be ominous (e.g., predators and the newfound ease of spreading the rationale for worldwide terror). Yet the Web is a real tool, and its impact is only going to become more profound.

Just behind a new communications technology is its marketing applications. The use of service-specific websites is now commonplace in healthcare, although such websites are often lacking in creativity.

THE WAY IT IS

I reviewed the websites of eight leading healthcare organizations, and guess what? They all left any notion of creativity at the front door. The typical service-level website tends to be a verbiage-laden, artistically challenged, feature-oriented, physician-centric bore.

We are constantly reacting to yesterday's news. There is a tendency to think: This is how a website looks. We should create one like it. Yet aficionados understand that good marketing requires constant creativity. Use your website to set your services apart from the pack; be an innovator, not a follower.

GUIDING PRINCIPLES

There are several principles for developing a website that genuinely serves your purpose. The website should:

- Make consumers **want** to go there
- Encourage consumers to **return** again and again
- Transmit your **message** in clear and simple terms

PRINCIPLE 1: Get them there.

Give people a reason for visiting *your* site in a website-saturated world and make it easy for them to get there.

Providing motivation to consumers to visit your website goes beyond assuming they are interested in learning more about your services. Sure, some will visit to check out the address of a clinic or learn a little bit more about your services, but not many. Incorporate three additional emphases on your website: (1) make it fun, (2) make it educational, and (3) have it serve as a portal to other websites.

1. **Fun, fun, fun** — Okay great marketing minds, here is your chance. Make your website interesting, more personal, add humor, whatever. A typical website provides unexciting bios of key staff, often limited to physicians. Juice up your bios by adding personal or entertaining information, such as "Why I love my job . . . " "Bet you didn't know that . . . " etc. Spread the wealth. Consumers like team efforts: include bios/photos of as many staff members as possible. This does wonders for internal esprit de corps. Check out our company's bios at www.naohp.com. (Gotcha!)

   Another option is to offer a quiz with a monthly prize: perhaps dinner for two at a local restaurant. Base the quiz on an educational piece or forum that your organization has recently offered. Include photo galleries from recent events, such as a health fair or educational program. Photos really are worth a thousand words. Check out our photo galleries at www.naohp.com. (Gotcha again!)

2. **Teach them something** — Play the education card to get consumers to your website. The more you teach consumers about occupational health, wellness, or women's health issues, the more receptive your audience is likely to be. Offer a monthly tip, provide links to other relevant websites and articles, or post a summary of the latest workers' compensation legislation from your state. I will go to a website far more readily for educational information than I will to read a litany of features about an organization.
3. **Serve as a portal** — Construct a website that serves as a one-stop link to other health and safety websites. If I go to your website to link to another website, it is likely that I will stay "in the neighborhood" and look at your website. The name of the game is to "get them there."

   Do not rely on consumers deciding to visit your website out of the blue. Nudge them whenever you can. Printing your web address on business cards and literature may generate an occasional visitor, but quality marketing is not about the occasional. Push consumers to your website by offering them numerous direct links. Our staff's email signature line includes the phrase, "Check out our website: www.naohp.com." And our tip of the week (distribution: 5,000) contains numerous links. It is far easier to make one simple click than to access a business card to check out a website.

PRINCIPLE 2: Encourage return visits.

A one-time visitor is good; repeat visits are better. Two principles encourage repeat traffic: (1) make the website dynamic and (2) advise your potential user universe that it is constantly changing. Many websites are designed and left relatively unchanged. Once you have seen it, you have seen it.

By comparison, a dynamic website offers new twists (e.g., weekly tip, new photos, a monthly regulatory update). It is important to let the world know that new information has been posted. Here is where periodical (biweekly, monthly) email blasts and updates come in: combine directions to your website links with other material ("Just added on our website! An update on recent changes in state workers' comp law . . . ").

PRINCIPLE 3: Transmit your core message.

If your website serves as an important adjunct marketing tool, transmit your core message in a clear, concise, and benefit-oriented manner. This approach tends to relegate features to the back burner.

The core message of your website should feature:

- A statement of your competitive advantages
- Testimonials from satisfied users
- Photos of smiling staff members (hint: retake that photo of Dr. Grouch)
- As many hints as possible regarding what consumers value: effective communication, friendly staff, positive return-to-work outcomes, experience, training, and expertise

Many websites look as if they were designed in a ninth-grade multimedia class. Invest a little money and have your website professionally designed. Your website's quality (or lack thereof) reflects the professionalism of your entire organization.

The World Wide Web era is still in its infancy—a Model T Ford waiting for SUVs to be developed. Be at the cutting edge, and do not retreat into the comfort of the status quo. If you have fun with your website, then others will have fun too—and they will also remember your organization.

Clinic Tours

Sales transactions involve some type of commitment. In most instances, commitments are **hard commitments,** such as signing a contract or making a payment. Others are **soft commitments** and involve little more than a well-intentioned, nonbinding promise. The majority of healthcare sales transactions are soft; there is no guarantee that the prospect will use your services or clinic. You must increase the likelihood of a binding close by emphasizing the value of your product.

Follow-up to a soft close is advisable. Follow-up can involve high-profile activities, such as thank-you notes and email correspondence. It is better to actually involve the prospect in some manner, because it is often the key to closing a sale.

A clinic visit is an excellent way to instill a sense of commitment. A visit provides an opportunity to meet with a prospect or new client on your own turf and establish processes that are likely to save time down the road. Most clinic tours tend to be haphazard or even counterproductive. Carefully plan and orchestrate a clinic tour.

RULE 1: Regularly schedule clinic tours.

Establish a weekly clinic tour schedule. You could schedule two tours every Thursday at 2:00 p.m. and 3:45 p.m. Fill your open slots rather than inviting prospects only as opportunities arise. Two tours per week result in one hundred tours per year—a surefire way to bring in numerous new clients.

RULE 2: Schedule tours at times that make sense.

Do not schedule tours during routinely busy times (e.g., Monday mornings), or during usually quiet times (e.g., Friday afternoons). If your schedulers know that every Thursday afternoon is clinic-visit day, they can schedule an appropriate volume of visits during these hours. If possible, try to coordinate your tour slots during your provider's "administrative time," as it allows the provider time to speak with the prospect.

RULE 3: Make it easy for the prospect.

Email prospects a confirmation of the time, date, and location of the visit, where and how to park (with parking passes as appropriate), and a map with basic written directions to your clinic. Mention that your medical director looks forward to the meeting. Cancellations are less likely if the prospects understand that you have set up an itinerary and blocked out time with your medical director. Finally, provide the prospects with your cell phone number in case they are running late, and include a basic itinerary of their visit so they will know what to expect.

RULE 4: Involve your program director.

A clinic visit is an excellent time to introduce the prospect/new client to your service line director, who would then provide the actual clinic tour. If the director is unavailable, the responsibility defaults back to the sales professional.

Exhibit 3-1. Chronology of a Clinic Visit

MONDAY Invitation	THURSDAY TOUR SCHEDULE	
Close a sales call by inviting the prospect for a clinic visit.	2:00	Clinic staff ensures that clinic area is clean and organized.
	2:15	Director/sales professional meets prospect at clinic entrance.
TUESDAY Confirmation		
Confirm visit via email; include map and/or directions to clinic.	2:20	Director introduces prospect to registration clerk.
	2:35	Prospect completes prototype registration.
Email confirmation of clinic visit with a short prospect overview to the Medical Director and registration desk.	2:40	Prospect reviews computerized patient/case management system.
	2:45	Prospect meets Medical Director; briefly discusses nuances of workplace.
Post name and affiliation of your guest on the clinic bulletin board.	2:50	Prospect walks through the clinic (waiting area, lab, PT, check-out).
	3:00	Prospect meets with billing department.
	3:15	Director recaps the tour and walks prospect to exit or their vehicle. Sales professional joins in as appropriate.
	3:45	Begin second tour.

RULE 5: Standardize the tour.

Orchestrate every minute of the tour. Provide a soup-to-nuts walk-through to demonstrate typical patient flow. Always associate a "why" with a "what" and make sure that the why implies value. Do not say merely that you have six exam rooms; say that you have six exam rooms, which expedites patient flow and offers patients more privacy, which leads to greater patient satisfaction.

RULE 6: Plan conversations.

Brief the service line director on the prospect's interests or hot buttons and focus his/her conversation on these issues (e.g., "I understand that you are concerned with waiting time. We attempt to address this concern by . . . "). Highlight exceptional procedures designed to ensure optimal client communication. Minimize chit-chat or reciting the obvious (e.g., "This is an exam room"). Focus on the prospective "win-win" relationship.

RULE 7: Make introductions meaningful.

Train staff members to ask the "right" questions and script the "right" answers for them. A medical director might ask the prospect about their company (e.g., "What seems to be your company's greatest health and safety problem?"). As a result, the prospect will sense that the medical director genuinely cares about the needs of their company and is capable of providing customized services. Similarly, clerical staff can be instructed to describe specific aspects of the registration processes. Train all staff members to explain what they do and exactly why their approach provides value to clients.

RULE 8: Involve your prospects.

As a consultant, I have been through literally hundreds of clinic tours. They are typically uninspiring. Involve your prospects in some type of hands-on activity. Ask them to complete a prototype registration or patient satisfaction form. Offer them a complimentary cholesterol check. Have them try a physical therapy modality. Let them experience your team in action.

RULE 9: Complete client paperwork.

Find time during the tour to review and complete all required information (e.g., client profile forms) necessary to expedite communications and information flow. Introduce the prospects to a liaison in billing and have them exchange critical information to facilitate subsequent billing processes. Provide the prospects with handout materials, including maps and appointment cards, which in turn can be distributed at the workplace.

RULE 10: Summarize your visit.

If feasible, walk the prospects to their cars or the building exit. Show them that extra level of respect by staying with them until they depart. Parting words are usually the most important aspect of a sales call. Summarize the new relationship and the next steps as you part company.

A carefully planned and well-executed clinic tour is an exceptional way to move a near-close to a real close, develop mechanisms that will smooth the way once the prospects move to client status, and cross-sell additional services as multiple members of your team become better acquainted with the prospects. Viable clinic tours occur too infrequently and, when provided, usually fail to fully seize the moment.

Open Houses

The first time I heard the phrase "open house" was when the Cohen twins, Jane and Sue, had an open-house party in their West Hempstead, New York, backyard one summer night in the 1960s.

Of course, I went. It was a free party, after all. I recall doing "the Slop" (aka dancing) to Jan and Dean's rendition of "Heart and Soul." Ah, those were the days!

The phrase "open house" means something different to healthcare professionals these days. In general, it means opening the doors to one of their facilities and letting the public come by to have a look. Sometimes such events coincide with the opening of a new facility or a new program. Other times an open house is offered as a marketing tactic.

Open houses are seldom carefully planned. The prevailing wisdom seems to be to open the doors, let visitors in, and good things will inevitably follow. Such a passive approach, however, is invariably an invitation for squandering a wonderful opportunity.

STEP 1: Get them there.

Maximize attendance by emphasizing that it will be worthwhile for employers to attend the entire event rather than to stop by for the last twenty minutes. Here are some ideas:

- **Offer options** — Offer three options for an open house date and time in a single invitation. Mix the options over different days and times of day:

Tuesday	7:00–8:30 a.m.
Thursday	6:00–7:30 p.m.
Saturday	11:30 a.m.–1:00 p.m.

- **Include an educational component** — Provide a twenty-minute presentation on a relevant health or safety related topic, followed by a brief question-and-answer session. Offer a different topic at each scheduled open house to attract the broadest possible audience.
- **Ask for pre-registration** — Pre-registration via email or telephone will lend importance and credibility to the process.
- **Cap attendance** — Limit attendance at each open house in accordance with the size of your facility. Assume a projected 25 percent no-show rate. If you would like to have twenty-four people attend your open house, cap attendance at thirty-two. Asking individuals to pre-register and noting there will be a cap on attendance stimulates interest and enhances perceived value.
- **Provide appropriate nourishment** — Mention on the invitation that light, healthy snacks will be served, so participants know they can miss their usual meal if necessary.
- **Offer freebies** — Publicize the availability of free educational literature. If the presentation will be on heart disease, consider offering a complimentary cholesterol screen. Do not provide much (if any) literature about your program. When marketing, providing valuable educational support is worth two merit points; offering self-serving material earns two demerits.

- **Proactively recruit** — It is not how many attend, but the mix of those who attend your open house that is important. Ideally, you want a blend of 50 percent of your most highly targeted non-client prospects and 50 percent of your most supportive clients. Mixing prospects with your most enthusiastic clients is an excellent way to let others tell your story for you.

There are many ways to recruit. Promote the open house as an opportunity one cannot afford to miss. Ask relevant staff to place telephone calls to top prospects and clients and encourage them to register. Such calls may also be essential to prop up one or more open houses that may have sub-par attendance.

STEP 2: Manage the event.

Outline your objectives for the open house. Examples include:

- Orchestrating one-on-one face time with guests
- Demonstrating staff competency and expertise without making an overt sales pitch
- Engaging your guests in some sort of hands-on activity
- Facilitating a clinic walk-through
- Gathering intelligence about your guests' primary health and safety challenges

Carefully hone your open house itinerary to ensure that each objective is appropriately met.

Face time: Make the first half hour of the ninety-minute open house a social period. This is when guests can eat snacks and meet your staff. Coach staff in advance on how to actively mingle in order to meet each of the guests. By scheduling the social period first, you can ensure that late arrivals do not miss the substance of the event.

Expertise: This is where the lecture comes in. Match a strong, knowledgeable speaker with a relevant, yet not overly esoteric, topic associated with your service line. Be certain that the speaker minimizes the "we" when talking and focuses on the "you" (the prospect or client).

Hands-on activity: A simple cholesterol screen is a hands-on way to bridge any distance between the visitor and the medical provider.

Clinic tour: Break into smaller groups for the facility tour. If there are twenty-four visitors, ask six staff members to escort four different guests. The secret is personal attention; avoid conducting a group tour similar to what one might experience at a museum. Make the facility tour brief (a one- or two-minute walk-though), unless a guest has questions. The purpose is to project an overall positive image, not to give a recital on every room or how every piece of equipment functions.

Learn about your guests: Ask staff members to gear small talk toward workplace health and safety challenges. The guest speaker should try to engage the audience by asking everyone to say something just before the presentation.

STEP 3: Follow up.

As a rule, following up with those who attend the open house is relatively easy and not particularly time consuming. However, it is often overlooked.

Follow up with your guests as soon as possible. Send a brief email message thanking your guests for their attendance within twenty-four hours following the event. Include appropriate links to your web page and other relevant sites and add any personal touch that you recall from your contact with the person either before or during the open house.

If a guest expresses interest in meeting with your sales professional or arranging a work-site visit with your program director or medical director, act promptly on that request.

A carefully orchestrated slate of open houses offers you multiple opportunities to inform and impress clients and prospects. Include them in your annual marketing plan.

Workplace Education

Taking your "show" on the road has traditionally been a good idea. It serves as a branding opportunity for your broader organization, allows your service line to connect directly with scores of individuals, and it often sets up an employer prospect for further sales activity. However, there can be numerous pitfalls, and many services fail to properly execute this tactic.

TIP 1: Create a finite package of educational offerings.

Be wary of going too far in one direction or the other. Many programs create a one-size-fits-all presentation that is offered to every comer, neglecting the possible priority needs and preferences at individual companies. Other programs create innumerable education programs, many of which are a one-time-only talk tailored strictly to an individual company. This is not an appropriate use of your time.

The middle ground works best. Design three different presentations, master each, and provide the one that is most relevant to a particular company.

TIP 2: Select a topic of interest to the potential audience and one that is relevant.

The choice of a topic is often dependent on who within your organization wants to speak. The speaker's pet topic may be a good one, and he or she may be a polished speaker, but if the topic is not relevant to the prospective audience, the size of the turnout and satisfaction of attendees may leave much to be desired.

Use the presentation to create greater awareness of broader healthcare issues. If you are trying to educate and motivate your audience, why not deal directly with work-related health and safety issues? Unless you are an urgent care clinic, you should save important personal health issues for a different audience on a different day.

TIP 3: Seize the moment.

Take advantage of your exposure. Obtain the name and email address of everyone in the audience. Send personal information-oriented email blasts to individual workers. At its core, outstanding marketing is basically a numbers game. Assuming an 80 percent success rate, one workplace lecture a week before fifty employees could generate 2,080 individual email addresses per year. That equals more than 10,000 new individuals in only five years, providing an excellent branding opportunity.

TIP 4: Make it fun and add some pizzazz.

Graduates of our sales training program recognize that the best way to teach something is to create an interactive and fun atmosphere. Ask your audience for their opinion, offer little contests with some type of prize or reward, or do a brief pre-talk and post-talk survey. (e.g., "Let's see if and how your perspective has changed.")

TIP 5: Talk the talk of the common man.

There is both a dissonance between "provider-speak" and "employer-speak" and rank and file "worker-speak." Frame your message with simple phrases and present concepts that can be easily digested by the typical employer. Many healthcare professionals who converse in provider-speak all day find it difficult to alter their dialect.

TIP 6: Learn something from your audience.

Education is a two-way street. Ask members of your audience to complete a mini-questionnaire (perhaps three to five multiple choice questions) and supplement the quiz with show-of-hands questions (e.g., "How many of you . . . ?"). Use this information to customize your presentation on the fly as well as to provide feedback to your employer client. Ask everyone to write down "the one thing that their company needs to do to make their workplace safer and healthier." Results from such questions are often an eye-opener for the employer and may lead to greater opportunities for your service.

TIP 7: Post results on your website.

Many healthcare service websites are pretty boring and rarely change once they have been created. Ask several of the same questions at every work site and publish the composite results (e.g., "Across 2,000 employees in Gotham City, 23 percent felt that poor communication with senior management is the number-one deterrent to optimal workplace health and safety.").

After a while your "N" will be large enough to provide fascinating cross tabulations comparing local companies by size or industry classification. The more prospect companies are exposed to such information, the more likely they will want you to teach at their work site—and the easier it will be to keep your on-site education card full.

TIP 8: Keep a few relief pitchers warmed up in the bullpen.

The numbers game again. If only a single person is your go-to educator, your goal of one on-site presentation per week may quickly dry up. In these not-a-minute-to-spare times, too many people are unavailable for one reason or another. A goal of fifty programs per year could easily shrivel to ten programs, and your entire on-site education plan can be rendered only 20 percent as successful as planned.

Stock your bullpen with a few relief pitchers that understand the topics and buy into your approach to on-site education.

TIP 9: Place your talks in context.

I am an advocate of the oft-stated idiom: "Tell 'em what you're going to tell 'em, tell 'em, and tell 'em what you told 'em." Make this structure central to all talks (and sales encounters, for that matter): place what you are about to say in the clearest of context, and end every presentation with a brief synopsis of your key points.

On-site education is an outstanding opportunity for your service program and organization to gain exposure and meet your obligation to effectively serve your community. An educated and appreciative population will likely view your service line in a more favorable light, and an informed population can only be good for both your organization and the community at large.

EDUCATIONAL FORUMS

Providing health education seminars, conferences, and short courses is also a viable marketing strategy:

- Buyers need to know more about the relevance of many healthcare services. Employer decision makers are still strikingly naïve about the value of a well-integrated, proactive approach to their company's health and safety activities.

- Education comes off as less self-serving and is perceived as a "kinder-and-gentler" form of marketing. In our information-saturated world, it is imperative to find a way to stay in front of your prospects in an unobtrusive, yet memorable manner. Educational programs do this.
- A service that positions itself as an educator is inevitably also viewed as an expert—an important image to foster.

SEMINARS AND CONFERENCES

Typically, seminars and conferences are held at a local hotel or in a hospital or clinic conference room. These sessions are usually free, or participants pay only a nominal charge.

Seminars and conferences are more valuable for a new service that needs to introduce itself to the community, or for a service in a highly competitive environment that needs to distinguish itself. Although there is intrinsic value in providing such programs, their value vis-à-vis their opportunity cost is often questionable.

Live seminars and conferences require planning and advance publicity. They tend to consume scarce financial and human capital that may generate a greater return if diverted to other activities, such as direct sales or targeted mailings.

Still, offering such programs can be valuable under certain circumstances:

- If your service is new to the market
- If your service is far from the market leader and needs attention
- If there is a hot new topic (e.g., a new federal or state regulation)
- If they are not done too frequently

DEVELOPING A SEMINAR

Considerable forethought should go into developing an educational program. Keep these six points in mind when developing your seminar:

1. **Make your topic market driven** — Ask prospective participants what they want to learn. Survey your top clients. Give them some choices and ask them to state their preferences. Solicit their ideas for topics not on your list.
2. **Offer the program at a hotel, restaurant, or conference center** — Programs held in your own facility have a tendency to come off as either self-promotional or a "budget production." The optimal day of the week and time of day are variable. Midweek morning sessions with a continental breakfast tend to be well received.
3. **Charge a token registration fee** — Forget the "if it is free, they will come" maxim. Charge enough to at least cover your expenses and create a perception of value. What is nominal varies by market; $39 a person is about right for most markets. When I am invited to a "free" investment seminar, I seldom attend, assuming that the session is little more than a thinly veiled sales pitch. Your clients and prospects are likely to feel the same way. No freebies!
4. **Use dynamic presenters** — Organizations tend to wheel out their own inexperienced speakers, assuming that if their organization is the sponsor, services should feature or rely exclusively on internal staff. This tendency is counterproductive if the speaker's presentation style is wooden. If a less-than-eloquent staff member must appear for political reasons, ask them to make a welcoming statement and introduce the speakers. Conversely, if you have a "hidden gem" on your staff, use the session as an opportunity to let this person shine.
5. **Publicize the event well in advance** — Using multiple modalities, start publicizing the event four to eight weeks out. Use direct mail, e-mail blasts, calls to prime prospects, and even radio spots in appropriate markets. A big turnout makes you look good; a dismal one has the opposite effect.
6. **If need be, throw it into fifth gear** — If attendance looks disappointing a week out, do something about it. Ask staff to call employers personally (or leave a voice-mail message) to advise them that it is not too late to sign up for your program.

WEBINARS

As the technology for hosting a webinar becomes more sophisticated and their cost declines, they become a valuable, more economically viable cost alternative to live seminars.

Webinars, like email advertising, are quickly becoming a victim of their own proliferation as too many people are being asked far too often to subscribe to a webinar.

Consider the following when you offer webinars:

1. **Charge for the webinar** — Free webinars are available everywhere you look, and their complimentary nature usually suggests a transparent sales pitch. I get invitations to a free seminar almost daily and seldom read beyond the first line of the pitch. Charge a nominal fee and develop value for your product.
2. **Use an experienced, well-spoken moderator** — More often than not, webinar moderators sound more like sixth graders reciting their first oral reports than savvy healthcare professionals. Your moderator need not be particularly knowledgeable about the subject at hand but must be smooth, self-confident, and articulate.
3. **Mix up the curriculum** — Nothing sounds worse than a speaker sitting alone in a room droning into the telephone for an hour (or more). Add pizzazz to your webinar. Use stunning visuals, conduct mid-webinar online polls, offer question and answer periods throughout the program, and use multi-perspective panelists more often than a single speaker.
4. **Archive and follow-up** — Webinars should be recorded, archived, and available for post-webinar review. Many would-be registrants that are not available to join the live broadcast will still register for the webinar if they can listen in at a later date.
5. **Shoot for the moon** — Don't underestimate your potential to attract the "best and the brightest" as webinar faculty. After all, webinar faculty require only a free hour and a telephone.

   Securing notable figures to participate is often easier than it might seem. By illustration, RYAN Associates has conducted in-depth telephone interviews with three U.S. Senators, Orrin Hatch (R-UT), Howard Metzenbaum (D-OH), and Bill Frist

(R-TN), and even used Dr. Frist as the keynote speaker at our 2007 national conference. All we had to do was ask.

EMERGING EDUCATIONAL TOOLS

As time constraints became more pronounced, alternative educational vehicles take on more appeal. The two most popular electronic media appear to be email correspondence and programmatic websites.

Astute use of email is a staple of strong marketing efforts. Yet caution must be taken to use this tool judiciously. There is a thin line between using email to your advantage and irritating your prospects with spam. You are less likely to overstep your boundaries when your messages are educational in nature. Clients and prospects are more likely to open and read email—and remember the sender (a central marketing principal)—if they feel they will learn something of value.

RULE 1: Keep it brief and do it often.

You are likely to see greater benefits if you send a brief (a few sentences) email educational piece once a week than if you send a lengthy message twice a year. People will read a short educational tip more readily than a lengthy feature. Save the feature-length presentations for your monthly or quarterly newsletters.

RULE 2: Make it relevant.

Offer tangible tasks (e.g., "track consecutive workdays without a reported work injury by posting the number of days in a prominent location") rather than offering trivial facts or meaningless statistics. Make your prospects want to forward your email to their colleagues.

RULE 3: Build your email address book.

A numbers game again—if you have one thousand email addresses rather than five hundred, you reach twice as many people, and it won't cost you any more.

WEBSITE STRATEGIES

Look for ways to use your website as an educational tool.

RYAN Associates publishes a "Tip of the Week," which is

transmitted weekly via email to thousands of healthcare professionals. Our website (www.naohp.com) contains a complete library of all previous Tip of the Week topics, categorized by subject matter. People who access our tip library become more familiar with our broader range of services.

You also should provide educational training via the Internet. Although this mode of training is becoming more common (and hence less unique), it still is not a widely accepted option in many companies. Recent RYAN Associates' focus-group research addressed this issue and found employers were cautious about such training for two reasons: (1) many employees lack access to the Internet at work, and (2) hands-on, personal interaction is well accepted and has greater impact.

The most appropriate use of the Internet for educational purposes at this juncture is to target key decision makers (upper management at client and prospect companies) rather than the rank and file. Even this strategy is not necessarily a winner since many potential subscribers remain uncomfortable with the technology.

Healthcare professionals are, by definition, educators: whether they educate at the employer, individual worker, or coworker level. We are not selling a rock-hard commodity, but rather an intricate concept: worker health and wellbeing.

There is a prominent place for education in our marketing efforts. The nature of educational outreach varies in each location depending on such variables as market size, market leadership, service maturity, and consumer preferences. Once you have defined a service's position in the marketplace, craft education into the service's broader marketing strategy.

USE EMAIL TO MAXIMIZE OUTREACH

Remember those days way back in the twentieth century when we actually spoke on the phone, wrote letters, and sent faxes? Seems like a long time ago indeed! Email and its cousins—voice-mail and text messages—have long since overtaken these modalities as the most expeditious way to communicate.

Consider some of the advantages:

- **Transmission is instant** — Time is money in sales; instant is good.
- **Email provides a record** — Effective sales are in the details, and email trails can preserve this detail in an easy, organized manner.
- **Messages can be personalized** — Even a generic email can quickly be tailored to make it personal. Developing highly personal contacts is vital in sales.
- **Short messages are easy** — It doesn't take a lot of time to write a short message. Are you always in a hurry? You can write an effective email in less than a minute, and who knows how many in an hour. Compared to the old days, you can become an icon of productivity.
- **Attachments supply critical information** — Email facilitates the use of attachments, which provides the sales professional with leverage to get critical information in front of prospects, clients, and internal personnel in a heartbeat.

What is necessary for the sales professional to become an email master, not just an email user? Consider four constituencies as central to your email strategy:

1. Individual prospects and clients
2. Collective prospects and clients
3. The service core team
4. The broader institutional support team

Send individual prospects an email before heading into a meeting, immediately following a meeting, and periodically throughout the full sales cycle.

Send clients a "just checking in" email from time to time. Use email at the collective prospect/client level, involving any client (list A) or prospect (list B) from which you can obtain an email address.

Email facilitates effective internal communication as well. Internally, make judicious use of electronic carbon copy (CC) and blind carbon copy (BCC) options in most of your external communications to keep colleagues up to date on successes, challenges, and information tidbits. The notion of the "right hand not knowing what the left hand is doing" should no longer be such a paramount problem. Double-check the send line to ensure that you are not inadvertently sending a sensitive message meant for internal distribution to an external recipient!

Email is a good way to stay on the radar screen of senior administration in your organization. A monthly sales summary email is a good way to get credit where credit is due and bring attention to a service that may be suffering from lack of visibility.

THE WHEN

Guidelines governing when emails should be sent tend to fall into two categories: rapid response and isolation.

The rapid response strategy suggests that sending an email shortly after an encounter is as important as the content of that email. Thanking a prospect for finding time to meet with you and summarizing key points from your meeting suggests diligence and professionalism on your end. Such a rapid response creates a halo effect of efficiency, which puts your entire organization in a favorable light.

The isolation strategy involves sending email or email blasts at a time and day of the week in which it is most likely to be read and absorbed. It makes sense to have your emails received during the day rather than early in the day when one's box may be cluttered with other overnight junk emails. Send email blasts on a Tuesday or Wednesday, after the Monday rush is over and before end-of-the-week fatigue has set in.

THE WHAT

Make your email short, and then even shorter, and create customized templates.

We live in an age of sound bites. People like their information short and sweet. Make your emails short, get in the spell-check habit, and proofread every word carefully.

Develop a set of frequently used email messages that can be modified slightly for individual recipients. In some cases, design an email message as a generic template from the start.

A well-written email can be archived to use later when similar conditions arise. The same rules apply: keep it simple and do it quickly. Use the time you save for other sales-enhancing activities.

THE HOW

An email-oriented marketing strategy begins with a commitment to make your email address library as large as possible. Equate the importance of obtaining an individual's email address with the importance of getting a person's name. Always ask for an email address, explain how and why you plan to use it, and be sure to confirm the address.

There are three other points to consider:

1. **Pursue correct email addresses** — Do not surrender when you get a rejected email (or a lengthy list of rejected messages following an email blast). It is worth the effort to call the intended recipient to get a correct address.
2. **Use your email program's address book** — I have over a thousand email addresses in my professional email address book and find that I save untold hours by not having to look here, there, and everywhere for an email address.
3. **Distribute specialized email messages to sub-groups** — Use distribution lists for subsets of prospects or coworkers, such as clients vs. prospects, former clients, or a special type of employer prospect.

Do not underestimate the power of an effective email strategy. Those who embrace email likely prosper; those who do not, do so at their peril.

Exhibit 3-2. Tips for Effective Use of Email

1.	Create a family of generic emails.
2.	Archive any email you particularly like for future modified use.
3.	Send a follow-up note to prospects after every meeting or call.
4.	Check in with clients periodically via email.
5.	Use educationally oriented email blasts to prospects and clients.
6.	CC or BCC staff on most external email correspondence.
7.	Periodically provide senior management with a sales status email update.
8.	Send follow-up emails within hours of a meeting.
9.	Send email blasts early in the week.
10.	Keep all email messages markedly short.
11.	Obsessively collect email addresses.
12.	Immediately follow-up on rejected email messages to get the correct address.
13.	Make extensive use of your email address book function.

Connectivity

The title of the popular soap opera *As the World Turns* is an apt way to describe the business world in which we now operate. We are in the midst of a period of rapid change that requires us to adjust to a new set of rules.

Three words tend to embody this new reality: **leverage**, **integration**, and **alliances**. These three words apply to sales and marketing as well.

LEVERAGE

Dictionary.com defines leverage as "exerting power or influence on." Assuming your organization possesses external and internal contact bases, the question becomes: How do you leverage these relationships in order to expand your book of business?

- **Ask your friends** — Ask human resource or safety directors at client companies with whom you have a good relationship to send an email blast to their peers at other companies recommending your program. Provide them with a sample script to jumpstart the process.
- **Obtain personal email addresses** — Obtain personal email addresses from key contacts at all of your client companies. With national personnel turnover rates in excess of 20 percent annually, many of your best contacts will be here today, gone tomorrow. By staying in touch via personal email, you become positioned to cultivate a relationship with the contact's next employer.
- **Ask your teammates** — Send an email note to multiple individuals within your own organization asking them for the names and email addresses of appropriate contacts they have with local employers. Depending on your colleagues' seniority and dependability, you can even ask them to call or email contacts on your behalf. After all, you play for the same team!
- **Ask your Board** — Leverage your own organization's board of directors. Board members tend to be well connected and highly respected, and they usually know a disproportionate number of CEOs. Ask board members if they are willing to send an email or letter or to make a phone call to several of their best business contacts.

Cause-Related Marketing

The opportunities in cause-related marketing are by no means restricted to specific affiliations. Stepping up to help deal with local (or national and even international) disasters can make sense on many levels. Consider a flood, an earthquake, or a major fire: Your program's marketing machine can be revved up to serve as an instant fund-raiser or awareness facilitator to help provide relief to victims. You could support community efforts to help provide relief, both monetary and non-monetary, to the cause.

A healthcare organization's inherent raison d'être is serving those in need. The more you visibly support this role, the more you will enhance your brand name throughout your community.

Marketing should evolve beyond traditional touches to a strategy that positions the organization as a true community asset. Social responsibility makes consumers take notice. Succeed in this regard, and only good things will follow.

BRANDING

It seems as if branding has been around forever. Create a common brand name and provide a halo effect for each delivery area or component. This silo mentality often gets in the way of pulling related services together. To offer products to customers via different avenues while branding them similarly is a contradiction in terms.

Of course, branding is a good idea—and an occupational health program is an ideal foundation for pulling together and levering multiple services under a common banner. It is another example of effective integration.

NEW ALLIANCES

Economic recessions tend to trigger new alliances. Alliances can be with other healthcare organizations (e.g., a local specialty group), a non-institutional healthcare player (e.g., the local chapter of the American Heart Association), or organizations outside of healthcare (e.g., the Chamber of Commerce).

Alliances can create win-win scenarios. A given organization can provide skills or expertise that the other organization lacks. The alliance can generate marketing economies of scale in which both entities double down on their marketing effort. An alliance offers an opportunity to merge each organization's client or prospect base, thereby creating a considerably larger and highly qualified universe.

The halo effect noted previously applies to alliance building as well. Assume your organization has created an alliance with your local Chamber of Commerce to jointly sponsor a community-wide wellness initiative. In most cases the Chamber's involvement would lend credibility and your organization would benefit from the good will the Chamber name is likely to engender.

Avoid being mired in the go-it-alone strategy of the previous decade. Challenging times call for innovative solutions. Organizations that master the art of leverage, integration, and alliance-building will significantly increase their likelihood of success.

EMPLOYER SURVEYS

"Keep your ear to the customer" is a central tenet of effective marketing. There are many ways to listen to the customer, and there are many customer subgroups—including patients, employers, carriers/payers, attorneys, specialists, and other entities.

Remain close to these constituents by using multiple modalities, such as meetings, emails, periodic phone calls, seminars, patient satisfaction instruments, and questionnaires.

WHY ASSESS?

Services often rely on intuition or anecdotal information to assess how they are viewed in their community. This information invariably lags behind the reality of recent events.

A simple questionnaire survey with any company that has used your services during the past year can:

- Indicate how well you are doing in a variety of service areas and be used to obtain suggestions for improved performance
- Produce accolades that may be used in marketing materials (testimonials, cost-savings outcomes) and to boost staff morale
- Identify cross-selling opportunities
- Provide you with a "heads-up" in areas that are slipping and, conversely, supply objective validation of service improvements
- Create enhanced public relations merely by asking clients to give you feedback (e.g., "Your opinion counts.")

HOW TO ASSESS

Consider the following when undertaking a questionnaire assessment:

- Conduct the survey annually, preferably at the same time each year.

- Offer the survey electronically. Survey Monkey is an example of a functional yet cost-effective service.
- Offer a "paper option" as well for respondents who are uncomfortable about responding to an electronic survey.
- Keep the survey simple and short.
- Ask respondents to review and update master company information from your database. The contact information can be included at the end of the electronic survey.
- Send out a second questionnaire or email alert to non-respondents after a few weeks.
- Offer the chance for respondents to win a prize. The prize can be something simple, such as dinner for two at a local restaurant or four movie tickets.
- Thank all respondents following the project via a letter or email and include selected findings from the annual assessment (e.g., "We appreciate your comments, and here is how we are responding.")
- Mix open-ended questions with scaled responses to obtain qualitative and quantitative information.

WHAT TO ASSESS

The sky is the limit, although there are some core issues that need to be addressed. Ask respondents:

- What they think of your service and what you can do better.
- If there are additional services that may be of value to their company.
- If there are one or more staff members affiliated with your program who warrant special recognition.
- What they think of various aspects of your service using a scale of 5 (excellent) to 1 (poor). Rank order the results of these aspects and compare them from year to year.
- How receptive they are to anything new in your service: a re-configured waiting area, changes in hours, a new marketing tactic during the previous year. What do your clients think?

- Any other pressing issue of the moment. Thinking about opening a new clinic or introducing a new product line? Seek insight from your constituents.
- If they are willing to let you use their open-ended comments for future promotional purposes. Add approved comments to a testimonial library that can be used in various ways in the future.

SATISFACTION SURVEYS

Survey data, particularly when it can be compared to prior years, is invaluable; but the value of the annual employer questionnaire can go beyond the numbers to the heart of program visibility.

Your constituents appreciate being asked their opinion. It does not hurt to make that point in your cover letter and email overview:

> *"As a valued client, your opinion is important to us. We are interested in your thoughts about, and suggestions for, our program. We hope that you can find the time to complete the enclosed (electronically linked) survey so that we might make our program even better for your company and others that we serve in the area."*

A questionnaire survey assessment provides you with as many as three more opportunities to stand before your best clients (initial survey request, follow-up request, and dissemination of results) in a professional client-centered way.

Similar to other productive marketing tactics, conducting an annual employer survey is not particularly time consuming or expensive. It provides an excellent way to stay in touch with your best customers, learn more about the community's perception of your services, maintain an up-to-date information base, and remain visible.

EXHIBIT 3-3. SAMPLE EMPLOYER SURVEY QUESTIONS

- *"What is your overall opinion of the WorkWell wellness program?"*
- *"What do you like best about the WorkWell wellness program?"*
- *"What does WorkWell Wellness need to do to be even more valuable to your company and other companies in the area?"*

EXHIBIT 3-4. CLINIC PERFORMANCE STRATEGY, 5-TO-1 SCALE

	5	4	3	2	1
Patient waiting time					
Parking					
Billing efficiency					
Staff professionalism and courtesy					
Results turnaround time					
Facilitating an early return-to-work					
The quality of medical care					
Overall cleanliness of the clinic					
"Bedside manner" of clinic physicians					
Effectiveness of sales staff					
Management of specialist referrals					
Coordination of after-hours care					
Appointment availability					

Employer Survey Data

The first of hundreds of RYAN Associates' survey research projects was completed in January 1986 on behalf of the Cheshire Medical Center in Keene, New Hampshire. The world has changed since then, but much of the value and focus of that first survey project holds true today.

A review of national survey data tells us a great deal. Employer surveys in different markets that ask the same questions offer a global perspective.

One survey question involves employers' preferences for various sales/marketing tactics. We typically ask respondents to rate the

Exhibit 3-5. Preferred Marketing Strategy, 5-to-1 Scale

OUTREACH METHOD	NATIONAL AVERAGE
A free workplace educational program	3.60
An open house at the clinic	3.59
A personal tour of the clinic	3.44
Worksite walkthrough by a physician	3.38
Receipt of written material via mail	3.33
A bi-weekly educational tip by email	3.31
Phone call introduction by a physician	3.16
An educational seminar at a local hotel	2.97
Personal visit by a sales representative	2.92
An educational seminar via audio/web hook-up	2.90
Phone call introduction by a sales representative	2.75

perceived effectiveness of an array of outreach methods on a scale of 5 to 1, with 5 very effective and 1 not at all effective. Although results vary somewhat by market, the aggregate results are notable (**Exhibit 3-5**). Several messages seem to emerge from these data:

1. Educational programs, particularly those delivered directly at the workplace, are popular and serve as an excellent marketing tool. Similarly, open houses and personal tours are favored by employers and should also be central to employer outreach.
2. Personal visits and telephone calls from sales professionals are at the bottom of the list. This result does not imply that calls should not be made; to the contrary, they are usually crucial to success. The take-away is that sales professionals must proceed gingerly and respectfully when scheduling and conducting sales calls.
3. Webinars, while gaining traction, still do not seem to be a preferred marketing tactic in the eyes of employers. Survey respondents may fear a hidden cost; emphasize low-cost access to your webinars.

SALES PROFESSIONAL CONTACT

We also ask respondents if they recall having contact with a sales professional representing a particular healthcare service. The aggregated

EXHIBIT 3-6. SALES PROFESSIONAL CONTRACT

RESPONDING EMPLOYERS	NATIONAL PERCENTAGE
Personally met the sales professional	20%
Only phone/email contact	11%
No contact whatsoever	32%
Do not know or recall	37%

data, presented in **Exhibit 3-6**, provide some interesting insights.

Whoa, Nellie! Fully 80 percent of responding employers across all sites do not recall engaging in a face-to-face sales call, and 69 percent do not recall contact of any sort. Virtually every company in your market should hear from your program at least monthly (e.g., monthly email blast).

PERFORMANCE MEASURES

Another question asks respondents who have experience with our client's sales professional to rate performance on a scale of 5 to 1, where 5 = exceptional and 1 = poor (**Exhibit 3-7**).

EXHIBIT 3-7. SALES PROFESSIONAL PERFORMANCE, 5-TO-1 SCALE

RESPONDENTS' RATINGS	PERCENTAGE
Exceptional performance (5)	45%
Very good performance (4)	28%
Average performance (3)	16%
Below average performance (2)	7%
Poor performance (1)	4%
Scaled response	4.03

When respondents were asked about qualities of the sales professional, common responses were:

"Professional"

"Very up-front and personal"

"Gave a ton of information . . . explained problems"

"Wants to make a big difference"

"Represents a well-run organization"

The prototype healthcare sales professional appears to be friendly, professional, and diligent. Typically, general product knowledge and poor understanding of classic sales principles appear to be weaknesses.

What might we gather from these data?

1. Bring education directly to the workplace.
2. Schedule as many clinic tours as possible.
3. Come across as the "un-sales person" by showing an ultra-professional side.
4. Reach out to all prospects so few employers can claim they have never heard from you or heard about your service.
5. Understand your product; knowledge is king.
6. Learn and practice basic sales skills.
7. Periodically take your program's pulse through professionally executed market research in order to obtain greater insight and address any performance limitations.

EMPLOYER-PROVIDER TASK FORCE

Creating an employer-provider task force (referred to by some as advisory councils) as an adjunct marketing vehicle is hardly a new idea. Heck, I helped put one together way back in 1982. Such groups run the gamut from exceptionally successful to barely functional.

WHY A TASK FORCE?

Whether you are starting a group or reinvigorating an existing one, first define why you want to have a task force.

The following values may apply:

1. **As advisers** — An employer group can provide your organization with an ongoing vehicle for insight, advice, and spot checks on your performance and growth plans.
2. **As a publicity vehicle** — In this age of cost-consciousness, provider-employer partnerships tend to play well with the media and in the community at large.

3. **As a retention strategy** — If a handful of high-volume clients really drive your program, a seat on your task force provides a hedge against losing them to a competitor.
4. **As an entrée to targeted prospects** — Are there a handful of prospect companies that you would like to bring on as clients? A seat on your task force is a good place to start.
5. **As a credibility enhancer** — Know a "mover and shaker" in the community? A slot on your task force would add credibility to the council and to your service.
6. **As a community outreach mechanism** — Multiple clinic locations could result in multiple councils plus a super council. Assume your network encompasses several clinics in several communities. Why not develop a different council per community (or clinic) and have one or two members of each council sit on a super council?

TASK FORCE MEMBERSHIP

Determine the composition of your task force and exactly how it will function once you have defined why you want a task force:

- **Optimize participation** — In addition to internal personnel, an average attendance of six to nine council members per meeting is about right. To get that many at a meeting, you probably need twice that number of council members. Shoot for a council composed of twelve to eighteen members at any given time.
- **Put a cap on** — A council seat should be viewed as a valued commodity. Limit the number of seats (e.g., sixteen maximum) and add new members only as other members withdraw.
- **Strive for balance** — The task force should reflect a balance among company type, size, geographic locale, job title, gender, worker bees, and prestige members.
- **Establish finite terms** — Define a council term as a finite period, such as two years. You are ensured of more active interest during the term, and it establishes greater value to the council seat. If you are starting from scratch with fifteen

council members, appoint five members for one year, five for two years, and five for three years. Establishing a rotating new membership of five council members each year ensures a continuous supply of new blood and energy.

- **Throw the bums out** — A certain task force member misses three meetings in a row? Unless there are mitigating circumstances, membership should be revoked. You are establishing value.
- **Elect a rotating chair** — Historically, a representative from the provider side chairs most employer-provider task forces. Ask employer members to elect one of their own every year to chair the meetings.

TASK FORCE FUNCTIONS

Creating a task force is the easy part; getting the most out of the task force is another thing altogether.

In developing a highly functional task force you should:

- **Give them a charge** — More often than not, councils digress into self-serving marketing vehicles (e.g., "We do this, we do that . . . "), which quickly breed disinterest and then disintegration. The task force should provide solutions to significant workplace health and safety challenges. It might look into such topics as reducing absenteeism, implementing a more efficient community-wide communications process, or recommending effective means to educate workers on wellness issues. Let the council focus on a different theme each year and recognize the beneficial nature of the task force findings.
- **Create committees** — Two or three working groups can, at a minimum, speak a few times by phone between meetings. This allows individuals to address various sub-issues.
- **Keep it going** — Groups that meet as often as six times a year tend to create and sustain momentum. Ninety minutes per meeting is about right, with appropriate nourishment (e.g., breakfast, lunch). The optimal time of day (breakfast, lunch, after work) and day of the week will vary. Poll council members for their preferences.

- **Meet on neutral turf** — To minimize a self-serving image, *do not* meet at one of your healthcare facilities. Rotate the venue to minimize the same ol', same ol' feeling. A series of private rooms in local restaurants makes sense, as do upscale conference rooms at task force members' workplaces.
- **Publicize your efforts** — Once you have determined a given year's theme, by all means, let the world know. Send a press release to local media (e.g., "Local provider-employer task force tackles worker absenteeism"). Send the media periodic updates, and broadcast email blasts to your distribution list detailing task force progress and findings. Add a section to your website that includes a roster of task force members, including their photos and biographies.

Make council members feel their work is important (it is!), and do not be shy about publicizing the endeavor.

Your employer-provider task force provides you with considerable new insights concerning the employer perspective and ideas for

EXHIBIT 3-8. DEVELOPING A TASK FORCE

1.	Define the purpose of the task force.
2.	Allocate a desired membership level and term limits.
3.	Develop a balanced list of prospective task force candidates.
4.	Invite candidates to join with a clear definition of task force purpose.
5.	Poll task force members regarding optimal meeting day and time.
6.	Locate appropriate external meeting venues.
7.	Elect a task force chair for one year.
8.	Identify the task force's charge for the year.
9.	Begin submitting task force information to the local media.
10.	Add task force information to your website.

new products and services, and it is an excellent vehicle for taking the marketing high road.

Provider-employer partnerships go directly to the heart of many healthcare services. A productive task force is central to this partnership.

Advertising

It was September 1985. Ronald Reagan had just begun his second term as president. An all-Missouri World Series between the Cardinals and thc Royals was about to begin, and earlier that year Villanova shocked the college basketball world. The Farm Aid concert took place in Champaign, Illinois, that month, and *Out of Africa* beat out *Prizzi's Honor, The Color Purple, Kiss of the Spider Woman,* and *Witness* for Best Picture. Actress Keira Knightly and Olympian Michael Phelps were born.

And I established RYAN Associates. "Back in the day" paid advertising reigned as the king of healthcare marketing. In larger markets, television advertising was in vogue, radio ads were ubiquitous, and billboard advertising seemed to appear everywhere.

Healthcare organizations had little reservation about putting dollars into advertising. Although enhanced brand awareness is seldom a bad thing, logic soon dictated that paid media was akin to using a shotgun approach when a laser was more appropriate. That is, paid advertising reached the multitudes when only a few hundred employer decision makers could make or break an employer-directed service.

Paid advertising soon lost its luster and was replaced by various marketing tactics that continue to evolve to this day. So, paid advertising is a relic of the past? Not so fast.

WHY ADVERTISE?

Paid advertising offers value when:

1. **The parent organization is involved in a brand recognition campaign** — If the parent organization is making media buys to enhance or reinvent its brand name, touting your services is a viable, if not advisable, adjunct to this effort. Ensure that your

services carry a brand identification that is consistent with your parent organization, such as logos and the corporate name.

2. **The public has a role in choosing your services** — If you offer blended urgent care/occupational health services, reaching out to the public makes sense.
3. **You are introducing something new** — Assume that you have made a commitment to adding wellness services to your program or are opening a new health and fitness center. Saturate the market with new product awareness and associated visual images.
4. **You are entering a new geographic market** — Healthcare organizations are increasingly establishing new urgent care clinics in new markets, such as an outlying exurb or an even smaller community twenty to forty miles away. In most cases you should buttress paid media that announces your entry into that market.
5. **You offer blended services** — When you introduce urgent care services to your occupational health services, you have expanded your prospect universe to just about everyone. Advertising makes sense.

WHERE AND HOW?

Where should your program advertise, and what should it say? Certain advertising mediums make more sense than others:

Television: Television advertising is expensive and makes more sense in midsize to smaller markets or as part of a larger outreach campaign. A visual message can have a strong impact. On the whole, an investment in television advertising is not likely to be cost-effective for many healthcare services.

Radio: Depending on one's market, there may be value in radio advertising. It is easier to reach out to targeted demographic groups via radio, such as likely users of a blended urgent care/ occupational health clinic. Because the cost for radio time is relatively modest compared to television time, radio buys tend to be more effective in reinforcing name recognition—a central tenet in marketing strategy.

Billboards: Billboard advertising has been a common medium for healthcare organizations for many years. The rental (if not creative) cost of billboard advertising is comparatively modest and can have a strong impact on viewers. Billboard advertising works best when it generates a strong and sudden impact, since many viewers see it for only a moment while speeding by. If you commit to a billboard ad, a single compelling photo and/or a few well-chosen words work best; conversely, details or phone numbers minimize the billboard's impact. Using billboards might be helpful if you hope to convey a basic message through visuals or a simple phrase.

Yellow pages: The ultimate value of yellow page advertising is related to the frequency with which potential users use yellow page listings to identify a service provider. When it comes to choosing a healthcare provider, yellow pages are not used all that often.

There are exceptions: market challengers and new market entrants are advised to buy better (larger) yellow page space than their more entrenched competitors; what better way to look equal to or better than the competitor?

Cause-based marketing: In a broader, institutional sense, cause-based marketing (supporting or partnering with a well-known healthcare advocacy group within the community) makes sense. If you offer wellness services, you might do well by financially supporting local events sponsored by the American Heart Association or similar groups.

Online advertising: Online advertising allows you to take the cause-based marketing concept a step further by advertising on various web pages of allied organizations whose mission is consistent with your own. Paid advertising is one option, as are various types of complimentary advertising space exchanges.

Online advertising also provides an option to utilize various technologies at a reasonable expense. Video snippets, virtual tours, and interactive sections are all increasingly mainstream. In addition, online advertising provides broad opportunities to link the viewer to various areas of your service and/or parent organization's website. Better yet, online advertising provides the viewer with an immediate opportunity to instantaneously follow-up, ask questions, or register for upcoming events.

WORDS OF WISDOM

My father told me that everything in life is circular: whatever it is will come back around if you wait long enough. This seems to be true for both occupational health and wellness programs. In the 1980s, paid advertising was considered a good value for the money. At the time, few really understood occupational health or how to market it.

Since then, advertising has made less sense for the typical, streamlined program (one or more clinics offering a core array of clinical services).

The healthcare landscape has evolved yet again. Many programs integrate new and oft-times different services; programs are extending into outer markets; and visual communication—including the Internet—overshadows more traditional marketing techniques.

Although advertising is unlikely to be central to employer-directed health services, there do appear to be appropriate roles for paid advertising in our brave new world.

Chapter 4:

Marketing and Selling Related Services

The principles set forth throughout this book apply to virtually any healthcare service that can be offered to employers. This chapter offers an in-depth look at the marketing of three common service lines: (1) wellness services, (2) women's health, and (3) urgent care. Similar sales and marketing tactics may be used as well for service lines such as executive health, travel medicine, sports medicine, and children's health.

Many healthcare organizations or systems send multiple sales representatives to a given company to sell different service lines. There are three problems with this approach:

- It is a costly duplication of effort.
- It tends to upset rather than encourage potential clients.
- It runs in the face of the central tenet that integrated, holistic healthcare services are more appropriate than discrete, fragmented ones.

Healthcare organizations need to centralize the employer sales function. A sales professional for an occupational health program, for example, is well positioned to represent many other services available at the organization and can serve as a central conduit between the organization and the employer.

WELLNESS SERVICES

Like the ocean flirting with the shore, wellness programs tend to surge ashore with vigorous force and promise, only to recede back before charging right back to the shore again.

Back in the late 1980s—an eternity ago in some respects—wellness services were thought to be an appropriate adjunct to many occupational health programs. History has not been kind to wellness services, whether they were bundled as part of a larger initiative or stood on their own. The 1980s wellness boom was short-lived, and the concept of wellness services as part of a larger organizational program faded into obscurity. Longtime industry observers have noted that for every boom there has been a bust, and that every new bust seems to involve the same missteps that caused the previous bust.

WHAT WENT WRONG

In order to sell wellness services, it is instructive to consider what seems to have gone wrong in the past. Numerous factors appear to have contributed to minimal market penetration:

1. For the most part, wellness services are offered as stand-alone, à la carte services, such as a lecture on nutrition or an isolated smoking cessation program. Meanwhile, experts in the field caution against any type of wellness intervention that is not developed in the larger context of a highly integrated, long-term systematic approach.
2. Wellness services were usually sold as a commodity, not as part of a broad, ongoing relationship with employers. Employer-directed services are inherently a broad-based, relationship-oriented specialty that spans the patient-care continuum (prevention, acute care, rehabilitation).
3. Services were seldom designed around the genuine needs of a company's employee population. Granted, health risk appraisals (HRA) have been available for decades, but they were rarely done in conjunction with a wellness program, and, when conducted, the connection between the results of an HRA and an ensuing intervention strategy was spotty at best.

4. Wellness services were seldom marketed (rather than sold), and in many cases the employer prospect universe was poorly educated about wellness concepts. Wellness services as stand-alone commodities invariably sat at the bottom of most sales professionals' portfolios, if they were there at all.
5. Sales professionals generally did a poor job articulating the value of a wellness program. The typical approach was to recite a series of platitudes such as "lowers cost," "increases productivity," "reduces absenteeism." On the rare occasions when actual data was rolled out to support the platitudes, the findings were often confusing or not meaningful to the prospective buyer.
6. More often than not, the person responsible for developing an occupational health program's wellness initiative did so as an adjunct to more pressing daily functions. The thinking goes something like this:

   > *"Of course we offer wellness services. Our nurse manager, Betsy Jones, possesses considerable skill in this area and can coordinate all requests."*

   Such a request pushes Nurse Jones and her organization into a corner; there are only so many hours available, and the resulting product is likely to be short on forethought and quality.
7. A fully objective evaluation of a wellness initiative is only as valid as the day that it is performed. For example, people lose weight and then gain it back. Habitual smokers quit for a while and then start again. New members join gyms and then rarely use the facilities. Results, per se, matter little, because they may be accurate only for today. Attitude change, on the other hand, may be more subjective and difficult to measure, but it offers more insight on the likelihood of a long-term effect on behavior change.
8. Data can be misleading. I recently reviewed a study that claimed a comprehensive wellness initiative saved a large company 600 percent in claims dollars in just two years; the purported cost savings claims seemed absurdly unrealistic. A 25 percent return on investment would seem to be more realistic, and therefore more impressive.

Unrealistically high ROI suggests slipshod methodology or hubris. Closer examination of the aforementioned study suggests an erroneous methodology that failed to account for a decline in workforce size, survival of the fittest among remaining employees, and a host of other potentially confounding variables that may have contributed to a dramatic reduction in claims costs. When it comes to using company claims data to support the effects of a wellness program, caveat emptor.

THE NEW WELLNESS SALES PARADIGM

One can hope that we have learned from our mistakes. The following principles support a new wellness services sales paradigm:

1. **Base each wellness package on needs** — A wellness program must be responsive to the genuine needs of a company's workforce. That is where HRAs and similar health assessment tools come in. A superior tool can provide a roadmap for a company to identify the highest-risk individuals, relate unhealthy health habits to lost dollars, and provide a multistage wellness intervention strategy. It begins, but does not end, with an assessment instrument. The results from an assessment instrument are often not interpreted, interpreted poorly, or do not lead to a prudent intervention strategy.
2. **Re-brand your product** — Wellness sales professionals are often victims of a legacy of errors. Many prospective buyers recoil at the mere mention of "wellness" because of previous experience. Do not enter the battle with one arm tied behind your back. Come up with a synonym that suggests a refreshingly new, modern intervention, such as "employee health enhancement."
3. **Wellness marketing drives wellness sales** — Marketing invariably drives wellness sales. The probability of success on a given sales call goes up immeasurably if the prospect is familiar with the sales professional's organization, services, and the inherent value of those services. Educate prospective buyers on the value of packaged wellness services and their associated ROI. There is not enough time in a typical face-to-face sales call to effectively walk a prospect through such concepts. A wellness initiative begins by educating your public. Think sound bites, testimonials, and the sharing of national success stories.

4. **Reflect your prospect's perspective** — When you sell something more conceptual than tangible, there is a tendency to offer a value-laden litany of features and rationale. Do just the opposite. Employ questions to understand the prospect's vantage point and encourage them to share their perspective. Useful questions might include:

   "How does your absenteeism compare with your expectations?"

   "How do you rate the overall health of your employees on a scale of five to one?"

   Followed up with, *"Why do you feel this way?"*

   Try to lead your prospect through a specific line of questioning:

   "Is the health of your workforce beyond reproach?"

   Which leads to, *"Why not?"*

   Which leads to, *"What can be done?"* and *"How will that affect your company's bottom line?"*

5. **Offer a taste** — I once sampled a tiny piece of cheese at our local supermarket. Going in I had not planned to buy any cheese, yet based on that taste, I purchased an entire chunk. A little taste of wellness might be just enough to pique one's interest. Consider offering a discrete service such as a weight-management program for up to five employees at each of twenty target companies. Granted, this is not the desired long-term, comprehensive plan, but decision makers tend to notice when participants return to their workplace as vocal advocates of your approach.

6. **Educate** — The more intangible your product, the more you become an educator rather than a salesperson. Rather than saying "you should" or "I suggest," use phrases such as "the data show," or:

   "It is understood within the healthcare community that a fully integrated approach generates the most significant long-term, positive impact on the health and safety of the workforce."

Do not necessarily ignore the negative in your approach. During an uncertain national economy, it may be better to bring it up, face it, and use it to your advantage than to ignore it. A compelling argument might be:

> *"In today's economic climate, companies are operating with leaner staff and limited resources. Their ability to sustain the health and well-being of every employee is exceptionally important. Your company's prosperity is contingent on sending the healthiest, most positive team to the playing field every day."*

7. **Go for it** — Many healthcare organizations' mission statements refer to the "good of the community," and we know that community wellness is an ultimate goal. In a nation beset by out-of-control healthcare costs and preventable mortality and morbidity, fostering wellness services appears to be mandatory. Every healthcare organization should place a high priority on wellness and ensure that they are tightly woven into the fabric of the organization's culture.

   The go-for-it mentality means resisting the temptation to dabble in wellness services. Every parent institution should ensure that there is a fully funded wellness department and that qualified personnel are in charge of wellness initiatives. It makes sense to create a task force that pulls together expertise from multiple areas (e.g., occupational health, employee health, behavioral health, women's health, consumer education) in order to create a genuinely integrated product.

8. **Aim for fewer/larger clients** — There seems to be a propensity in healthcare to view success in terms of the "number of . . . " The number of different clients receiving wellness services is often viewed as more important than a well-orchestrated wellness program at a single company. Base a long-term commitment to employer-based wellness programs on a successful model that can be replicated at other companies over time.

9. **Emphasize partnerships, not programs** — A wellness program needs to be more than just superbly conceived; it must be fully compatible with the culture of a client company. Such compatibility requires a careful assessment of a company's culture

done both subjectively through staff interviews and objectively through the gathering of intelligence. Detailed planning, ongoing mini-analyses, and a willingness to switch gears and revise a program midstream are essential.

10. **Cultivate workplace-based champions** — Avoid the "we understand/you don't" attitude that many bring to workplace-based wellness programs. Long-term commitment by the employer and their workforce is necessary in order to go beyond initial buy-in, maintain momentum over the long haul, and smoothly integrate new employees into the program. A wellness program should be viewed as perpetual, not finite. This paradigm shift is more easily accomplished when a client company appoints an in-house wellness coordinator to work with your organization on planning and implementation.

    The external wellness program's role should emphasize ongoing support and services. Outcome monitoring should be a joint effort. Once a prototype program is in place at a client company, your program can maintain contact with the company's wellness coordinator and simultaneously move on to develop similar programs at other companies.

11. **Blend objective and subjective analyses** — Many work site-based wellness programs use tired parameters to measure the success of their interventions. Such measurements often ignore potentially more salient measures such as attitude and behavior change. A balanced analysis should measure and blend traditional core metrics such as claims dollars per employee, absent workdays per employee, and the percentage of at-risk workers by multiple measures, with subjective findings such as understanding the relationship between risk factors and health status, program commitment, satisfaction, and attitude. A healthy worker population is essential to the health of our nation, and the workplace is an ideal venue to provide a comprehensive slate of wellness services. Driven by increasingly mature healthcare consumers and considerable economic pressures, wellness services will inevitably become a more pronounced aspect of our healthcare delivery system.

    The issue is not if, but how and when.

Women's Health

Women's health services provide another compelling example of how occupational health sales and marketing can redirect revenue to another service unit. In this instance, as in many others, the overriding objective of the healthcare organization is as much related to **generating demand** as it is to **usurping existing market share**.

As of 2012, for the first time in history, there are more women than men in the national workforce. Women have increasingly assumed roles in senior management, particularly human resources, and are more often than not responsible for healthcare consumption choices for their household.

Face-to-face or high-touch outreach to women is the best way to generate demand for women's services. The workplace provides an immediate venue to come in contact with thousands of women.

The logic of creating awareness in women's health services through the workplace is compelling. A package of reportedly excellent women's health educational lectures is available within many healthcare organizations. Increased direct educational and other outreach to women would enhance the number of annual gynecological examinations performed within the organization and would likely generate large volumes of screening examinations, procedures, and admissions directed to the system.

The volume potential is compelling. Assume that your organization conducts an educational program at four companies every month, each of which enrolls 100 women in the program. Thus, 4,800 women (12 x 4 x 100) would have access to information and would be more likely to schedule an annual gynecological examination within the women's health service.

Although the workforce population is arguably relatively healthy, one can safely assume that many women lack the awareness or will to schedule an annual examination. Even if only 10 percent of those exposed to an annual educational program opted to access services within the system, the result would be 480 annual examinations, hundreds of screenings, and a significant number of procedures and admissions.

Once a woman begins the process of using system resources for an annual gynecological exam, she is likely to return in future years. Hence, considerable new business generated for the system would be ongoing rather than episodic.

EXHIBIT 4-1. COMMON SCREENING EXAMS

SCREENING EXAMINATION:	FREQUENCY
Blood pressure	Once every two years
Blood glucose	Once every three years after age 35
Mammograms	Once every one to two years after age 40
Clinical breast exam	Once every three years
Cholesterol screen	Once a year after age 20
Blood pressure	Once every two years
TSH (thyroid test)	Once every five years after age 35

In addition, numerous other screens are common, driven by age (STD, HIV), family history (various cancer screens), or symptoms (fibroid screens).

Women's health is a prime example of a service line that can be promoted at the workplace and has the potential to generate considerable high-margin revenue.

MARKETING WOMEN'S HEALTH SERVICES

Several marketing strategies are recommended to employers for women's health services:

1. Offer live and/or audio seminars on women's health issues. Educational programs drive awareness and help educate the consumer base.
2. Reach out to individual companies to ensure that topics are geared to the specific needs and desires of that company and its workforce. Popular topics include alternatives to hysterectomy, incontinence, sexual function, and age-specific health services.

3. Create a massive email network using contacts from women's health outreach campaigns in combination with all relevant occupational health contacts.
4. Use an extensive database to distribute email messages containing women's health tips and updates. The format should encourage forwarding by recipients to other groups of women not yet in your database.
5. Sponsor women's health chat rooms for free-form discussion and on specific topics.
6. Emphasize one-on-one referrals, as appropriate, from occupational health and other primary care providers to women's health services.

Integrated women's health and occupational health services could become the next big thing in healthcare, especially if the workplace is astutely used as a vehicle to reach women with the message that their health and the health of their friends and family members really matters.

Urgent Care Services

The twenty-first century has seen a marked increase in urgent (or immediate) care centers. As in the past, many are freestanding and independently owned. Many others are hospital affiliated, or have emerged from occupational health clinics that wish to diversify.

In many instances, urgent care clinic marketing has not grown with the times. Two old marketing dinosaurs still seem to populate the urgent care marketing landscape:

1. **Direct mail** — The notion persists that if an urgent care center selects the right zip codes and demographically correct households within that district, business will follow. This ignores the reality that direct mail has minimal impact nowadays. Given its costs (printing, postal, distribution) and questionable impact, it is usually a poor marketing strategy.
2. **Paid advertising** — Advertising is another relic from a bygone era. Paid advertising, whether it is radio, television, billboards, or

print media is costly, does not target a narrow base of potential urgent care clinic users, and is largely forgotten.

STAND-ALONE URGENT CARE CLINICS

Stand-alone urgent care clinics, that is, those whose services *are not* blended with occupational health services, should consider the following marketing tactics:

- **Word of mouth** — If real estate is all about location, location, location, urgent care clinics are all about reputation, reputation, reputation. Word of mouth praise travels quickly to many quarters, and word of mouth criticism travels at an even more rapid rate. Consumers frequently choose urgent care centers based on convenience and price. Convenience largely means exceptional patient service and location, although factors such as hours of operation and the qualifications and persona of its providers are also important. Consequently, stand-alone urgent care clinics are encouraged to place greater emphasis and resources on strict patient service protocols and training than on paid media and other traditional marketing tactics.
- **Signage** — An urgent care clinic's best marketing can be done simply and inexpensively by ensuring that the clinic is in a visible location and that clinic signage is clear, professional, and memorable. Signage should:
    - Use large block letters that can be easily read
    - Include little more than the clinic name for branding purposes
    - Ensure that signage is large enough to be seen from as far away as possible
    - Be positioned toward heavy traffic coordinators, such as freeways, highways, or mall entrances
    - Be visible at night through various lighting methods
- **Email** — Other chapters of this book tout the wisdom of gathering email addresses at every turn and sending educationally oriented email blasts periodically. Urgent care

centers should adapt this strategy. Ask every patient for an email address. Privacy issues require that you get the patient's signature before you begin sending email blasts.

Staying visible and providing useful information to the consumer is a vital way to build market share through repeat business, family referrals, and positive word of mouth.

BLENDED URGENT CARE/OCCUPATIONAL HEALTH CLINICS

The marketing tactics recommended for stand-alone urgent care clinics apply equally well to blended clinics. There are several additional tactics specific to a blended urgent care/occupational health clinic:

- **Brand awareness** — A blended clinic provides name reinforcement and brand identification on both sides of the urgent care/occupational health corridor. As users of occupational health or urgent care services become more familiar with a particular brand name, they are more likely to feel comfortable receiving services from that brand. Mercy Occupational Health patients, for example, are more likely to become walk-in patients at Mercy Urgent Care, particularly when the latter is in the same building.
- **Email exchanges** — If the urgent care side of a blended clinic actively accumulates email addresses, it can exchange these addresses with the occupational health side so that both have a considerably larger base. Email blasts from the urgent care side to occupational health patients (who can include employees that attended educational programs or received flu shots and other inoculations) create greater awareness of the availability of urgent care services and lead to more urgent care traffic.
- **Cross promotion** — By including both sides of the house on the blended clinic's logo, you get double the publicity from every advertisement, brochure, letterhead, or email. Urgent care traffic is largely based on familiarity and confidence. Never cede an opportunity for cross promotion. A blended logo might look something like:

Mercy URGENT CARE

Mercy OCCUPATIONAL HEALTH

- **Employee education** — Most occupational health educational forums can be used to promote urgent care services and vice versa. Educational forums can include company-based education, multi-company educational conferences and seminars, online training, and webinars. A topic such as "Developing a Multi-faceted Prevention Program," for example, can appeal to both occupational health and urgent care constituents.
- **Overlapping clinic tours and open houses** — Unless a new or remodeled blended clinic has just opened, most clinic tours and open houses are likely to be on the occupational health side of the house. Yet any visitor who sees one side of the house either can see the other side or can frequently be apprised that it is there:

  "We also have six exam rooms and full x-ray services down the hall in urgent care, and our urgent care clinic hours are even longer than our occupational health hours."

Chapter 5:

Selling to Employers

Sales is the process of dealing directly with individuals or small groups to secure some or all of their business. Many services employ one or more full-time sales professionals with such titles as Sales Representative or Account Executive. Many smaller programs combine sales positions with other roles, most commonly Program Director. Far too often, programs tend to come up short in terms of a unified and effective sales strategy.

More Than One Way

Generating incremental business from employers can be accomplished in one of four basic ways:

- Through adept marketing only, in which there is no sales presence
- Just by showing up at a prospect's door
- Through a classic sales process
- Through detailed negotiations that may involve both oral and written presentations

APPROACH 1: Marketing only.

The first plateau can be misunderstood and is often undervalued. Considerable new business can be brought in without engaging in any sales whatsoever—that is, by executing a strong marketing plan. As discussed in previous chapters, if you can enhance brand awareness, define your services, and emphasize your competitive advantages, new business will follow. At the end of the day it may be more effective to design and execute an astute marketing plan than it is to meet face-to-face, one-by-one with prospective buyers.

The value of strong marketing in supporting the sales effort usually does not stop there. Effective marketing paves the way for subsequent sales even if marketing, per se, does not bring in incremental client business. The more familiar a prospect is with your organization's name, the more likely that a sales professional will get in the door and be shown respect.

APPROACH 2: Just showing up.

The second plateau embodies the famous Woody Allen quip, "Eighty percent of success is showing up." Even my beloved Labrador Retriever, Brava, could probably close a number of sales simply by showing up and wagging her tail. Often a given healthcare sales professional is the only person *ever* to visit a company. If so, why would the company want to consider any other program?

So far, so good. Market your services aggressively from afar and keep on "just showing up."

Not quite. The odds are that the larger companies that use a disproportionate amount of healthcare services are the ones that are going to make or break your organization, and these same companies are unlikely to be the type that will make a decision based solely on name recognition or a brief drop in.

APPROACH 3: The classic sales process.

The third plateau is the process where selling really begins. At this level, success is often contingent on being in the right place at the right time, or targeting your prospects.

Targeting means that the sales effort should be directed at the prospect companies most likely to use a large volume of your services. Although it is difficult to pinpoint projected utilization with precision, it is not difficult to estimate likely utilization. The classic approach for estimating service utilization has changed little during the past twenty-five years: it involves estimating work-related injuries by multiplying a company's anticipated injury rate (by standard industrial classification or SIC code) and the number of full-time employees (FTEs) at that company. Hence, an industrial classification that yields 6.1 injuries per 100 workers per year projects to an estimated 18.3 injuries per year at a company with 300 employees.

Two other predictors should be used to further refine the rank ordering of prospect companies by their potential value to your program:

1. The distance between the company's headquarters and your clinic
2. The company's history with your service and/or others in the area

You are going to stand a better chance of securing the business of a company close to your delivery venues than one that is more distant and closer to one or more competitors. A review of the company's history usually involves a subjective analysis of any previous relationship (either as a sales prospect or client) that your organization has had with a prospect company and their degree of loyalty to one or more of your competitors.

APPROACH 4: Detailed negotiations.

You are now ready to sell. Employ the following tactics:

1. **Keep your pipeline full** — Once again, the numbers game. If you increase the number of contacts in your database, your gross revenue should increase proportionately.

   A full pipeline means never having to say you are out of prospects. At any given time prospects are at various points in the sales cycle (e.g., initial contact, first meeting, follow-up meeting, closing activity).

   At some point you will have a good feel for how many new contacts you need to initiate each week in order to keep the pipeline full. At such a time a specific number of new companies can be added to the pipeline every week.

   Action step: *Develop an electronic sales pipeline summary report that denotes how many active prospects are in the pipeline and the status of each prospect.*

2. **Maintain an accurate database** — Your sales process will grind to a near halt if your contact database is filled with outdated or incorrect information. In an economy in which perhaps 20 percent of the workforce changes employers every year, it does not take long for a flawless contact base to go sour. Proactively update your contact base at frequent intervals.

   Action step: *Set aside a specific month each year to ask someone to call every employer in your contact database. Often a clerical, part-time employee or summer intern is assigned to this task. Confirm the accuracy of names, job titles, direct phone numbers, and email addresses.*

3. **Hire the right person** — I have provided sales and marketing training to more than one thousand would-be sales professionals since 1985 and have found many of them ill-suited for sales. The ideal sales professional should have a genuine sales persona, direct sales experience in some industry, and be able to relate to an employer's typical view of their own world.

   Reality is frequently quite different. Healthcare organizations are not accustomed to supporting a sales function and often seem unaware of what such a position requires. Healthcare services sales positions are frequently a landing place for someone within an organization with nowhere else to go or a fresh-faced newcomer with no sales experience. Total compensation is often low, which means the candidate pool is proportionately inexperienced.

   Hire an experienced sales professional. It is easier for an experienced sales professional to learn the healthcare product than for otherwise sharp healthcare professionals to learn how to sell. Set standards. Ask questions during a preliminary phone interview to elicit a candidate's fire for the job, and hire someone with a genuine ability to connect with personnel at the workplace.

Action step: *Make sure that a newly hired sales professional has previous sales experience. Compensate them in an appropriate manner. You get what you pay for!*

4. **Train well and supervise** — Whether or not the "right" candidate has been hired, the odds are good that a healthcare sales professional is not going to receive enough or even proper guidance.

   Many sales professionals have "graduated" from RYAN Associates' sales and marketing training programs since the first one was offered in 1988. Most end the course on the right track, but they often lack sufficient supervision or accountability to make the most of their newly honed skills.

   Meanwhile, sales professionals who have not gone through the training are prone to play the game with both hands tied behind their backs. No rules for the road, no fine-tuning newly acquiring insights, and, invariably, little or no guidance from within their organization.

   Every healthcare professional should be responsible to a direct report who also tries to master the principles of healthcare sales and marketing. It is all about collaboration and teamwork.

   Action step: *Healthcare sales and marketing professionals should meet with their direct report to establish detailed protocols for developing goals, working together, monitoring progress, and ensuring full accountability.*

5. **Provide appropriate performance incentives** — I have lived two different professional lives. In the first life, I was an employee on a fixed salary. I worked hard, but rarely after 5:00 p.m. Weekend warrior? No way!

   My second life, since 1985, has been as the owner and President of RYAN Associates. My income is entirely based on the company's performance, which has a great deal to do with the amount of effort I put into the business. During these years, neither time of day nor day of the week has mattered much; my work has been a 24/7 commitment.

Guess which life was most productive? The lesson could not be more vivid: provide appropriate financial incentives, and you are going to get a stronger, more focused performance.

Sales professionals tend to be under-compensated, and many either have no or misconceived incentives as part of their compensation plan. The National Association of Occupational Health Professionals (NAOHP) 2010 national survey of provider-based programs shows a median compensation level of $58,315 for an occupational health sales professional, with considerable variance by geographic region. Such compensation is markedly low compared to many industries and suggests the position is not structured to attract the best and the brightest.

Simplify compensation models. A sales professional's role should be to increase a service's gross revenue. Their incentive model should be based strictly on incremental gross revenue by comparing performance to previous years' norms or budgeted expectations.

> **Action step:** *Provide sales professionals with a base salary plus a performance incentive based on gross revenue generated above a baseline norm. Forget meaningless metrics such as number of new companies or number of sales calls.*

6. **Develop and maintain quotas** — The need to establish mileposts and due dates for all of your program's marketing activities is discussed in chapter one. Goals and quotas are as vital in sales.

   The only number that really matters is gross revenue. Metrics such as the number of telephone calls, introductory letters, or first sales calls help maintain a salesperson's sense of focus, but they are not an appropriate way to measure sales success.

   Setting goals, establishing quotas, and monitoring metrics are not necessarily inadvisable. Measures such as phone calls per week, initial meetings, follow-up calls, and percent of closes per live sales calls may be interesting but do not translate to gross revenue.

Action step: *Establish metrics that will keep your sales process focused, but do not mistake such numbers as an indicator of success.*

7. **Acquire the necessary tools** — Imagine a barber without scissors, a plumber without a wrench, etc. We all need certain tools to do our job well. Yet healthcare sales professionals often lack a full or appropriate tool kit.

   Do not let a sales professional into the sales zone without a full complement of supporting tools and materials. At a minimum, the sales professional should possess:

   - A company car or appropriate compensation per mile driven for work-related travel
   - A laptop computer with files that summarize relevant services and your complete sales universe database
   - A personal cell phone with email capability

Action step: *Avoid merely putting your toe in the water. Be certain that your service supports success by having the tools that will make it easier for you to achieve that success.*

8. **Create an electronic library** — An earlier recommendation emphasized the value of wowing your prospects with timely follow-up. Rather than leave a heavy stack of printed materials with a prospect, promise customized follow-up materials as appropriate.

   Electronic libraries can feature many elements. Include pages that describe each of your services, being certain to emphasize the value and benefit to the buyer rather than merely a description of the service. Similarly, maintain specialized client reference sheets and testimonial letters that may be sent to prospects who are looking for certain attributes.

Action step: *Create a directory entitled "prospect/client library" and add product descriptions, value statements, and opinion pieces as they become available. Constantly update and add to your library.*

9. **Involve your physicians and other senior professionals** — Timely involvement in the sales process by a physician, service line director, or senior administrator frequently seals the deal. Their presence at a sales call suggests to the prospect that your service is being managed by competent personnel, your teamwork is impeccable, and the service has a full blessing from the top. It is a great idea to bring non-sales professionals to such meetings—sometimes.

   Much depends on the interest and "stage presence" of the staff member. If they are eager to help, that will usually show in their demeanor and be a positive addition to the sales call. Likewise, some people light up a room with their presence, whereas others, despite admirable technical expertise, tend to turn the lights out. Be selective when involving personnel depending on their interest and personal presence.

   When you deem it appropriate to involve a senior staffer you should:

   - Brief them in advance on the objectives of the sales call.
   - Define everyone's roles and limits at the meeting.
   - Emphasize the value of brevity in any presentation or response to any question.
   - Conduct a debriefing session following the meeting (e.g., what went well, what did not go well, and what lessons did we learn).

   Action step: *Using email, inventory the amount of time that key professional support might be willing to contribute in order to assist with the sales effort. One hour per week, one hour per month, once or twice a year? Develop a mutual understanding of time availability and document that understanding.*

The Sales Call Cadence

Although every sales call is unique, seasoned sales professionals tend to recognize and practice a routine cadence in their calls.

THE STRUCTURE

The "Tell 'em what you're going to tell 'em, tell 'em, and tell 'em what you told 'em" axiom applies to live sales call as well:

> **Phase I: The first thirty seconds** — Articulate the objective for your sales call and provide your prospect with a "roadmap" for the course of the call. ("Tell 'em what you're going to tell 'em).
>
> **Phase II: The interview** — Conduct the sales interview ("Tell 'em").
>
> **Phase III: The last thirty seconds** — Summarize key points, reiterate action steps, and depart on a high note ("Tell 'em what you told 'em).

Remember the punch line in the shampoo commercial, "You only have one chance to make a good first impression"? What about the saying, "People say the most important thing as they are walking out the door?" These concepts should not be lost on the sales professional. The Golden Minute provides a structure for you to address the important first and last thirty seconds of a sales encounter.

PHASE I: The first thirty seconds.

As in any meeting or communication, the first thirty seconds of a sales encounter should be so well structured, rehearsed, and standardized that the sales professional begins every encounter with confidence.

The following constitute a recommended structure:

- The handshake
- The sign of respect
- The purpose
- The roadmap

The handshake: I recently shook hands with one of the handful (no pun intended) of people I respect the most in my industry and noted that he was looking beyond me at the next person as he shook my hand. If Mr. Perfect was fallible in this regard, what about the rest of us?

The rules of handshake engagement are simple but often overlooked: Strike a balance between dead fish and big fish, and do not be overly passive, weak, or insecure. Do not hold on too long, try to break the other person's hand, or go into fraternity/sorority rush mode. Like Goldilocks said about Baby Bear's porridge, your handshake should be "just right." Couple the handshake with eye contact. If your handshake is three seconds long, sustain eye contact through the duration of those three seconds.

Make the recipient of your handshake feel like the most important person in your universe for those two or three seconds. Saying the person's name and offering your most natural smile are added extras.

Show respect: After the handshake, the most important thing you can do is thank the other person for taking time to meet you. As a sales professional, you inevitably carry the baggage of every other sales professional who has preceded you, and that baggage can be pretty worn. Find a way to ease tension and minimize resistance.

I like to provide a realistic time frame and ask if it is "acceptable" to the other party. "This meeting should take no more than ten minutes. Is this still a good time for you?" If you have already established a time frame, ask if it is still applicable.

State your purpose: Once you have put your prospect or client at ease by showing respect for the person's most valuable commodity—time—and by placing a limit on how much time you may require, let your prospect know in one crisp sentence exactly why you are there and why it is worthwhile to pay attention.

Succinctly state the purpose of your call. How often does someone talk to you at length without first stating a purpose? Put that uncertainty to rest from the start.

Include a "What's in it for you?" benefit statement. The purpose of your visit should not be to "learn about their company and tell them what you can do to minimize their problems." It is to learn more about their company and to provide them with sufficient insight to help them lower costs and make life easier.

The roadmap: Remember, a roadmap keeps your prospect focused on your message, provides rationale and continuity for each segment of your meeting, and offers assurance that you are moving through the itinerary. Seeking acceptance of your proposed roadmap provides your prospect with yet another courtesy and ensures you that the prospect is reasonably comfortable with your plan.

> *"I normally like to ask a few questions about the challenges that are facing your company, advise you if and how WorkWell might be able to help you address these challenges, and then discuss where we go from here. Is that format acceptable to you?"*

Let's put the first thirty seconds together:

The intent of the first thirty seconds is to quickly dismantle the inherent sales suspicion barrier prospects have toward sales professionals by showing respect for the prospect and stating your intentions up front. These thirty seconds are extremely short and vitally important; meticulous care must be given to fine-tuning your approach to a prospect during this phase.

EXHIBIT 5-1. THE SALES CALL: THE FIRST 30 SECONDS

(While shaking hands for two to three seconds): *"Good morning Mr. Shultz, I'm Don Rust from WorkWell. You mentioned on the phone that you had about fifteen minutes. Does this time frame still work for you?"*

"Great."

"As the Service Representative for Work Well, my job is to learn more about your company and see if and how we might be able to help you minimize unnecessary health and safety costs and make your job a lot easier. I normally like to ask a few questions about the challenges that your company is facing, advise you if and how WorkWell might be able to help you address these challenges, and wrap it up by discussing where we go from here. Is that format acceptable to you?"

PHASE II: The interview.

The core objective of a sales calls is to identify a problem and encourage a dialogue that moves you to a position where you can provide solutions to that problem.

- Talk less than you may wish, especially at the outset.
- Ask broad, open-ended questions intended to uncover a problem.
- Probe actively in order to remain focused and ensure the optimal degree of accuracy. Look for statements that beg for a greater degree of specificity (e.g., "Quality is important to me"). Probe for more information (e.g., "How do you define quality?").
- Take notes to reinforce your apparent interest in what the prospect has to say and help you retain your concentration.
- Summarize key points continually throughout the sales call.
- Move toward an "If we could, would you . . . ?" conclusion to Phase II.

Phase II is the longest phase and the heart of the sales call. It is when the general principles of effective sales are called into play.

PHASE III: The last thirty seconds.

The crucial last thirty seconds of a sales call has the potential to turn around an otherwise lackluster sales session. Conversely, a poorly executed last minute can nullify a good effort that occurred earlier in the sales call.

Three steps should be routinely included in Phase III:

1. Summarize the key points of your meeting and verify your action step (what both parties are going to do next).
2. Offer a sincere, and enthusiastic, final comment (e.g., "I am really excited about the possibility that your company may work with our program").
3. Repeat the handshake regimen that was used at the outset of the meeting.

If Phase I creates the crucial first impression and Phase II encompasses the business discussion, Phase III is the anchor of the sales call. In an effective call, body language (both yours and theirs) rings true, and sincerity, specificity, and professionalism reign supreme.

Summarize: This is where careful note taking comes into play. Briefly review the meeting by summarizing the situation, your proposed solution, and the benefit to the prospect:

> *"You advised me that your lost day experience has increased by more than 10 percent over each of the last three years, resulting in a workers' comp bill that is twice as high as it was ten years ago. We agreed that your company will use 'Back-to-Work-Plus," and we will provide you with monthly and annual reports that document lost work time. Such tight control of your workplace injuries should increase the likelihood of fewer lost workdays and reduce your expenses. Are there any key points I left out?"*

The next step: Every encounter should have a next step that can be enunciated in your closing statement.

> *"As we discussed, our next step will be to schedule a visit for you to tour our facilities. It is my understanding that we can schedule such a tour through your assistant. Is there anything else?"*

Knockout punch: Develop a carefully scripted final statement: the final words that you say as you are "walking out the door." Get right to the point and say it with confidence.

> *"At WorkWell, we take great pride and interest in each of our clients. We genuinely feel that we are likely to make a measurable difference to our clients and look forward to working with every client as a true partner and not as a number. I really hope we can have the chance to provide services to your company."*

Another handshake: If you only have one chance to make a first impression, you have only one chance to leave a lasting impression. Conclude your encounter in the same sincere, warm, and focused manner as you began, and thank the prospects for their time.

The Golden Minute consumes only about 5 percent of a typical twenty-minute meeting, yet may account for 80 percent or more of the meeting's impact. Proactively plan your approach to the beginning and end of every sales call or other business encounter.

A self-confident, methodical approach is central to success in most professions. In sales, the first impression is often the only impression; the sales professional must capture the moment.

Exhibit 5-2. The Sales Call: The Last 30 Seconds

"You advised me that your lost day experience has increased by more than 10 percent over each of the last three years, resulting in a workers' comp bill that is twice as high as it was ten years ago. We agreed that your company will use our 'Back-to-Work-Plus' program, and that we will provide you with monthly and annual reports that document lost work time. Tight control of your workplace injuries increase the likelihood of your achieving less lost workdays and reduce your expenses."

"Are there any key points that I left out?"

"As we discussed, our next step is to schedule a visit to tour our facilities. It is my understanding that we can schedule such a tour through your assistant."

"Is there anything else?"

"At WorkWell we take great pride and interest in each of our clients. We genuinely feel that we are likely to make a measurable difference to our clients and look forward to working with every client as a true partner and not as a number. I really hope we can have the chance to provide services to your company. (While shaking hands) It was pleasure meeting with you, Mr. Shultz. Thank you again for finding time for me."

Executing a carefully planned routine during a sales call can have a marked influence on the success of your sales effort.

EXCEPTIONAL RELATIONSHIPS

Relationships are an integral part of healthcare sales. In some sales, relationships mean less, if they have any value at all. The more one's product is a commodity that can be purchased online, the less relationships matter. On the other hand, the more complex a product and the more education required to make the buyer understand the product's worth, the more a buyer-seller relationship comes into play.

WHY DO RELATIONSHIPS MATTER?

As return on investment associated with core clinical services is decreasing, astute programs are expanding their product portfolio to offer more services to a relatively static client base. Most add-on products (e.g., wellness services) tend to be part of a larger whole that contribute to the health and safety of the workforce. Hence, they are not commodities, but rather another piece of an increasingly complex puzzle.

The healthcare sales professional is becoming far more of an educator than a commodities dealer. But there is a catch: the greater the need to educate, the harder it is to get the "I do not have a second to spare" prospect to sit down. Uneducated prospects are likely to revert to being commodity buyers, and your chance of an in-depth relationship with the company is tarnished.

What to do? The best way to get a prospect's attention is to establish credibility and trust with that prospect *before* you attempt to educate them. This requires patience, foresight, and often a considerable dose of innovation.

WAIT, THERE'S MORE!

There are some additional reasons for honing exceptional relationships with clients and prospects:

1. **Word of mouth** — Never underestimate word of mouth. Develop only "good" relationships with clients or prospects

and they are unlikely to be singing your praises to the masses. Develop an extraordinary relationship, and word is likely to spread quickly; everyone you meet along the way has the potential to be a subcontractor for your sales effort. Leave an indelibly strong impression.

2. **Follow the bouncing ball** — Annual employee turnover hovers around 20 percent and is even higher during a recession. Hence, up to one third of your contacts are likely to be employed elsewhere a year from now. Over the years, numerous healthcare CEOs from RYAN Associates' client organizations have left the organization we served only to hire us again at their next stopping point to replicate what we did at their former organization. These "out-of-nowhere" overtures would not have developed had we not walked out of the door with an exceptional relationship.

BUILDING AND DEVELOPING RELATIONSHIPS

How do you build exceptional relationships? Although it varies somewhat based on the sales professional's persona, there are some general rules of the road:

1. **Be yourself** — In many walks of professional life, the professional's manner is different on and off the playing field. You may wear a professional hat from 8:00 a.m. to 5:00 p.m. and a personal hat the rest of the time. In many cases such a dual personality is correct and even commendable; in healthcare sales it often is not.
2. **Learn what is really important . . . and remember it** — Achieve exceptional relationships by focusing on "them." Learn what is really important to a prospect/client, both professionally and personally. Repeatedly revisit these issues. Sales is always about "them."
3. **Check in frequently** — Many sales professionals establish contact with clients and prospects only when there is a professional objective. An exceptional relationship implies frequent contact. Balance sales-oriented contacts with no-obligation "social calls."
4. **Do the little things** — In the email era it takes little effort to send a short note, a relevant attachment, or a timely link. Yet

sales professionals rarely take the time to do this. Once you know what is important to one or more of your prospects/clients, you can scour for relevant material and send it on to them. If you do this frequently, you are likely to grow quickly from "just another" sales professional to an "exceptional" sales professional.

5. **Acknowledge critical dates** — Are you sentimental about your birthday? I am (aside to readers: mine is September 5, hint, hint . . .). Gather birth dates and acknowledge them (a personal email will do). Pay careful attention to any hints you may pick up such as, "I'm getting married on June 11."
6. **Be selective** — Unless you operate in a small market, you cannot cultivate exceptional relationships with every prospect/client. Be selective. "Red hot" prospects that offer great professional opportunity for your program warrant a seat at the front of your bus.

   What about chemistry? There are certain people whom I am unlikely to cultivate an exceptional relationship with: I am from Mars and they are from Pluto. In such circumstances, avoid trying to fit the square peg into a round hole and consider even a "fair relationship" victory.

Sales professionals are, or at least should be, "people people." Building strong relationships with others should be an inherent aspect of your professional life. Do not try to do too much too quickly and lose track of key relationships.

SCRIPTING

Avoid reinventing the wheel in sales call after sales call, whether you are describing your service's benefits, explaining a service, or responding to objections. Prepare and memorize (script) an appropriate response to frequently asked questions or common objections, service features, and your service's most compelling benefits.

Scripting serves three critical functions. You:

- Are assured of saying exactly what you want to say, time after time.
- Can concentrate on visual cues such as eye contact, tone, volume, and body language.

EXHIBIT 5-3. COMMON SCRIPTS

CIRCUMSTANCE	SCRIPT
Opening Statement	"It is a pleasure meeting you. I appreciate your taking the time to meet with me. About how much time do you have available for this meeting?"
Roadmap	"As a representative of WorkWell, it is my responsibility to meet with employers such as yourself. I want to learn more about your company's health and safety practices to determine if WorkWell's services can help you enhance your workforce's health status and lower unnecessary health and safety costs. I would like to ask you a few questions and then discuss how we might be of help to you. Is this acceptable to you?"
Benefit Statement	"WorkWell is unique in that we focus on eliminating work-related illnesses and injuries before they occur and minimizing lost work time when illnesses and injuries do occur. As we achieve this we both lower your unnecessary direct and in-direct costs and enhance the health status of your employee population."
Value of Care Management Program	"Our computerized care management system allows us to move your company's cases through the system more quickly, get your employees back to work sooner, and thereby save you money."
Basic Close / Action Step	"We traditionally initiate a relationship with a new employer client by conducting a one-hour orientation session with key department heads and first line supervisors. We would like to schedule the session within the next week. The sooner we begin, the sooner we can begin to address your health and safety costs."
Final Comment	"WorkWell creates a win-win-win relationship between our program, your company, and your employees. I look forward to working with you toward this end."

- Will appear more self-assured and knowledgeable, and the prospect will be more likely to feel at ease in dealing with you.

Typical scripted statements are featured in **Exhibit 5-3**.

WHAT YOU ARE SELLING

I am reminded of the Miller Lite commercial where the two young women argue over what makes the beer the best: "Great taste!" "Less filling!" "Great taste!" "Less filling!"

Sales has its own version of the Miller Lite debate: "It's a commodity!" "It's a relationship!" "It's a commodity!" "It's a relationship!"

Many professionals tout health sales as relationship selling. In other words, the product is a highly integrated series of workplace health and safety services. Sales trainers, including myself at times, advise against selling discrete services as commodities, because that is not what healthcare sales is about.

Commodity sales continue to be the norm in healthcare. It is easier to revert back to sales 101: tell your prospect what you have to offer and hope for positive buying signals. It also is more immediate and concrete, whereas relationship selling often requires a lengthy sales cycle and tends to be more complex.

So, exactly what are healthcare services sales? Is it commodity-based or relationship-based? My answer is that it depends on the circumstances and often involves a little of both.

COMMODITY / RELATIONSHIP

Once the sales professional understands the basic product, he or she must determine how best to present the product. Here is where the commodity vs. relationship issue comes in.

In a world that is more gray than black and white, the line that separates commodity from relationship is often blurred. A sales professional is likely to be more commodity oriented when dealing with a certain prospect, or at certain points in the sales process, because of market positioning. Sometimes the sales professional will focus on products at different points during a given sales call, depending on the prospect's expressed needs.

Key determiners affect how best to present the product:

1. **By prospect** — You can preach relationship to certain prospects until the cows come home, yet they will never get it. Others will immediately embrace the value of a broad relationship with a highly respected healthcare organization. Others are likely to fall somewhere in the middle.

   Test the phrase "relationship" early in the sales process; assess where the prospect appears to fit on the commodity-relationship continuum and proceed accordingly.

2. **By the sales process** — Many sales transactions are made only after a long sales cycle. This cycle can begin with name identification marketing, continue with a broad differentiation campaign, and involve an introduction, meeting, follow-up, and at times, a written proposal.

   The commodity-relationship emphasis sometimes changes several times during this process. Depending on other variables, the cadence of these changes can vary as well. Your differentiation campaign could emphasize the partnership, whereas the actual sales call might zero in on specific products. Conversely, early marketing might familiarize prospects with your services, while the actual face-to-face call would emphasize how each product is part of an integrated package.

3. **By market position** — The relative emphasis on commodity vs. relationship can also be affected by a service's position in the marketplace. A long-standing service with a stable client base is likely to be more interested in vertical expansion—that is, adding new commodities to the existing service mix. In that case, you would be more likely to emphasize the commodity, since the relationship already exists.

   What if you are a second-tier market challenger or a new entrant in your market? An emphasis on relationships then becomes disproportionately more important because your service needs to differentiate itself from better-established competitors who offer similar commodities.

4. **By competitor style** — Apart from market position is competitive style: your organization's style vs. the style of your competitor, regardless of market share position.

Assume that you are affiliated with a long-standing community healthcare organization, and your primary competitor is a faceless national chain. Employers may see your organization as warm and fuzzy and the competition as cold and remote. In that case, emphasize the relationship side of the continuum.

Conversely, imagine you are small and intimate and your competitor is large and complex. In this case, position yourself toward the commodity side of the continuum.

5. **By product** — Although many healthcare commodities are inherently linked to each other (to achieve an optimally healthy and safe workplace), some are easier for prospects to digest if presented as commodities.

   A pre-hire screening process is an appropriate adjunct to a comprehensive health management approach, but many prospects see it as little more than a commodity. Sell with that perspective in mind.

   On the other hand, placing personnel, such as a nurse or physical therapist, at the work site is inherently relationship-oriented and in almost every circumstance has to be presented that way.

6. **By the sales call** — There is nothing wrong with bringing both your commodity hat and relationship hat to a sales call and switching hats as necessary. In other instances, a natural flow exists.

   There may be a need to explain your services as a series of commodities and why all of these commodities are integrated into a systematic whole that results in a genuine long-term relationship.

   No matter how hallowed dogma may be in sales lore, adherence to such dogma can be a sales professional's downfall. The effective sales professional needs to be nimble and ready to adapt to the realities of the moment.

"It Depends"

I often begin my response to questions with the qualifier, "It depends."

At first I felt a bit guilty about using this phrase because it can be perceived as a dodge. I now recognize it has a place as a core sales and marketing principle.

Sales and marketing is an art, not a science. Rules, few though they may be, are meant to be stretched, even broken, as circumstances change. Do not view your world in black and white but rather in gray and as part of a full spectrum of tactics and approaches.

Note the following examples of the types of variables that justify an "it depends" response:

MARKET SIZE

Question: *"How much emphasis should we place on marketing vs. sales?"*

Answer: *"It depends. Market outreach strategies vary markedly depending on whether a market is urban, suburban, semi-rural, or rural. The larger your market, the greater your emphasis on marketing; the smaller the market, the greater the emphasis on sales."*

In a larger market, sales and marketing are more likely to be approached as a "numbers game." In larger markets you should keep in close written contact (email as well as traditional correspondence) with hundreds of employer prospects and place proportionately greater emphasis on marketing rather than direct sales. The larger the market, the more time and money one should spend on marketing.

As one moves along the continuum toward smaller markets, the opposite occurs: less emphasis should be placed on multiple high-touch marketing techniques, and proportionately greater use should be made of direct correspondence and face-to-face sales calls.

MARKET POSITION

Question: *"How should we prioritize our marketing tactics?"*

Answer: *"It depends on your position in the market."*

If you are the market leader, your tactics should reflect your market leader position, the track record of your service, and an attitude of "why take a chance with a lesser option?" If you are a "market challenger" (that is, an active program that is not the market leader), focus on key points of differentiation (e.g., twenty-four-hour service) and hammer away on the benefits of this unique feature. If your program is a recent market entry, position it as something new and fresh.

DELIVERY SITE OPTIONS

Question: *"As a hospital-based program, how do we best compete against free-standing clinics and clinic networks (or vice versa)?"*

Answer: *"It depends."*

If you represent a health system or hospital, you probably have perceived competitive advantages, such as breadth of services, short term, if not immediate, access to specialists, and (hopefully) a history of long-standing respect within your community. If you represent a non-hospital-affiliated free-standing clinic, your perceived advantages are likely to include ease of access, fast service, and direct focus. There are hybrid models between these extremes that require some blend of these differentiation points.

INSTITUTIONAL CULTURE

Question: *"How should we deal with an organizational culture that is not particularly hospitable to sales and marketing?"*

Answer: *"It depends on the deeper roots of your organizational culture."*

Is your parent organization ultra-conservative and resistant to change, or is senior management innovative and willing to introduce new services with a splash? What if it is somewhere in between the two extremes? How firmly held and changeable is this cultural bias? Your services ultimately need to align with your organizational culture while remaining on the lookout for signs that the culture is open to change.

PERSONNEL CHARACTERISTICS

Question: *"What sales and marketing responsibilities can I add to various job descriptions for personnel in our program?"*

Answer: *"It depends."*

Assume you are a basketball coach, and your team is composed primarily of small, quick players. Your strategy would be to run, press, and play the game at a frenetic pace. If your team is composed of slow, tall timber, you would most likely slow the game down and work to get the ball inside. The same principle is true in sales and marketing: play to the strengths of your personnel by designing marketing tactics that fit the collective personality of your team.

VISION

Question: *"You suggest addressing both short-term goals and long-term positioning strategies in our marketing plan. What percentage of the plan should address long-term strategic goals?"*

Answer: *"It depends."*

Go back to square one and reflect on why your organization made a commitment to the particular service in the first place. Is your raison d'etre to serve as a basic clinic, or was your organization established as a foundation for a highly integrated and continually evolving series of services? Finding the proper place on the integrated service continuum allows you to place the correct emphasis on the short-term/long-term balance in your marketing plan.

PORTFOLIO MIX

Question: *"How thoroughly should I describe our services during a sales call?"*

Answer: *"It depends on your portfolio of services and what mix of services you deem most appropriate for the prospect."*

If your prospective arrangement focuses entirely on core services such as injury management and screening exams (and even with screenings "it depends"), comparatively little discussion is necessary. New or complex services such as wellness offerings or the provision of on-site personnel usually provide the sales professional with license to discusses services in greater depth.

The common thread of this discussion is that your approach to selling is contingent on assessing your unique place in the market. Think of every variable as a continuum upon which your services may be at either end or anywhere in the middle. When it comes to sales and marketing, one size does not fit all. It just depends.

PUBLIC SPEAKING SKILLS

I waited all day to ask my first crush to my high school freshman prom, and when I finally saw her, the words wouldn't come out. Such was the plight of a chronic stutterer; although largely overcome, it remains somewhat of a challenge to this day.

Fast forward to the early 1980s. I looked around and saw some enormously accomplished individuals with relatively modest intellect who seemed to have made their way because of their ability to speak in public. I vowed then to become an accomplished public speaker. Now I relish the opportunity every time I am in front of an audience.

If you become proficient in public speaking, it can greatly enhance your sales performance. There are several reasons why:

- A sales encounter is little more than speaking publicly to an audience of one or a small group. The same rhythm, hand gestures, eye contact, and volume control that are instrumental to public speaking are equally as important in a one-on-one or small-group encounter.
- The art of preparing a presentation—an integrated beginning, middle, and end—is also a well-advised approach to a sales encounter.
- The more you speak publicly, the greater your confidence as a communicator—a level of confidence that readily translates to success.

You need to genuinely want to become a more effective public speaker. Unless that desire exists, it would be foolish to incorporate public speaking into your career-building approach.

PUBLIC SPEAKING GUIDELINES

The effective public speaker should employ the following guidelines:

1. **Practice, practice, practice** — The best way to become a public speaker is to do it over and over again. Seek out opportunities to speak before any type of group—regardless of whether the group is related to your profession—and work on your skills.
2. **Prepare, prepare, prepare** — The better you know the content of your talk, the more effort you can put into your delivery. Take more time than seems necessary to refine and practice your presentation. Know your material so well that you can give your talk without notes or audiovisuals.
3. **Structure your talk and offer a roadmap** — Let your audience know where you are taking them and offer a crisp summary at the end.
4. **Involve your audience** — At the outset of your presentation, assume that your audience is tight, unmotivated, and lackadaisical. Thaw them out and get them involved.

   The audience needs to be aroused both physically and mentally. I like to get an audience to stand up, turn around, or engage in some similar method to get their blood flowing. I also want to get them thinking about the subject at hand. With a larger audience, I often ask a simple question such as, "What's the greatest challenge you face in dealing with the workers' comp system?" Then I ask the audience to share their answers with their neighbors. Even in a one-on-one setting, a thought-provoking question about the company's experience can be used to break the ice.
5. **Be yourself** — Many emerging public speakers seem to think that humor has to be part of any public talk. Problem is, if you aren't funny, your attempt at humor can fall flat. If in fact you are a funny person, go for it. If you tend to be more of a no-nonsense type, do not try to be a comedian.
6. **Don't force your movements** — Beware of the two extremes: the Wooden Indian and the Energizer Bunny. The former tends to hide behind a podium and maintain a rigid posture. No wonder their audience usually finds the presentation boring. The

latter tends to race back and forth across the stage or within the audience. Unless you are a budding evangelist, your audience would likely find such a technique forced and distracting.

7. **Speak from the heart** — I am amazed how many talks seem so canned and rehearsed as to come off as blatantly insincere. Always include a "from the heart" segment in your presentation. Use a phrase such as, "Let me speak from the heart for a moment," and slow down your pace and delivery. You are likely to connect better with your audience and ensure that your most important points come through loud and clear.

8. **Minimize or eliminate audiovisuals** — Although I (begrudgingly) use PowerPoint for educational sessions, I almost always refrain from audiovisual support during major presentations. Use a single index card that might list the major eight points of your talk, but even that becomes unnecessary after a while. Why? Eye contact with an audience is crucial, and the use of audiovisuals compromises such contact.

   Audiovisuals can be a distraction: you will be tempted to turn toward the screen, read words that are plainly seen by your audience, and periodically have to address errors in the audiovisuals or equipment. Focus entirely on your talk and send a message to the audience that you truly care about them.

9. **Present a challenge** — Make an audience think during your presentation. Ask questions that are associated with your next thought (e.g., "When was the last time that you . . . ?" or "What do you think is the best solution to the problem I described?"). If you lecture to your audience, you will quickly compromise their attention span.

10. **Show sincere appreciation** — No matter how small or large an audience, I am genuinely touched that each person found the time to hear me speak. Most speakers feel the same. Let your audience know how appreciative you are at both the beginning and end of your presentation. Be certain that your appreciation is not only mentioned in passing ("I appreciate your being here") but from the heart ("You know, I never take for granted that busy people such as yourselves can find the time to hear what I have to say; it means a great deal to me. Thank you.")

EXHIBIT 5-4. PUBLIC SPEAKING: A PRIMER

Here is a "starter kit" for a budding (or even self-professed) public speaker.

- **RE-ARRANGE THE ROOM IF NECESSARY** — Do what you need to do to make the room comfortable for you. Re-arrange tables, put people closer to one another, narrow your sight line, etc.
- **REPEAT QUESTIONS AND KEEP ANSWERS BRIEF** — Repeating the question gives you a pause to think and clarifies things for your audience. Keep your answers brief; they may be of interest only to the person who asked the question.
- **NEVER TURN YOUR BACK ON THE AUDIENCE** — Do not turn around to look at a screen or walk into an audience to make a point.
- **STATE FACTS, SHOW REMEDY, APPEAL FOR ACTION** — Use this as the core of a presentation: (1) the issue or problem, (2) the solution, (3) action steps.
- **REPEAT KEY POINTS** — Drive home your most important points by repeating them.
- **DON'T FEAR SILENCE** — Nobody likes a motor mouth. Give audience members a chance to catch their breath. Often, silence is golden.

If you make a commitment to becoming an effective public speaker, you will find that it enhances virtually every other aspect of your professional activity.

WORDS MATTER

Question: What do the following quotes have in common?

"It gets a little dicey from here."

"And now for the bad news."

"But we're improving in that area."

Answer: They were all said by senior healthcare sales professionals during sales calls that I personally monitored. They were all blatantly counterproductive. Ouch!

The art of using the "right" words and avoiding words that tend to harm the effort of a sales professional is vastly undervalued in healthcare sales.

BECOME A WORDSMITH

Be proactive in your quest to be a strong wordsmith.

Use strong, descriptive, positive words: Your choice of words should reflect the image you wish to project (e.g., energy, confidence, focus, and warmth). Ask your colleagues to list the ten words that reflect the most positive things about your organization and create a composite list of those words. Use these words extensively in any conversation, telephone call, or sales encounter with a prospect or client.

Avoid weak, ambiguous, and negative words: Sales professionals frequently use weak or negative words during sales calls. Avoid words that might be construed as negative or critical or ones that suggests lack of confidence. It is better to be silent than to call attention to a negative.

Use euphemisms to convert a negative to a positive: Common negatives can be converted to positives provided you take the time to consider the conversation in advance. The statement "you have a problem" becomes "you have an opportunity." Or, "your injury rate is too high" becomes "if we can help you bring your injury rate down to historic levels for your industry type, this would result in lower workers' comp costs for your company."

Reflect the word choice of the other party in your dialogue: If one man's drink is another man's poison, then one man's words are another man's meaningless phrases. Some words resonate well with some, and other words resonate better with others. Encourage prospects to discuss their needs, wishes, and fears. Make special note of recurrent or key words, reflect positive words back verbatim, and convert negative words into a meaningful euphemism.

Qualify, always qualify: I have either written or reviewed more than seven hundred consulting reports that have left our office since 1985. Rule one is and has always been, qualify, always, qualify.

Short of mathematical certitude, nothing is certain, and the word "never" covers a mighty long time. As a consultant I try to project an image of humility and provide cover for the inevitable times that I miss something or offer a nonviable recommendation. I pepper my suggestions, both written and oral, with phrases such as "in my opinion," "it appears to me," and "if I were you, I would . . . " Conversely, I avoid such phrases as "you must."

Keep coming back to your competitive edge: Succinctly describe your competitive edge (what sets your service apart from everything else available in the marketplace?). Synthesize each competitive edge down to a word or two and find a way to repeatedly use them in your discourse. Competitive-edge words include "experience," "locations," and "proven outcomes." If your program has "the edge," do not be shy about frequent repetition of the word or phrases.

Never promise: Sales professionals quickly learn how important cost savings and return on investment are to employer clients and prospects. It becomes tempting to "promise" a specific level of savings or a projected return on investment using unrealistically high or arbitrarily developed numbers. Phrases such as "We should be able to reduce your costs by 20 percent," or "We will provide you with a positive return on investment" are not only risky but are also far from guaranteed.

Qualify any statement regarding cost savings or return on investment with phrases such as:

> *"Although we cannot be 100 percent certain that we can make a difference, I am confident that our program's management of your employees' health will help you reduce unnecessary costs and result in a positive return on investment."*

Exhibit 5-5. The Healthcare Sales Professional's Dictionary

POSITIVE WORDS *(Use often)*	NEGATIVE WORDS *(Avoid)*	EUPHEMISMS *(Substitute phrases)*	QUALIFIERS *(Integrate them)*	COMPETITIVE EDGE WORDS *(Use often)*	NEVER PROMISE *(Resist the temptation)*
value	problem	problem = opportunity	In my opinion . . .	experience	I am confident . . .
return	bad	concern = opportunity	It seems to me . . .	location	We found that most of our clients . . .
savings	high costs	high costs = cost savings potential	If I were you . . .	communication	It is our intention to . . .
healthy	negative	inconsistent = more integrated	We have found . . .	outcomes	We believe we offer you the greatest likelihood of . . .
quick	issue		In my experience . . .	proven	
time-saving	threat		I suggest . . .	expertise	
opportunity	concern				
enhance	crisis				
positive	expensive				
assist	error				
	inadequate				
	poor				
	weak				

Applicability of basic principles extends far beyond the workplace. The astute use of words can have far-reaching value under any circumstances, whether used with a spouse or significant other, child, parent, neighbor, friend, or coworker.

Simplicity and Repetition

Have you noticed how complicated our world has become? I routinely receive more than seventy-five email messages each day, have about three hundred cable television stations to choose from, can look up or read about virtually any topic on the Internet, receive hundreds of mail pieces each week, and have an untold number of voice messages daily on my office phone, cell phone, and home phone.

It is not surprising that the average person is receptive to but a fraction of the information before them. Therein lies a quandary: How do you get YOUR message across in such an information-saturated world?

Consider the following recommendations for increasing the likelihood that your message will be heard by most of your intended audience most of the time.

MASS COMMUNICATION

Understanding how to reach your audience begins with an understanding of mass communication.

In competing for an audience's finite attention:

- Keep your message simple.
- Keep repeating the message.
- Use multiple modalities to communicate the message.

SIMPLICITY

Communicate with short, simple, and focused messages. Think of it as the "forest through the trees"—the more you clutter your message with information tangential to the core message, the more likely the core message will be minimized or overlooked.

Sales professionals often exhibit a tendency to go "on and on" and overpower the other party with the sheer volume of their information. The opposite should be the norm. Concentrate on making one or two key points in one or two sentences to convey a message. When I review something I wrote (e.g., email, letters, reports) my first objective is to shorten it by deleting nonessential words, sentences, or concepts. You should do the same.

REPETITION

Express a key point for ten seconds six different times rather than make the same point once for sixty seconds. Simplifying a point and then repeating it often significantly increases the odds of that point's lodging in the prospect's mind.

MULTIPLE APPROACHES

Use multiple communication modalities to deliver a message. If you plan to communicate a message to someone four times, communicate once by phone, once by voice mail, once by email, and once by letter. People respond in a variety of ways to different communication modalities. By using all four modalities you are hedging your bets that you will use the one modality that proves most effective to the recipient.

TIME EFFICIENCY

A perception reigns that there is not enough time in the day to get the job done, and no time for another sales pitch. Be more efficient and show appreciation for the prospect's time constraints:

1. **Make every communication shorter** — Email can be two sentences, not five paragraphs. A voice-mail message should take ten to fifteen seconds, not several minutes. A letter can be one or two short paragraphs, not multiple pages. In every instance the central point of the communication will be more clear. The aggregate time savings for the prospect, and the sales professional who writes the message, can be dramatic when measured over a year.
2. **Use generic documents or scripted messages** — Customize documents to address a client or prospect's specific needs. Many email messages or letters are a variant on the same theme, such as

a thank-you note following a sales call. Take the time to craft one well-written note and avoid re-inventing the wheel. Likewise, voice-mail messages that say roughly the same thing can be scripted and easily repeated:

> *"Hello Mr. Myers, a brief thank you for finding time to meet with me this afternoon. I will review your company's data and get back to you in writing within twenty-four hours."*

It is far better to have a series of prepared voice-mail messages (scripted) you can pull out and use when appropriate.

3. **Deliver voice mail outside normal business hours** — Indeed, there are times when you prefer *not* to reach the other party, as a dialogue consumes valuable time, and talking with a prospect may not be particularly important at that juncture. These types of voice-mail messages can be delivered with confidence (you know going in that you will be leaving a voice mail), and a large number of messages can be delivered in a short time.
4. **Deliver a voice-mail blitz** — Assume you would like to do a low-cost/big-impact public relations blitz. Set aside one hour starting at 6:00 p.m. (or over a weekend), and leave fifty or more employer contacts the following voice-mail message:

> *"Hello, this is Dana Maginnis calling from WorkWell. I'm calling to check in to thank your company for your business, find out how we are doing, and see if there are any problems that we can address. I am available most afternoons at 453-1834; please call me if I can be of help."*

GETTING STARTED

Develop a personalized list of communication actions amenable to using a generic document or a scripted and memorized statement. (**Exhibit 5-6** offers one such list.)

"Reach out and touch someone," applies more than ever in an increasingly impersonal, frenzied world. You can execute hundreds of personal contacts in a timely and efficient manner by planning

EXHIBIT 5-6. SAMPLE COMMUNICATIONS STRATEGY

GENERAL RULES:

1. Proactively develop a communications plan
2. Develop generic documents and scripts in support of each plan component
3. Execute the plan as an integral part of each workday

Use generic email messages to:

1. Confirm a meeting
2. Follow-up on a meeting
3. Confirm a "closed" account
4. Just check in
5. Announce a new service, location, or employee

Use generic letters to:

1. Offer an annual thank you and questionnaire
2. Introduce yourself or your service
3. Serve as a contractual cover sheet

Use scripted voice-mail messages to:

1. Just check in (alternate with email)
2. Confirm a meeting
3. Thank you for meeting/summary follow-up
4. Announce a new program feature

Use generic documents to:

1. Submit formal proposals
2. Provide reference lists (updated constantly)
3. Present staff profiles

ahead and using generic yet customized templates and scripts. Such an "in their face" approach increases the probability of potential clients knowing who you are and using your services when the time is right.

Sales Negotiations

Ask the ten people who know me best what my worst trait is, and eleven will answer, when it comes to time, "He's the most impatient cuss I have ever met!" I have been known to periodically (okay, daily) sit alone in my car yelling at a red traffic light to change. My time is my life, and so it is for many others.

THE WORLD IN WHICH WE LIVE

For starters, "We aren't in 1939 anymore, Alice." We live in a vastly different world in which virtually all of us feel information-saturated, overburdened, and pressed for time.

It is a world in which long dialogue is a nuisance and short, to-the-point interchange is embraced. It is a world that values *Headline News, USA Today,* and Internet blogs more than traditional news shows or in-depth books.

We live in a world in which people want things short, simple, and digestible. Learn to prosper within the confines of the sound-bite world. Develop a plan to succinctly get your core message across.

RULE 1: Mince the written word.

Whether you are writing a proposal, designing promotional material, or sending an email, eliminate unnecessary words to improve results. I write what I want to say (phase I) and then carefully scrutinize and tighten the verbiage to the fewest possible words (phase II). Take time to review everything you write and eliminate any paragraphs you can. Then review the text and eliminate any sentences you can. Finally, review the remaining sentences and eliminate any words you can. The shorter the written document, the more likely a reader will absorb your central point.

RULE 2: Enhance your verbal communication style.

Cleaning up written material is comparatively easy—provided you take the time—because you can revisit your document before you distribute it. Not so with spoken words; once said, they cannot be revised. Be vigilant about streamlining your verbal communication. Develop a simple, proactive plan, and be mindful of the plan during your various communications.

RULE 3: Set the stage.

State your objectives up front in clear and concise terms. Begin sales calls, phone calls, or meetings with a clear declaration of your intent. Define exactly what you are doing (e.g., "My objective is . . . " "The purpose of this call is . . . "). Be honest and keep it brief.

RULE 4: Speak sparingly, but carry a big stick.

Limit each comment to two or three sentences. We invariably, if subconsciously, rate depth of detail ahead of being concise when the opposite should be true. Make the other person *feel* they are controlling the conversation, although in reality you are by asking leading questions and knowing when and how to close.

The best way to create a perception of buyer-control is to let the buyer do most of the talking. You are creating the verbal equivalent of the aforementioned dictum for written communication: eliminate paragraphs, then eliminate sentences, then eliminate words.

RULE 5: State the reason.

Tie a reason to everything you say—usually within the same sentence. Use the word "because" as often as possible. Rather than say, "We would like to have you come for a tour of our clinic," say:

> *"We would like to have you come for a tour of our clinic because it is the best way for you to understand the quality of our services and permit you to compare us to other options."*

RULE 6: Call a close a close.

Many sales professionals are uncomfortable asking for the business because they fear rejection. The close often becomes hesitant, meandering, or even disingenuous. The best way to ask for the business is to ask for the business as directly as possible.

RULE 7: Learn from your written edits.

If you conscientiously edit written correspondence (rule 1), you begin to see patterns in your words and phrases. I have found that these written tendencies tend to crop up in verbal communiqués. My first drafts and my vocabulary tend to be overpopulated by adjectives such as "extremely" and "extraordinary." Note tendencies to be excessively expressive and minimize these tendencies in conversation.

RULE 8: Silence is golden.

Sales professionals often consider even a few seconds of silence an unacceptable void that must be filled with a stream-of-consciousness discourse. To the contrary, sit still or steer things back to the prospect with such open-ended queries as, "Anything else?" or "Your thoughts?"

RULE 9: Tighten your response.

People tend to ramble when answering questions. Tighten your response to questions by:

- Repeating the question. This gives you time to organize your response and to ensure that you understand the question.
- Pausing between sentences. Give the other party a chance to clarify or accept your answer.
- Asking at the conclusion, "Does this adequately answer your question?"

RULE 10: Straight talk—above all.

Here's a novel thought: look someone in the eye and say exactly what you are thinking. Create win-win situations in which your service's capabilities address a prospect's needs. No hocus pocus—learn a prospect's needs, describe your solution, define, quantify the win-win, and begin service. The more quickly and precisely you get from point A to point D, the better off you will be.

RULE 11: Use the buyer's language.

Use language that the other party understands. If you are speaking to an employer, use "employer-talk" rather than "provider-talk" in crafting your messages.

RULE 12: Adjust complexity based on your audience.

Be mindful of your audience's (whether an individual or a group) presumed level of understanding. Although your inherent messages may be consistent, be prepared to alter them depending on your audience. Although the ability to communicate by using the listeners' language and sizing up their comprehension level is subjective and takes time to cultivate, rules 11 and 12 can yield immeasurable results.

EXAMPLES OF CUT-TO-THE-CHASE PHRASES

Certain phrases are useful at the beginning of a thought:

"The purpose of this call . . . "

"It is my hope that . . . "

"In summary . . . "

"It seems the win-win is . . . "

"The bottom line is . . . "

"Did I answer your question?"

"To briefly explain . . . "

"Key factors to consider are . . . "

"The most valuable thing we can do for you . . . "

"I recommend . . . "

"Consider these options because . . . "

"How do you feel about . . . ?"

PERSONALITY PROFILING

Effective sales professionals have the ability to "read" and connect with their prospects. This is not always easy for the sales professional who is dealing with numerous personality types, many of which are markedly different from their own personality.

Personality profiling has been around for some time and is described in various ways. In general, the four personality types are descried as follows:

Domineering (or "High D"): High D personalities are assertive, controlling, impatient, and no-nonsense Type-A individuals. Think of former New York Yankee boss George Steinbrenner or General Alexander "I'm in charge here" Haig.

Influential ("High I"): High I personalities are warm, creative, enthusiastic, visionary, and personable. High I personalities are often disorganized and/or behind schedule, but invariably upbeat. Think of your typical talk-show host such as Johnny Carson or Jay Leno.

Steady ("High S"): High S personalities tend to be precise, thorough, prudent, and task-oriented. They tend to be slow to make decisions, carefully weighing every option. They are not overly communicative. You are likely to see a roomful of "High S" individuals in your finance department.

Compliant ("High C"): High C personalities are also highly analytical, but are more idealistic and susceptible to group dynamics. They have time for everyone and prefer to avoid confrontations. Typically, a High C is a quiet, analytical sales prospect. Think of this prospect as a quintessential team player.

To effectively employ personality profiling:

1. Know your own personality type (D, I, S, or C) and the degree to which you fall into each quadrant (are you a "High I" or a "Moderate I"?) Determine what variance there might be between your self-image and how the public is likely to see you.

2. Learn to quickly assess into which quadrant your sales prospect is likely to fall. Signals as apparent as the neatness of a prospect's office, intensity of their emotions, and voice volume are often strong clues.
3. Address each prospect differently depending on your perception of their personality type.

High D prospects: With "domineering" prospects, be well organized and get right to the point. Ask a lot of questions to determine the prospect's needs and "hot buttons." Reflect their personality by being brief, to the point, and extremely benefit-oriented. Emphasize your service's potential impact to the bottom line. Make them feel that using your services is their idea.

High I prospects: Be lively, forward thinking and more relationship-oriented. Emphasize the value of a true provider-employer relationship between the prospect's company and your service. The relationship is everything.

High S prospects: Be patient, thorough, and methodical. Ask a lot of questions and gather data. Emphasize the logical value of a comprehensive approach to workplace health.

High C prospects: Be patient. High C prospects tend to be highly analytical and cautious. Emphasize a step-by-step approach to health and safety. The availability of outcome data is also likely to be of interest. It is a good idea to try to get to know the typical High C prospect personally. Determine who else from their company should be involved in reviewing your proposal; High C individuals tend to prefer a consensus-driven review.

COMMUNICATION PRINCIPLES

Whom among your network of professional colleagues and personal friends do you consider to be great communicators? What characteristics do they seem to have in common that make them qualified for this exalted status?

Although by no means confined to sales, learning how to communicate effectively is paramount to a successful sales effort.

COMMUNICATION PRINCIPLES

Incorporate the following principles into your verbal communications:

1. **Keep it simple** — Break your message down to a simple, easy-to-digest concept. Avoid too much detail. Do not try to jam too many concepts into a single verbal interchange. Use basic, short words. Assume the individual with whom you are speaking has a minimal attention span. Leave the flowery prose to Shakespeare.
2. **Be brief** — The effective communicator is a person of few words. The more you say, the more likely your essential message is lost or muddled amid a sea of extraneous verbiage. Know when to stop talking. (Hint: It is sooner than you think.)
3. **Identify a clear objective** — Determine the objective of your comments before you utter a word. Let the other party know exactly what your objective is. Use phrases such as "My goal today is . . . " or "The purpose of my call is to . . . . " When you state a feature, advise the client or prospect exactly why it is valuable to them. Constantly associate a "why" with a "what."
4. **Focus on your message** — Stay "on message" and keep your focus on the objective and the theme of your communication. Repeat this core objective frequently. Always be wary of diversions in conversation.
5. **Master pace** — Conduct your communication like a fine symphony orchestra. Vary pace, volume, and emphasis in a well-crafted and self-confident manner. Pause frequently (and usually right after key points) and do not be afraid of silence. Above all, avoid droning.
6. **Maintain eye contact** — Ah, those eyes are the window to the soul. In many ways what they say is as important as the words you are using. Concentrate on eye contact and learn to interpret signals from your subject's eyes as a guide to alter, maintain, or cease your communication.
7. **Ask questions** — Listen far more than you speak, but maintain control of the conversation by leading the subject where you want to lead them, often through artful and effective questioning. Ask broad, open-ended questions such as, "In a perfect world, what

type of relationship would you like to see develop between your company and a healthcare organization such as ours?"

8. **Articulate mutual benefit** — Conceive the likely win-win scenario prior to your conversation and focus on articulating the scenario early, often, and convincingly during a face-to-face meeting. Do not be shy about getting to the heart of the matter by using a statement such as "It seems to me that our relationship with your company is likely to be mutually beneficial." Set things out in clear terms.

9. **Probe for detail** — Probe to obtain more specific and insightful information. Classic probes such as "Tell me more . . . ," "Exactly what do you mean by . . . ," or "Why do feel that way?" provide you with clarification and more specifics with which to frame the ultimate win-win scenario.

10. **Repeat key points** — If an idea or point is twice as important as everything else you are saying, why not say it twice? Ensure that the most important thing you say is the one thing that the subject remembers following the interchange.

11. **Involve your subject** — Involve your prospects and clients continuously through your discourse. Pepper your comments with frequent mini-closes such as "Do you agree?" Such questions prompt responses throughout a conversation or presentation. If you want an individual to really absorb your message, keep it fluid and active rather than static and stiff.

12. **Use verbal bookends** — Remember the Golden Minute? The first and last things you say are likely to become your one or two most important comments. Your opening comment should articulate the objective of the conversation, and the last statement should provide a clear summary of key points.

13. **Use nonverbal cues** — Master the art of nonverbal communication. If a picture is worth a thousand words, so too is body language, including facial expressions and hand gestures. Nonverbal communication begins with preparation and forethought. The more prepared and focused you are, the easier it becomes to work on delivery. Simplicity and brevity rise to the fore. The less time you are "on stage," the less time you have to "perform."

> Try a simple test to address your nonverbal communication skills. Ask one or more of your colleagues to critique the nonverbal aspects of one of your sales presentations. Ask your colleagues to ignore what you are saying and rate you instead on your eye contact, gestures, signs of self-confidence, apparent sincerity, and other nonverbal expressions.

There is surprisingly little complexity in being a great communicator. Indeed, the opposite is true: the more simple, controlled, and focused the process, the more effective the communication stream.

Even the most dedicated sales professional frequently assumes a defeatist manner when it comes to being a strong communicator. With adherence to a relatively short and simple array of principles, your communication skills are likely to improve multi-fold.

COMMUNICATOR: FROM GOOD TO GREAT

Many are mediocre communicators; few are exceptional. Strive to be exceptional. Note the difference between a great and a mediocre communicator:

> **The great communicator** is someone of few words who expresses even the most complex topic in a simple and direct manner. Great communicators vary their pace, listen and probe intently, and maintain a focus on their inherent message.

> **The mediocre communicator** is a person of many words who advances thoroughness over simplicity. They drone on in a steady voice and pace and are easily distracted into tangents. They are detail-oriented and often substitute detail for focus. Their basic message is lost in a sea of words.

EMPHASIZE THE POSITIVE

I have reviewed hundreds of mock sales presentations at RYAN Associates' sales training programs since 1988. Although the mock presentations are intended to provide a hands-on experience in designing and delivering a sales proposal, individual styles also are scrutinized.

EXHIBIT 5-7. OUT WITH THE NEGATIVE, IN WITH THE POSITIVE

OLD PHRASING	NEW PHRASING
We hope to work with you.	We believe we can have a positive impact on health and safety at your company.
We specialize in addressing your health and safety problems.	We specialize in working with employers to enhance the health and safety of their workforce.
You can reduce lost work time by developing a strong pre-placement screening program.	We have found that companies like yours often reduce total lost work time by developing a strong pre-placement program.
If you work with us, we will reduce your total workers' comp costs by at least 10%.	We feel confident that we can reduce your total workers' comp costs by 10% or more.
Develop a drug-testing program.	In my opinion, your company should develop a drug-testing program.
Is it possible to schedule an orientation meeting with your frontline supervisors next week?	We have found that an orientation meeting with frontline supervisors is a critical first step in developing a productive relationship with our clients.

Speakers invariably choose inappropriate words at critical moments. If you think you are immune to this problem, invite a colleague to sit in on one or more of your sales calls and write down every negative or weak phrase you say. Alternatively, consider taping a day's worth of telephone calls and critique yourself. Or do both.

Inappropriate words seem to fall into two categories: (1) calling attention to a negative or (2) exhibiting uncertainty or hesitation. Both tendencies can be overcome by focusing on positive, active words and phrases.

I recently sat in on a sales presentation in the Northeast. The sales professional was amiable and possessed considerable product knowledge. Further, the prospect was engaged and appeared to be a relatively "easy sell." The following is an exact quote from the sales professional: "Now to the unpleasant part . . . Where do we send the bills?"

Needless to say, the word "unpleasant" is unnecessary. A far better way to address the same point would be to say:

> *"We take pride in our program's ability to manage your billing process in a smooth and seamless fashion. What type of billing arrangement would work best for your company?"*

Another quote from the same meeting: "We can address your workplace health and safety problems effectively." Here, too, we have a negative word, "problems." Better to replace the word problems with opportunity, as in, "I think you have a real opportunity to enhance the health and safety of your workplace."

Negative words abound in our vocabulary. Common negative words include "bad," "poor," "problem," "complication," "unacceptable," and "difficult." Replace these words with positive words such as "opportunity," "success," "improvement," and "progress."

Another common behavior is a tendency to tread lightly when a firm, positive demeanor would be more effective. Examples of tentative phrases include "Is it possible that . . . " "Perhaps . . ." "Is it okay if . . . ?" "Do you think . . . ?" "Hopefully . . . "

Seek agreement by expressing yourself with action-oriented, confident phrases. It is acceptable to seek agreement by associating the request with past experiences.

"Is it possible for me to meet with your Chief Financial Officer to get a better handle on your real costs?" could be re-phrased as, "We have found that meeting with a company's CFO at the outset provides us with an opportunity to better focus on your unique experience."

Several ad hoc rules should govern sales interactions:

1. **Respect the prospect** — There is a narrow line between criticizing a company's performance and calling attention to their shortcomings in a graceful, positive manner. Rather than "your injury rate is above the national norm for your type of industry," say, "It appears there is a real opportunity to make a difference in your workers' compensation expenses."

   Do not *tell* a prospect they should do something; *suggest* that they do something. At the same time, tell the prospect what

EXHIBIT 5-8. SAY THE RIGHT THING

COMPETITIVE ADVANTAGE: We believe our program's focus on generating excellent return-to-work outcomes that result in direct cost savings for our clients sets us apart.

OPENING STATEMENT: My role is to meet with employers such as yourself to learn more about your company and determine how we might best be able to support your company's health and safety needs.

CLOSING STATEMENT: We value working with employers such as you. We believe there is a strong likelihood that we can make a difference and look forward to working with you.

RESPONDING TO A PRICE OBJECTION: We believe that the most sensible and cost-effective approach to workplace health and safety is a comprehensive approach that minimizes incident rates and lost work time through astute prevention and injury management.

they are doing right. As Dale Carnegie advised us more than seventy years ago in his legendary text, *How to Win Friends and Influence People*, "offer honest and sincere appreciation whenever possible."

2. **Qualify your suggestions** — Qualify anything other than a fact as your opinion or understanding. My favorite phrases in this regard are "in my opinion," "from my perspective," or "in my experience." You not only cover yourself in those exceptionally rare instances when you are wrong, but such qualifiers suggest a healthy and much appreciated dose of humility.
3. **Little is guaranteed** — Do not guarantee anything such as, "We will reduce your costs, lower your lost work days, or increase your (and your employee's) satisfaction level." You are better off telling the prospect something like,

   > *"Although we cannot guarantee that we will lower your healthcare costs, we are confident our focus will provide your company with the greatest likelihood of making a positive difference."*

GETTING TO YES

Do you know the feeling of coming extremely close to making the sale only to see "defeat snatched from the jaws of victory"? Conversely, have you celebrated a "confirmed" sale only to never hear again from the new customer?

These two scenarios can be minimized when you follow a logical sequence of events along the way to closing a sale.

An ability to close the deal is integral to success in any kind of sales. Every sales professional should master the universal principles that apply to closure. On the other hand, closing in occupational health sales presents a relatively unique set of challenges that requires specific techniques.

CLOSING STRATEGIES

Closing is seldom as easy as it might appear. Consider the following:

1. "**Always be closing" or "ABC"** — Fans of the 1990s movies *Glengarry Glen Ross* or *The Boiler Room* are likely to remember this principle. To me, ABC implies two things:

    - Conceptualize a closing strategy prior to meeting with a prospect and work toward that close during each step of the sales cycle. Better yet, develop a series of closing strategies and selectively choose the most appropriate strategy for that particular sales encounter.
    - Effective sales calls proceed through a series of small closes. Learn how to walk a prospect through a series of increasingly meaningful agreements.

2. **Know when to close** — Your antennae should always be attuned to buying signals. Buying signals can come at any time and often occur when one least expects them. It is as grievous an error to ignore a buying signal and continue with a sales presentation as it is to force a close too early in the sales process. Be alert for buying signals such as expressions of strong dissatisfaction with the status quo, an identified product or service need, or concerns about falling short in terms of regulatory compliance in a specific area.
3. **Avoid closing jargon** — Nearly everyone is on guard against stereotypical sales behavior. Eliminate tired Willy Loman-esque closing phrases such as:

    "Shall I sign you up for Plan A or Plan B?"

    "If I can show you . . . , will you sign today?"

    "Give us a chance right now, and we won't let you down."

4. **Don't "ask for the order"** — Contrary to common dogma, I do not believe that an effective closer is necessarily one who routinely asks for the order. Rather, a good closer is one who facilitates a process in which the prospects progressively understand their own needs, want to buy in order to meet those needs, and invariably reach that conclusion autonomously.
5. Use questions to elicit interest — The most effective way to get a prospect to move toward closure is by posing effective questions.

"Mr. Prospect, is there anything that might prevent your company from working with our program?" Or, "Mr. Prospect, off the record, what do you think of the proposal that I described?" (The "off the record" qualifier often elicits a more candid response). Both questions tend to shorten the sales cycle.

EMPLOYER SERVICES SPECIFIC CLOSING

Employer-directed healthcare services are unique in that a sales professional usually is not selling a tangible product. Unless a contract is involved, such as the provision of on-site services, the prototype sale usually involves a smile, a handshake, and a prospect's promise to send the company's workers and job applicants to your clinic. Such sales require an emphasis on softer closing techniques that increase the likelihood that the prospect will, in fact, use your services.

Establish a sense of urgency: Start by subtly eliciting a sense of urgency on the part of the buyer, because inertia rests deep in the soul of any decision maker. Why should XYZ Company start using your services tomorrow when the status quo is a far easier alternative?

Assume that your prospect told you that the company's estimated annual direct workers' compensation expense was $600,000 last year and another $600,000 in indirect expenses. That's $1.2 million per year by your prospect's own accounting, which is a large figure—a figure that may seem more abstract than real to the prospect. The challenge to the sales professional is to whittle that figure down to manageable, meaningful terms. Given a traditional 250-day work year, an annual expense of $1.2 million equates to $4,800 per day or $600 per hour. Once Mr. Decision-maker realizes that his company is spending $600 every hour rather than an abstract amount each year, there is a greater sense of urgency to change behavior and address the problem now.

Distinguish between quick and extended closes: Some closes can be little more than a verbal agreement, while others require formal follow-up. You need to learn how to distinguish between these two options.

Two variables tend to drive the rationale for initiating a quick close: (1) a sense of certainty that the prospect will use your services without further persuasion, (2) a calculation that the prospect's business volume potential is not commensurate with the time commitment required to take your prospect through an extended closing cycle.

The former is largely intuitive: Is the prospect so disillusioned with their current provider or enamored with the idea of working with you that they will almost certainly move their business your way? The latter involves a cold calculation on the part of the sales professional: Does the possibility of not getting the prospect's business exceed the projected value of your time in selling to new prospects with potentially higher volume? (calculate it at 25 percent times the projected volume, or $1,000 a year). After a while such calculations become intuitive.

EXHIBIT 5-9. CLOSING PRINCIPLES

1. Always be closing (ABC)
2. Know when to close
3. Avoid closing jargon
4. Don't ask for the order
5. Use questions to illicit interest
6. Establish a sense of urgency
7. Distinguish between quick and extended closes
8. Get your team to the work site
9. Conduct meaningful clinic tours

Follow-ups to closing: When a prospect agrees to use your services—and there is little doubt their company will do so—or you are dealing with a sufficient book of business to warrant formal closure, one or both of two follow-up closes are appropriate: (1) bring your team back to the workplace, (2) bring the decision maker to your delivery venue.

The former makes sense under any circumstance. Suggest that one or more team members, as appropriate (e.g., medical director, clinic manager, service line director), visit the prospect's work site, meet with key supervisors, and even make a short presentation about the new relationship between your services and their company. Such exposure and time commitment can only serve to increase the company's confidence in your organization and increase the likelihood that they will embrace your services.

Closing requires preparation, discipline, adaptability, and intuition. As that legendary sales professional Kenny Rogers once vocalized, "You've got to know when to hold 'em, know when to fold 'em, know when to walk away, and know when to run."

EFFECTIVE QUESTIONING

You need to learn about prospect needs that can, in turn, match with your services. You must elicit interest on the part of the prospect to engage in conversation with you in the first place. Both requirements are predicated on your ability to know when, how, and what kind of questions to ask a prospect.

WHY ARE QUESTIONS IMPORTANT?

Your initial challenge is to get to first base with a prospect. You need to say something that instills a sense of curiosity. Anyone who has tried to sell anything recognizes how difficult it is to pique interest from a non-qualified prospect. Conversely, when we are the prospect, this is easy to understand: How often do we immediately squelch sales inquiries (e.g., "Hi, this is Roger Johnston calling from Best Communications . . . ") because we view Roger as yet another annoying salesperson?

What if you could secure the interest of twice the number of prospects than you currently do? Almost assuredly your productivity would go up. Icebreakers do little more than place you in line with every other sales professional. Do not begin your quest with a prospect carrying the baggage of all of the salespeople who have called on that prospect in the past. Set yourself apart from the start.

Breaking the ice is one area in which a well-constructed series of questions can secure the active interest of a prospect.

What you could say: *"Hello, this is John Bargetto from Wellness Works and I would like to talk to you about our services."*

What you should say: *"Hello, this is John Bargetto from Wellness Works. We work with employers to enhance the health status of their workforce. Are your company's healthcare costs higher than you would like?"*

In the latter approach, the prospect is more than likely to answer yes. If so, the prospect might be curious enough to want to know how Wellness Works might make a difference. In two sentences, the sales professional has piqued interest (e.g., "Tell me more . . . ") and elicited a need (e.g., "I'd like to lower our costs . . . ").

THE HEART OF THE MATTER

After you break the ice, your questions should continue to play a significant role throughout your entire sales call interview. And it is an interview. Do not be a "feature preacher" who does little more than recite an endless list of virtues ("WorkWell is open twenty-four hours a day. We have three locations in town. Our Medical Director is board certified in occupational medicine.").

Do not spend the majority of your sales call/interview reviewing the history of your service. ("Wellness Works started three years ago with a focus on providing comprehensive wellness services to the workers of Canton. We now have more than fifty companies as valued clients.")

Do not be a modern day Chatty Cathy by talking 80–90 percent of the time while the bewildered prospect thinks of ways to get you off the phone or out of their office as soon as possible.

To the contrary, speak 10–20 percent of the time and use most of that time asking relevant questions, probing (asking the prospect to expand on vague, yet critical, terms such as "quality" and "responsiveness"), and moving the prospect through a logical sales process: generating interest, establishing credibility, identifying needs, attaining commitment, and closing.

PHASE I: Generating interest.

Seek permission to continue with your call by asking the prospect, "Is this a good time for you, or would you prefer to schedule our call/meeting at a time that would be more convenient for you?" This basic courtesy tends to take the prospect off the defensive. If you quantify the expected time allotment (e.g., "This should take no more than five minutes . . ."), you may be pleasantly surprised how many more prospects are willing to speak with you.

Secondly, advise the prospect why you are calling and the planned course of the conversation. Securing a desired level of focus and interest from the respondent is dependent on their understanding the reason for your call from the outset.

> *"Hello, this is Roger Johnston calling from Wellness Works, an affiliate of Mercy Health that provides healthcare cost management services to Canton employers. Our call should only take about five minutes. Is this a good time for you or would you prefer that we schedule the call for a later time or date? Typically, I like to ask about a company's health and safety management practices and briefly review the services we offer that might address your specific needs. Is this approach acceptable to you?"*

PHASE II: Establishing credibility.

Once you have engaged your prospect's interest, establish your service as a credible resource to address any needs their company may have. You may describe your service or ask a prepared set of questions.

The latter approach is particularly effective. A series of brief questions works well to gain insights about the company while appearing engaged in what the prospect has to say. Remember, it is difficult to disagree or object to a question. Effective questioning keeps objections to a minimum while you are building the case for your service. Statements, as opposed to questions, can be more easily contradicted or misinterpreted and put the prospect on the defensive.

PHASE III: Identifying needs.

As you ask more detailed questions and dig deeper into a prospect company's experience, policies, and strategies, you become better positioned to identify needs. The need may be simple and easy to match with your services (e.g., improved coordination for work injuries, an enhanced screening of new workers) or may require broader, more innovative programs.

PHASE IV: Attaining commitment.

Commitment involves obtaining a prospect's buy-in to your proposed solutions. A typical sales presentation presents the solution and waits for the "buy" green light. It is usually more effective to move toward commitment by asking a series of questions.

Examples include:

> *"What do we have to do in order to secure your business?"*
>
> *"If we were to work with your company for the next year, what would we have to accomplish in order to secure your greatest level of confidence?"*
>
> *"Is there any reason why you think our suggested approach might not work for your company?"*
>
> *"We have dramatically lowered health and safety costs at many companies in the area. Would you like to know how we did this?"*

PHASE IV: Closing.

Closing employer-directed services usually involves enhancing the likelihood that the prospect will use your services rather than ensuring it.

Examples of questions that could be used in the closing phase include:

> *"Do you have any concerns about our proposal?"*
>
> *"Is there anyone else who needs to review our proposal before we can move forward?"*

"We agreed that a 10 percent reduction in your average lost workdays would save your company as much as $300 a day. Is there any reason why we shouldn't get started as soon as possible?"

A typical shortcoming of sales calls is a dependence on canned presentations rather than using questions as a tool for moving a prospect through the sales process. Different types of questions tend be more appropriate during different phases of the sales process (piquing interest, establishing credibility, identifying needs, attaining commitment, and closing). Well-structured questions can be to use to identify opportunities, qualify prospects, uncover needs, understand a company's decision-making process, and provide insight on how to position your recommendation. Learn how to ask questions, determine how to ask the right question at the right time, and understand why you are asking each question.

Crafting Responses

In October 1984, I attended a reception for one of the most well-known politicians of his generation. I seized the moment by standing up and asking him a simple question.

As his answer dragged on for the better part of five minutes, I stood aimlessly shifting my feet and nodding in forced agreement.

This famous politician is not alone. I am amazed at how poorly many sales professionals respond to questions.

Here are some of the primary culprits:

The Wind Merchant: Virtually everyone answers a question with too long of a response. When asking a question in a one-on-one situation, the person answering the question should give the other party ample opportunity to control the conversation. When speaking to a group, the individual asking the question may be the only person in the room who really cares about the question.

The Wanderer: My contemporaries likely recall Del Shannon's 1961 hit, "The Wanderer," who "wandered around and around and around and around and around." Many sales professionals are modern day wanderers who meander about a seemingly endless list of tangential topics in responding to a simple question.

The Know-It-All: Ask them a question and you can count on their personal opinions quickly morphing into indisputable facts.

The Garbage In/Garbage Out Specialist: These are the folks who habitually misunderstand a question and provide an answer wholly irrelevant to the inquiry.

EXHIBIT 5-10. A QUESTION-ANSWERING PORTFOLIO; SELECTED QUOTES

SET THE STAGE:

"I would be more than happy to address questions at any time during my presentation, or if you prefer, you may speak with me privately after my talk."

OFFER THANKS AND PRAISE:

"That is an excellent question. Thank you for asking."

REPEAT OR PARAPHRASE THE QUESTION:

"Let me try to paraphrase your question. What I hear you saying is, '. . . . ' Is that correct?"

QUALIFY YOUR RESPONSE:

"In response to your question, it seems to me that . . ."

CONFIRM YOU ARE ON THE RIGHT TRACK:

"Did I adequately address your question?"

CONCLUDING REMARKS:

"Is there anything else?" or *"Does anyone else have anything they wish to say on this topic?"*

Your ability to answer questions exceptionally well is imperative to effective sales. A question may represent a strong buying signal, a latent objection, or a lack of understanding. Your ability to answer questions can often push your sales effort over the top.

THE ART OF ANSWERING

To some extent, responding to questions is an art. But it also involves skills that can be learned.

Here are some rules for your consideration:

1. **Set the stage** — Advise the other party of your willingness to take questions and when such questions might best be asked.
2. **Say thank you** — Thank the person asking the question and, within limits, praise them for the value of the question. It is the professional thing to do and buys you a few precious seconds to help craft your response.
3. **Restate or paraphrase the question** — In a one-on-one encounter, this provides an opportunity for clarity; in a group setting it ensures that everyone in the room heard and understands the question.
4. **Qualify your response** — Pepper your response with phrases such as "in my opinion" and "it seems to me." Establish an image of humility and credibility from the outset.
5. **Reflect for a moment** — Before you respond to a question, reflect to ensure that your answer is concise. In most cases, condense your response to no more than three or four sentences.
6. **Pause early and often** — Ask the individual who asked the question whether you appear to be on the right track.
7. **Ask a final question** — Always conclude your response to a question by asking "Is there anything else?" In a group setting, always ask, "Does anyone else have anything to say on this topic?"
8. **Limit your comments** — If you have a lot of information to share with an individual or a group, only give a quick summary. If more detail is requested, suggest that interested individuals confer with you after the session or schedule a follow-up phone call.

BE ALERT

Most of us tend to underestimate how often we are asked an important question in our professional or private life. Few professionals conscientiously work on their technique for answering questions. As with many things in sales, a proactive plan including a step-by-step routine can make a difference.

FALLBACK OPTIONS

We tend to operate in a black-and-white world: win or lose, succeed or fail, make the sale or do not make the sale, achieve your objective or do not achieve your objective.

If only life were that simple. In reality our world is not one big sporting event, but one with shades of gray in which success can, and should, be measured along a continuum and not always viewed as win/loss.

The concept: There are many reasons why even the best sales professionals fail to make the sale. Prospects may not be ready for the service or may be in a bad mood that day. Prospects may be satisfied with their current provider only to change their minds at some point in the future. Prospects may be pressed for time or may not have all the information they need to make a decision.

None of these reasons should shut the door on the sales professional. Seldom accept rejection as final.

The variants: Fallback options need not be restricted to face-to-face sales calls. Indeed, the "fallback option" concept can be applied to almost any stage of the sales cycle, as well as virtually all inter-personal activities.

The phone call: Attach a purpose and objective to every business call. You might be calling a prospect to learn more about their needs, qualify the prospect, set up a meeting, or actually close a sale.

What if you fail to achieve your core objective during the call? Your instinctive reaction is to chalk one up in the loss column and move on to the next prospect. But such a reaction closes the door and assumes that you will never achieve your initial objective.

EXHIBIT 5-11. OPTION 1: DISTRIBUTING HAND-OUT MATERIALS DURING A FACE-TO-FACE MEETING

ADVANTAGES	DISADVANTAGES
• Provides instant information to the prospect	• Suggests you are "pre-programmed"
• Suggests to the prospect the sales professional is well-prepared for the meeting	• May distract the prospect as they review the handout
• Prolongs the encounter, which allows more time to achieve the original objective of the call	• May suggest to the prospect the meeting is over

EXHIBIT 5-12. OPTION 2: SENDING HAND-OUT MATERIALS AFTER A FACE-TO-FACE MEETING

ADVANTAGES	DISADVANTAGES
• Allows you to fine-tune and customize the material	• Gives the prospect time to consider other options (e.g., "A bird in the hand").
• Fast turnaround indicates efficiency and responsiveness	• If the materials are not sent promptly, it may suggest poor organization and/or lack of responsiveness.
• Buys time to think of additional information you can send	• The prospect may receive the materials at a time when they are not focused on the subject (e.g., "Out of sight, out of mind").

There are fallback options.

The preparation: Prepare your fallback option *before* you place the call. Ask yourself three questions:

1. What is the real purpose of my call? If everything goes my way, what do I want to achieve?
2. If things do not go my way, what is the next best (fallback) option or options?
3. If I get channeled to voice mail, exactly what message do I want to leave? Do I even want to leave a message, or would it be more effective to call back at a later time or date?

EXHIBIT 5-13. KEEPING YOUR OBJECTIVE ALIVE

UNSUCCESSFUL PRIMARY OBJECTIVE	FALLBACK OPTION
Learn more about the prospect's needs	Send a self-assessment questionnaire
Qualify the prospect	Assume they qualify and move on
Set up a meeting	Ask if they will agree to speak with you again in three months
Close a sale	Suggest they visit your clinic or facility

The same principles apply during a one-on-one or group meeting. The primary difference between a telephone call and an in-person meeting is that you can actually see your prospects, gauge their facial expressions and body language, and provide them with appropriate material right on the spot.

Review and answer the same three questions before a face-to-face meeting. In such meetings, a fourth question arises: What, if anything, do I need to bring with me if I get the opportunity to provide collateral or informational materials? Perhaps you should not bring anything, knowing that you can send them something quickly upon your return to the office or via a quick call to support staff at your office.

Just as you maintain a portfolio of services that you can mix and match to suit the needs of prospective clients, maintain a portfolio of sales-process options that allow you to adjust favorably to unforeseen circumstances during the sales process.

Over time, a second option may in fact turn out to be the preferred option.

THE FEAR FACTOR

Electing the President of the Free World is one thing, and selling healthcare services is another. However, there are similarities. Avoidance-over-appeal is a real part of decision making at every level. Given sufficient probing, most prospects will express inner fears that can be successfully addressed.

Buyers of healthcare services typically have two basic motivations:

- Helping their parent company save money
- Making their own lives easier

Most sales professionals view the former as fundamental to their sales challenge: enhance health status, save the employer money, and everyone is happy.

The second motivation is often ignored. Many people are inherently parochial. They are concerned about *their* finite time, *their* daily burdens, and *their* professional success. Sales professionals often minimize these factors or ignore them completely. Determine the relative importance of professional vs. personal motivation and structure your sales approach accordingly.

> **PRINCIPLE 1: Do not minimize the potential importance of a prospect's parochial interests.**
>
> In many instances, both professional and personal factors should be incorporated into a benefit statement.

> *"Our proposed program would provide your company with a compelling opportunity to reduce lost workdays and enhance the health and well-being of your workforce. Further, it should make life easier for you, as we provide the tracking, reports, and verbal updates that you have been receiving piecemeal."*

PRINCIPLE 2: Include a clear personal "what's in it for them" point in every benefit statement.

Know when and how to play the "personal" card. Prospects run the gamut of personality types, from those who genuinely place the welfare of their company above all else to those who are card-carrying members of the "me, myself, and I" club. Assess where each prospect seems to fall on this continuum and position the sales approach accordingly.

Professional factors:

- Save the company money.
- Enhance worker health status.
- Instill a new corporate health ethic.

Personal factors:

- Save the prospect time.
- Save the prospect hassle.
- Make the prospect look better.

The key to a successful sales encounter involves the application of three communication principles: (1) asking the right question, (2) listening, and (3) probing.

Crafting questions: Questions should be crafted to readily identify a pressing problem that can be placed on the table to elicit a solution. Typically, the sales professional will ask about purely professional problems (the company's most significant health and safety problems). As part of this process, investigate the potential personal ramifications of professional problems.

Classic questions might include:

"What is the most frustrating aspect of your job?"

"What activity causes you to lose the most amount of valuable time?"

"When it comes to healthcare costs, what do you personally need to achieve to really be successful?"

"With regard to the health and safety of your workforce, what is your worst nightmare—what keeps you up at night?"

This line of questioning serves two valuable purposes:

1. If you listen carefully, you can usually place the prospect in a pretty reliable place on the "care about my company/care about myself" continuum.
2. If the prospect doesn't offer much in response to the preceding questions, there is a strong likelihood that you can safely retreat to the "best for the company" arena.

On the other hand, prospects who relate to personal challenges are more likely to respond to solutions that will be helpful not only to the company but also to them (save them time and/or make them look good). Suddenly, the sales process is all downhill from there.

PRINCIPLE 3: Use questions to determine where the prospect sits on the "care about my company/care about myself" continuum.

Once you have detected the importance of personal issues, your benefit statement can be crafted. In almost every instance, touch on both sides: the professional impact and the personal impact. The art comes in determining the proper emphasis to place on respective sides of the continuum.

If there is a heavy **company** orientation:

> *"I feel confident that our unique computerized focus on return-to-work outcomes will provide your company with the best chance to reduce unnecessary costs and enhance the health status of your workers."*

If there is complimentary blend of **company and personal**:

> *"Our approach serves two vital purposes: we emphasize early return to work, thereby reducing unnecessary lost work time and your workers' compensation-related costs while at the same time allowing you to spend more time addressing other important issues."*

If there is a heavy **personal** orientation:

> *"Our injury/illness prevention programs and our focus on early return to work will dramatically reduce the time that you have to spend on such cases, providing you with more time for other matters and making your life a lot easier."*

Do not minimize or ignore the potential importance of a prospect's personal fears and self-interests. Learn to identify those fears and self-interests and craft your recommendations and benefit statements accordingly.

HUMOR

A gleam in one's eye, a smile on one's face, and a skip in one's step often is as beneficial as the most cogent sales presentation.

Healthcare is undoubtedly a serious business that requires a serious approach. Given this caveat, do not dismiss the value of a little levity when performing sales and community outreach.

As the years go by and I become older (indisputably) and wiser (disputably), I seem to take life less seriously. Guess what? Everything seems to work out fine, arguably even better than when I took a more no-nonsense approach.

If you take yourself too seriously, you assume the risk of projecting a stiff, insincere image to your current and prospective clients. I like to run an office in which lightheartedness and humor are staples. I do not recall a single weekly staff meeting that did not include a solid dose of laughter and good cheer.

Mixing serious matters with frivolity:

- Makes for more cheerful and committed employees
- Engenders an upbeat spirit that extends out to sales calls and other marketing contacts
- Helps keep staff focused throughout a meeting

Group and one-on-one meetings, and even formal presentations, require a cadence not dissimilar to a concert, movie, or book: fast/slow, dead-serious/upbeat. Such a cadence stimulates a creative, innovative urge among all participants. Like an athletic team, a sales team that feels relaxed and confident is usually a successful one.

What better place to gain insight on modern marketing than by reviewing the commercials shown during a Super Bowl telecast? What did these commercials—which cost advertisers about a gazillion dollars a minute—have in common? That's easy: they all tried to transmit their core message through humor.

Not surprisingly, people made a point of watching the commercials during the game and even looked at their favorites again later on the Internet. A considerable number of viewers will recall at least some of the products that were touted and will be subliminally programmed to buy them because they found the commercials amusing.

This lesson should not be lost on all of us who wish to get the attention of employers. Although outright side-splitting comedy would not be appropriate in a healthcare setting, a toned-down version of humor can go a long way toward breaking the ice.

Here are two suggestions:

1. **Add humor to your website** — Websites all more or less look the same: information-laden and boring. If you really want to make your website catch people's attention, you have to make it different and fun.

   There are many ways this can be done. Photos work well, as does the inclusion of simple contests, audio overviews, or music.

2. **Use humor in your promotional materials** — B-O-R-I-N-G. There's that word again. Most promotional packets are little more than a jam-packed, overweight litany of services and features; it is unlikely that one person in one hundred spends any time at all reviewing the material. To get the reader's attention, marketing materials need a hook—something humorous, something fun, something intriguing, something different.

HUMOR IN THE SALES PROCESS

Is there such a thing as a funny sales professional who does not take himself or herself all that seriously? The thought of it! Remember this when you are trying to separate yourself from the myriad of salespeople who have preceded you.

Do not underestimate the likability factor in a prospect's buying behavior. I am instantly drawn to someone who makes me feel at ease. I am more comfortable in dealing with that person. (As my old friend Jim Madden often said, "Nervous people make me nervous.") A jocular sales professional is likely to get both my ear and my business.

HUMOR IN PUBLIC PRESENTATIONS

This gets a little tricky. Inherently unfunny people who try to be funny in public presentations tend to be worse off than the humorless wooden soldier. If you are a genuinely funny person and have a funny story to relate, by all means, bring it on.

There is a basic rule to keep in mind: save the last half of a talk for serious business. Humor is best provided at the outset or intermittently throughout the first half of your talk. The last half needs to be reserved for serious business, a cogent summary, and an emotional close.

Although there are many related resources for presentations readily available on the Internet, humor in public presentations need not always be canned. A good speaker is one who can generate ad-lib humor during a public presentation. As a public speaker, I have experienced both sides of this suggestion: untamed guffaws with one group, blank stares with another. After a while you learn to move forward and be yourself.

RETURN ON INVESTMENT (ROI)

It began with two cavemen, or even before: bartering, fair trade, an exchange where both parties (theoretically) walk away satisfied. This concept persists to this day: spend money on something and receive something of equal or greater value. Better yet, enter into a transaction with the belief that you are receiving the greatest possible return on your investment, given all the available options.

A sales professional's activities are really no different. The heart of every sales encounter is to provide value to the buyer and to ensure that the service provides the greatest value available. In sales, words to that effect are not sufficient. You must genuinely believe in the value of the product and articulate this value in the most honest, persuasive, and appropriate manner possible.

Let's take a look at ROI principles for common health services.

WORK INJURY MANAGEMENT

At the most fundamental level, an employer prospect has a basic goal: to get workers back to work as safely, quickly, and inexpensively as possible. A properly conceived service should do more by decreasing the likelihood that the worker will get re-injured and preventing other workers from sustaining similar injuries.

Any discussion concerning the value of a program's work injury management services must take into account the program's injury management proficiency as well as its prevention skills. When selling "work injury management" services, illustrate your service's ability to ensure a rapid return to work at a manageable cost. Rapid and sustainable return to work must be more than an idle promise; it requires meaningful justification.

Numerous attributes can lead to a more rapid return to work:

- **Care management software** facilitates faster and tighter control over the care management system.
- **Targeted case management** ensures that the cases most amenable to prompt coordination will get priority attention.
- **Modified duty programs** promote more rapid reintegration into the workforce.
- **Continuity with occupational rehabilitation** services provides interventions to reduce the likelihood of lost work time.

The second half of the equation—lower costs—is more challenging because buyers frequently cannot see beyond average fees. You need to lead a prospect through a process that results in an understanding of the difference between price and value (return on investment). The discussion may go something like this:

> *"At WorkWell we recognize that your company's costs are best addressed not by pricing alone, but by your company's overall return on investment.*
>
> *You might work with another provider that charges, on the average, $15 less per visit than WorkWell. Over ten visits, you would save $150 by using that clinic rather than ours. Based solely on price, the other clinic would and should be your choice. But rapid and safe return to work of your employees should invariably be more important to your company. Earlier, you estimated that every lost workday costs your company about $2,000 in direct and indirect costs. If our services save your company even one lost workday, you would save more than you would if you used the lower cost provider for 133 patient visits."*

So far, so good. The sales representative has stated the difference between price and value. Next comes the **rationale** that is used to illustrate why your service is the best option to achieve that value. This requires an emphasis on the *likelihood* of your service making a difference, rather than a *guarantee* that your service will make a difference:

> *"We believe that our services offer your company the greatest likelihood for reducing lost workdays and thereby reducing your overall costs. We base this belief on our confidence that we are unique among other options in the area. We have been doing targeted care management for more than five years. We use a dedicated patient tracking software system and track outcomes on a daily basis. We are truly focused on reducing lost work time, which has the most marked impact on your bottom line costs."*

If the emphasis is on prevention, the sales professional might say something like this:

> *"We believe that our services offer your company the greatest likelihood for reducing lost workdays and thereby reducing your overall costs. We base this belief on our emphasis on minimizing injuries and illnesses. Our physicians and other clinic personnel are trained to investigate the environmental origin of work-related conditions, investigate that origin thoroughly, and provide appropriate recommendations to the company. In this way, we usually reduce injury incidence, lost work time, and overall costs."*

PRE-PLACEMENT PHYSICAL EXAMS

Unless a service proactively addresses the return on investment concept, it is likely to find it difficult to compete with lower cost providers who offer pre-placement examinations more as a low-cost commodity than as part of an integrated approach to workplace health management.

A typical human resources officer is likely to purchase pre-placement physical examinations on price alone if he or she assumes there is little qualitative difference among alternative providers. The human resource officer may factor in convenience, such as a clinic closer to the work site or with extended hours. Unless prompted, the prospect may be unlikely to think of return on investment when selecting a provider of pre-placement physical exams. Is there a difference between "fair" and "excellent" pre-placement physicals? If so, how can one convey that value?

Pre-placement physical examinations are done to determine one's physical suitability for a prospective job. If the prospective hire does not meet the criteria set for the job, they are more likely to become injured on the job and thereby cost the employer money. An exceptionally well-conceived and delivered pre-placement physical exam is usually one that is based on an astute job analysis and performed by a practitioner who is skilled at matching job requirements to the applicant. Some practitioners do this well; many do not.

Thus, the value statement:

> *"At WorkWell we believe that the value of a pre-placement physical examination is not based on price alone, but on the quality of the exam itself; that is, we understand the criteria for the position and can effectively match that criteria to the job candidates. If prospective hires who are not physically suited for the job slip through the pre-placement exam process, they have a greater likelihood of being injured, costing your company, by your estimates, about $2,000 for every day they are out of work."*

And the rationale behind it:

> *"All pre-placement physical examinations at WorkWell are performed by a provider who has received specific training in matching job criteria to applicants. Our dedicated software allows us to carefully review job criteria before the exam to ensure that the exam is thorough and focused. We believe that our physical exams provide your company with the greatest likelihood of ensuring that all candidates are physically suited for their jobs, and the best return on your investment."*

The concept is simple on the surface but rarely practiced: sell on value, not price, and support the value of your product with meaningful and concrete examples. It is the heart of effective sales.

WELLNESS SERVICES

It is virtually impossible to adequately measure Return on Investment on wellness service in the short term. Certain evaluation parameters such as claims cost and per capita lost work time may make some sense on the surface but are tainted by confounding factors (e.g., non-work related conditions, skewed data) and the possibility, some may say likelihood, that newfound healthy behaviors will abate in time. Offering effectively measured and well-documented successes elsewhere (e.g., a large national employer) is generally of little interest or seemingly inapplicable to your prospects.

What to do? Some percentage of prospects will instinctively buy into the wellness services concept and be amendable to a relationship. Keep your antennae focused to identify these prospects. Others may respond to word of mouth or references from happy wellness services clients in the community. Once you establish a few core clients, monitor them closely and seek permission to use them as referrals.

The more your prospects are encouraged to view wellness services as a critical component of a broader health and safety initiative, the more likely they will contract for wellness services. When it comes to wellness, it is all about total health management.

URGENT CARE SERVICES

In general, ROI is less important than convenience, price, and total health coordination in selling urgent care services. Of course, you can tie each one of these three variables into a general ROI context.

- An urgent care clinic close to the workplace means that workers spend less time away from the workplace, thus saving the employer costs associated with lost work time.
- Even though the cost of urgent care services is not directly borne by the employer, urgent care is viewed as a lower cost alternative to episodic care.
- Blended occupational health/urgent care clinics can offer employers a one-stop option for their employees. Having both work-related and personal care coordinated under the same roof suggests more expeditious, focused, and ultimately less costly care.

Several principles apply when you use ROI to support the sales effort.

EXHIBIT 5-14. ROI IN SALES

1. Never be "beaten" on price alone.
2. Ensure that every component provides a unique value to prospective buyers.
3. Persuade prospects that return on investment is more important to them than unit price.
4. Provide concrete rationale that your program's approach provides the greatest likelihood for optimal return on investment.

Chapter 6:

Sales Techniques

Once you have mastered core sales tactics, you are ready to walk into a prospect's office and sell your services. A sales call, however, is not as simple as it may seem on the surface.

Sales Techniques: An Overview

Shape your sales strategy by:

1. **Leaving written materials at home** — People do not have as much time for the written word as they once did. You exude greater self-confidence when you can look a prospect in the eye, discuss the prospect's needs, and offer solutions to these needs.

   Distribution of written materials preceding, during, or immediately following a sales call is often counterproductive. Such materials are not likely to be reviewed. They suggest a "one size fits all" mind-set and draw attention away from your core message.

   Learn more about your prospect's needs, offer solutions, and follow-up with customized email attachments. By placing relevant material in a prospect's hands shortly after your meeting, you are likely to project an image of customization and responsiveness.

> **Action step:** *Create and continually expand an electronic library of files that include summaries of your services and their value, client reference lists, and selected research findings that suggest they were created "just for the prospect."*

2. **Preparing for your call** — Make "prepare, prepare, prepare" your mantra. In most cases adequate preparation does not require a lot of time and is telling at the sales meeting. Prepare for the call by:
   - Reviewing the prospect company's website
   - Learning the title and core responsibilities of the person or people you will meet
   - Crafting your basic introduction
   - Identifying the core objective of the meeting
   - Creating a Plan B fallback objective
   - Planning for your close or follow-up plan

   > **Action step:** *Develop an electronic template/form that outlines the preparation activities noted above. Take a few minutes to complete the form before every sales call. Review the information that you have entered on the form before your meeting.*

3. **Learning to communicate effectively** — During a sales call, you need to:
   - **Ask questions rather than offer advice** — In sales it is all about the other person. Ask open-ended questions (that is, few, if any, yes-or-no questions) to help illuminate the prospect company's needs, concerns, and practices. Ferret out the negative (e.g., "What is your biggest concern with regard to healthcare at your company?").
   - **Listen . . . and listen some more** — Most of us think we are genuinely good listeners; most of us are wrong. In a sales call, the traditional 80:20 rule tends to apply: let the prospect do 80 percent of the talking. And listen carefully—focus and take notes.

- **Learn to probe** — What do astute trial lawyers, primary care physicians, and journalists have in common? Answer: They all know how to probe effectively. A probe is a request for the prospect to provide greater specificity to an issue that they have addressed only generally.

  Statement: *"I look for quality first and foremost."*
  Probe: *"What does quality mean to you?"*

- **Be concise** — Learn to express every question and every response with as few words as possible. Every superfluous word takes away from the core message. In golf the temptation is to swing as hard as you can, but the reality is that a slow easy swing works best. In sales, the temptation is to fill the air with your words, but the reality is that the fewer the number of words, the better.

  > **Action step:** *Select a day in which you have scheduled numerous sales calls or other types of meetings. Dedicate that day to saying as little as you can. See how it works for you.*

4. **Being a wordsmith** — Even experienced sales professionals have a difficult time choosing the right words. Several examples are illuminating:

   - **Using platitudes** — This is public enemy number one. Do not make claims without credible justification. Do not suggest your service offers the "best customer service" in the absence of quantifiable justification, such as the results of patient satisfaction surveys. Avoid saying that your service has the most experience unless you can prove it. An expression such as "We have managed more than 30,000 injuries since 1995" is a tangible, persuasive and legitimate statement. I often throw back the phrase, "Sez who?" when I encounter a platitude during our training programs; do the same.

   - **Using negative words and phrases** — As previously described, a negative word contributes to a negative atmosphere. The words "bad" or "poor" should always be "an excellent chance for improvement." A negative word here and there may not make much of a difference, but in the aggregate such words fail to create the optimistic, productive mood that is critical in a sales call.

- **Talking in a way your prospects understand** — As a member of the healthcare sector, you likely see the world differently than your prospects in the corporate world. Listen carefully to the phrases that employer representatives use to describe their circumstances and be poised to reflect these words back as part of your proposed solution.

    Action step: *Review a sample of your collateral material or another promotional piece and write down every phrase that strikes you as either a platitude, negative word, or an example of "provider speak." Substitute a word or phrase for each example that you find. You are likely to be surprised at how many inappropriate words you discover.*

5. **Preparing for objections** — "Objection" is among the most feared words in many sales professionals' daily lives. However, an objection is more likely to elicit a positive response from experienced sales professionals who are prepared to deal with common objections.

    The four most common objections to healthcare services are:

    - Price
    - Your service delivery location compared to other options
    - A prospect's satisfaction with their current service provider
    - A prospect's dissatisfaction in receiving your service or working with your organization in the past

    If you know these objections are coming, logic dictates that you be prepared for them by writing out—or scripting—a response to each one.

    Scripting involves preparing and memorizing the optimal response to questions or concerns you hear frequently. In preparing a script, write down the words, carefully review them, and edit them multiple times. When you have developed a response that is concise and justifiable, memorize it verbatim, so you are free to fully concentrate on such visual cues as eye contact, volume, pace, and overall body language.

Take the price objection. Many buyers act on the basis of the price, minimizing or disregarding patient service, continuity of care, and value. In these instances, you need to change the focus from "price" to "return on investment."

> *"I can certainly understand why price is important to you. I encourage you to consider the bigger picture. In the long run, return on your investment should be more important to your company than the price of individual services. We believe that our experience and integrated continuity of care are best suited to address your concerns and save your company more money in the long run."*

Develop a series of different scripts, commit them to memory, and proceed to deliver each, as appropriate, with unmitigated self-confidence. Scripts can be designed to address:

- The price objection
- The location objection
- The satisfied with current provider objection
- The dissatisfied with your service objection
- Your service's competitive advantage
- The reason your location is valuable to a prospective company
- The reason why your program's extensive experience is valuable to a prospect company
- The reason why extended clinic hours are valuable to a prospect company
- The reason why a sophisticated care management software platform matters to a prospect company

> **Action step:** *Prepare an appropriate response to the location objection. Rework the objection several times to ensure that is as concise and appropriate as possible. Memorize it.*

6. **Learning how to close** — Closing a relationship-oriented sale is vastly different from closing a typical commodity sale. There are (usually) no contracts to sign, no credit cards to process, and no cash to exchange. Without appropriate follow-up, a typical close reverts to little more than a smile, a handshake, and a promise.

   Enter follow-up. A close is not a finite moment per se, but rather asking your prospect to complete an action that will increase the likelihood that their company will use your program.

   Classic follow-up closes include a private clinic tour, which should be meticulously planned and orchestrated. It may be a workplace visit by one of your senior providers or a conference call involving your coordinator, medical director, yourself, and key coordination personnel from the company. The more it appears that you are ready to begin services for the prospect company, the more likely the company will, in fact, use your services.

   > **Action step:** *Review the section on clinic tours that is included in this book. Outline a plan for orchestrating a clinic tour at your facility, and then try it!*

7. **Practicing the Golden Minute** — Responses to objections and the mechanics of a clinic tour are not the only sales activity that should be meticulously planned. As discussed, the first and last thirty seconds of every sales call should be carefully planned as well. This Golden Minute represents the sixty seconds that often make or break sales calls.

   The first thirty-second segment is easy to plan and, with a little practice, not difficult to execute:

   - Offer a firm handshake, smile, use the prospect's name, and look your prospect in the eye.
   - Thank them for their time (e.g., "I recognize how valuable your time is . . . ").
   - Restate the objective of the meeting. (e.g., "My role is to find out what health and safety challenges your company is facing and to suggest ways that we might provide possible solutions to those challenges.").

- Provide a roadmap (e.g., "I would first like to ask you a few questions about your company's health and safety practices, and then . . . ").

The last thirty seconds of a sales meeting also are critically important because they capture the mood of the meeting:

- Briefly summarize the gist of the meeting (e.g., "In summary, it is my understanding that . . . ").
- Reiterate any action steps (e.g., "Our next step will be to . . . ").
- Offer your "knockout punch," or why obtaining their business will mean a great deal to you (e.g., "I personally take great pride and interest in every company that I bring into our program . . . ").
- Repeat the handshake before you leave the meeting.

> **Action step:** *Develop your own unique handshake, greeting, and departure regimen. Practice it with friends and coworkers. Carefully note how others introduce themselves to you. What did they do well or poorly? Perfect it!*

8. **Dazzling them post meeting** — How quickly the warmth of a given moment can fade away! During my college days, a girlfriend travelled one thousand miles to join me for our homecoming weekend. What a romantic three days! The euphoria quickly died when we went back to our respective college lives in Nashville and New York City. It was an early lesson on the need to proactively sustain a moment.

   In healthcare sales, follow-up is critical. It should be rapid and customized, such as the electronic library I described, which gives you greater latitude to say, "I have something that addresses that issue. May I email it to you later this afternoon?" Once such an agreement is made, your next objective is breathtaking turnaround. Send the promised attachment within hours, even if it requires a call back to your office to ask someone to send it on your behalf.

   You can dazzle your prospects in other areas as well:

- Send a brief post-meeting email thanking the prospect for their time and reiterating any action steps within hours of your meeting.
- Ensure that any other promises are honored as expeditiously as possible. (e.g., "I will ask our medical director to call you as soon as she possibly can.")
- Keep your word when you promise to contact a prospect at some later date. If your sales encounter is unsuccessful, in most cases you will want to ask if you may call back in, say, six months. If that is acceptable to your prospect, calendar the call right at the six-month mark. ("When we last spoke on January 5, we agreed that I would check in with you six months later.")

> **Action step:** *Develop a simple "thank you for your time" email. Create a second version for unsuccessful sales calls. Refine them and leave room in the email template for information specific to the recipient (e.g., "In follow up, I will . . . "). Save the base documents and use them as the starting point for every email follow-up to a sales meeting.*

Sales Pipeline Maintenance

Any reader close to my age is likely to recall "Pipeline," the 1962 hit song by The Chantays. Since it was a spirited instrumental sans words, I was never sure what the song meant—that is, until now.

The song obviously refers to a necessary, but all-too-often lacking, ingredient for a sales professional: active prospect pipelines.

PIPELINE DEFINED

A sales pipeline is an ongoing array of prospects in various stages of the sales process. When you have a consistently full pipeline, you have other options whenever a decision-making delay or a rejection occurs. Failure to keep the pipeline primed impedes progress at any point in the sales cycle.

Maintaining a vibrant pipeline sounds easy—akin to keeping your gas tank somewhat above empty. The science of pipeline maintenance is more complex, requiring strategic planning and a proactive approach.

1. **Multiple pipelines** — Do not confine your pipeline solely to prospects that are in various stages of the sales process. Numerous other pipelines such as active or former clients should be activated as well.
2. **Complex pipelines** — Most pipelines contain several variables or segments such as company size or type, each of which needs to be managed.
3. **Equilibrium** — A pipeline that is too large is as worrisome as one that is too small. Develop an appropriate level of equilibrium for each market segment and every pipeline.

PIPELINES PLURAL

Your core pipeline is your sales prospect list. Develop and maintain a comprehensive and accurate list of employers in your service area from the get-go and segment those employers according to their revenue potential.

Other potential employer pipelines include:

1. **Current clients** — Depending on your service mix, your client base is likely to offer numerous opportunities to cross sell new or expanded services. Create a pipeline to stay in touch with this segment in a consistent manner.
2. **"No" prospects** — A decision not to buy is not necessarily a permanent rejection. Maintain a pipeline of employer prospects who said no, and schedule periodic times to reconnect with them.
3. **Referral candidates** — Do not underestimate word of mouth from individuals who are your most enthusiastic supporters. Fill one of your pipelines with the universe of your best supporters and create mechanisms for staying in contact with them, such as an email message.

COMPLEX PIPELINES

You must account for the inherent differences among pipeline members. Avoid mixing apples and oranges.

Assume that you sell three different levels of service: (1) a relatively complex on-site service program, (2) a core clinic, and (3) an inexpensive "get to know us" service such as a newsletter or advisor.

Segment your prospect universe into three analogous groups: (1) employers who are candidates for on-site services, (2) traditional employers, and (3) employers who are not likely to become full-fledged clients any time soon.

Ensure an adequate number of prospects in each of these three categories, rather than focusing on the aggregate size of your pipeline.

Depending on the program, other segmentation variables may be important. Consider each prospect's position in the sales cycle. A functioning pipeline maintains a balance between the various stages of the sales cycle, ranging from new prospects to those that are near close.

EQUILIBRIUM

It is as counterproductive to become trapped in a pipeline that is too large as it is in a pipeline that is too small.

An inappropriately large pipeline invariably means that you will be unable to move many of your prospects through the sales cycle at an appropriate rate of speed. An inappropriately small pipeline means that you are likely to run into unproductive downtime. Maintaining a nearly perfect sense of equilibrium is advisable, but how?

It is largely a question of trial and error:

- Begin with a certain number of prospects.
- Ensure that they are divided properly among relevant segments.
- Constantly assess the size of your pipeline.

If your pipeline is too small, increase the number of your initial weekly contacts (e.g., rather than send out ten letters of introduction, mail fifteen). If the pipeline is too large, decrease the number of introductory letters.

Set aside a specific time each week to review your pipeline, commit to a routine, and act accordingly. Friday morning is as good a time to send out letters because they will arrive early the next week (on a day when the recipient is likely to be more energized and able to focus on your correspondence).

Ask yourself each Friday how much "juice," if any, you want to add to your pipeline (and pipeline segments), and then act.

A full pipeline is your ally. What appears easy and obvious cannot be optimized unless it is managed in an aggressive and astute manner. Make pipeline maintenance a way of life.

SUMMARY: STEPS TOWARD AN EFFECTIVE PIPELINE

Creating and maintaining an effective pipeline provides you with clear direction and saves time.

Consider:

1. Have an up-to-date, comprehensive employer universe.
2. Stratify your universe by sales potential.
3. Examine and assign segments to your pipeline as appropriate.
4. Develop or refine your vehicles of introduction (e.g., direct referrals, introductory letters, calls, site visits).
5. Set aside a day of the week to review your pipelines.
6. Initiate contact with new prospects per your assessment in step number 5, above.

The Numbers Game

"Hedge your bets." "Increase your odds." "Play the percentages." We have all heard these phases and others like them and may recognize that they apply equally as well to gambling, business investments, and healthcare marketing. The quantitative (sheer degree) can often be as important as the qualitative (tactics) aspects of the plan.

Assume that 50 percent of incremental business comes from face-to-face direct sales, while the remaining 50 percent (or so) of incremental sales come as a result of marketing tactics that do not involve human contact.

Four numbers should govern your marketing effort:

- The size of your universe
- The number of email addresses you have captured within this universe
- The frequency of memorable contacts within this universe
- The number of marketing tactics you deploy each year

EXPAND YOUR UNIVERSE

Include every possible user of your services in your prospect database. The larger your employer database, the more incremental business you are likely to receive as a result of your marketing tactics.

Expand the size of your universe by broadening its geographic breadth. We often hear of primary, secondary, and tertiary service areas. Too often a healthcare organization and/or its individual service lines fail to look beyond their primary service area, or at the least, ignore their tertiary service area. Yet employers in such tertiary areas—usually far from the madding crowd—invariably feel ignored and seem to be disproportionately anxious to work with any provider who shows interest in working with them. Although your penetration potential may only be 10 percent of employers in a tertiary market, 10 percent of something is 10 percent more than nothing.

EXPAND YOUR CONTACTS PER PROSPECT

The math is again painfully simple, yet the reality is that actual marketing touches are often fewer than appropriate. Just as a 20 percent increase in your prospect universe is likely to generate a 10–20 percent increase in volume, a 20 percent increase in actual, memorable employer touches promises to add 10–20 percent more volume.

EXPAND YOUR EMAIL BASE

E-marketing, if conducted in a sensitive manner, is an exceptionally cost-effective way to gain exposure for your program, and many programs are moving in that direction.

Build as large and accurate an email address base as possible:

1. Seek email addresses on every form and at every opportunity.
2. Do not limit your email address file to one contact per company; endeavor to get as many addresses as you can.
3. Obtain both personal and work email addresses. With national employee turnover hovering around 20 percent, many of your best contacts will soon be at another company. Do not lose track of them.
4. Follow up on email addresses that bounce back because of an incorrectly entered address, an outdated address or a spam blocker. The email recipient is invariably impressed with your tenacity, and you will dramatically increase the number of transmittable email addresses in your file.
5. Gather employee/patient email addresses that can be used for general health advisories and other announcements. Provided you receive signed permission to use an email address for educational purposes, such a practice is within the law and provides a marketing edge at the individual patient level.

EXPAND YOUR TACTICS

The fourth number worth considering is the actual number of tactics you execute on an annual basis. Many services try a tactic or two and call it a day. Not every tactic resonates with every prospect. Add variety to your tactic mix.

EXPAND YOUR SALES TIME

Numbers matter in healthcare sales:

Face-to-face sales calls: Healthcare sales professionals fall far short of seeing as many prospects as they should in a given week. A quota of at least fifteen face-to-face calls per week is a reasonable expectation.

Average length of sales call: The average length of a sales call is often an overlooked time eater. Assume the average length of your sales call is thirty minutes and you could reduce that time to twenty minutes through a more condensed routine: ten minutes less per sales call times fifteen sales calls per week times fifty weeks = 7,500 less minutes per year (10 x 15 x 50 = 7,500), or enough time to conduct another 375 sales calls.

Telephone time: The time that a sales professional spends on the telephone can dramatically diminish the time available for other sales and marketing activity. Even a 20 percent reduction in telephone talk time can produce considerable incremental time for additional sales calls.

Exhibit 6-1. A Ten Step Plan to Make the Numbers Work for You

1.	Add new employers to your core prospect list.
2.	Expand your contact base to secondary and tertiary markets.
3.	Expand your annual number of touch contacts you have with every prospect.
4.	Aggressively gather email addresses from client contacts.
5.	Gather both personal and work email addresses when possible.
6.	Constantly follow-up on email bounce backs.
7.	Gather patient email addresses (with permission).
8.	Establish a quota for live sales calls per week.
9.	Reduce your average length of time per sales call.
10.	Reduce your average time per telephone call.

Leveraging Client Relationships

In many cases there is a greater opportunity in selling new items to existing clients through cross selling (vertical expansion) than there is in approaching new prospects.

ARE YOUR CLIENTS HAPPY?

Do not to assume that a client is happy with your services because you have not heard anything to the contrary. Seek multiple opportunities to periodically assess how happy your clients are before attempting to cross sell services. Make quarterly "check-in" calls, send an annual questionnaire to all employer clients, and conduct informal inquiries. Assess your program's performance and readily identify your greatest supporters.

CROSS SELLING

The long-run viability of most services rests with their ability to expand and integrate the services for employers. Do not feel confined to placing too much emphasis on core occupational health services that are likely eventually to perish. Selling additional services to your existing client base becomes a central survival strategy

There are numerous advantages in dealing with an existing client:

1. You know the client and presumably have generated a reasonable amount of trust. Once your trust and credibility has been established, a large hurdle has been successfully navigated.
2. A client is a previous buyer of your services. They have pulled the buy trigger in the past; they know that, and so do you.
3. You know the client's business and are well positioned to understand how a new service is likely to fit into the larger picture.

Build on the positives of working with an existing client. Learning how to leverage this relationship by emphasizing the inherent merit of a systematic, integrated approach to your client's healthcare needs.

You might word your pitch in the following manner:

> *"Our primary goal is to make the greatest possible impact on your employees' health status and your company's bottom line. We recognize that the best way to make such an impact is through carefully integrated, systematic delivery of services. To date, we have provided xxx to your company. Now that we know your company better, we realize that if you also utilized yyy, the impact on your workforce's health status and your company's cost savings could be even more dramatic."*

GENERATING MARKETING LEVERAGE

Marketing can also be enhanced by leveraging existing relationships. Marketing leverage does not have to be limited to existing clients; other relationships can also be leveraged, including those with referring physicians (and other non-physician specialists), payers, and even patients themselves.

You can obtain leverage by:

1. **Securing employers as references** — Remember the phrase, "Don't call me; I'll call you"? Such proactive thinking is central to creating a deep inventory of employer testimonials. Do not wait for testimonials to come to you. Aggressively seek them out.
   - Ask *every* employer client to serve as a reference and build as long a list as possible.
   - Overwhelm reference readers with volume. If one hundred employers are willing to serve as a reference for your services, list them all; it provides your services with exceptional credibility.
   - Provide as much information about each reference as makes sense (e.g., name, title, company, phone, email address).
2. **Asking employers for testimonials** — Employer testimonials provide the glow of others' words rather than the usual transparent, self-serving boasts. Systematically request testimonials (e.g., through an annual employer questionnaire). Archive the questionnaires and select quotes as appropriate for various audiences.

3. **Asking for direct employer referrals** — Employers know other employers, and Human Resource officers know other Human Resource officers. Ask a happy client if they can make a call (or send an email) on your behalf to one or more of their selected colleagues.
4. **Working with referring physicians and payers** — Although you have to be selective depending on the nature of your relationship with the physician or payer, both groups offer the opportunity to obtain considerable leverage and, in the case of payers, access to numerous clients. Ask for a referral or a call to be placed to another client once a good relationship has been attained.
5. **Reaching out to patients** — Depending on the market, word of mouth travels either fast or lightning fast. Hence, any plan to reach out to patients makes sense. They talk and, in many cases, may be with a new employer soon.
6. **Mining your own organization** — Considerable leverage is often available not too far from home. Board members may work for a given company or, at the least, have friends in high places throughout the community—so may senior management or, for that matter, virtually anyone in your organization.
7. **Mining close to home** — How about your own staff? Staff members may have a family member who works at a target company or a friend or neighbor at one of your high-profile prospect companies. Potential entry points may be right under your nose.

COMMUNICATION IS KEY

If the word "communication" filters through every aspect of healthcare service operations, the word "leverage" should filter through every aspect of sales.

Do not limit yourself to bilateral communication with prospects, or you are likely to short change yourself. Leverage every relationship that you have within or beyond your organization in order to have the broadest possible impact.

Most healthcare organizations have a base in place and are poised to leverage that base in a manner that is beneficial to their service, the service's employer client base, and the end users of their services.

The Herd Mentality

The Merriam-Webster dictionary defines herd as "a group of individuals usually having a common bond," or "a number of animals kept under some type of human control." So let us think of bulls, a seemingly fitting metaphor for any book on sales. Incorporate the herd mentality into your marketing strategies and sales approach.

For every early adaptor or resistor contrarian, there seem to be ten others who prefer to follow the crowd. For every buyer who buys offensively out of desire, there appears to be ten who buy defensively out of fear.

Thus two secrets of herd mentality selling:

1. Discern to what degree your prospect is a defensive buyer.
2. Employ the "herd mentality" selling approach when you identify a defensive buyer.

I am disappointed with Hollywood movies that simplistically portray characters as either heroes or villains. Realistic, balanced portraits of the human spirit are rare. We also have squeaky clean heroes in entertainment and sports or the hapless antihero who becomes everyone's "whipping boy." In short, we seem to live in a world in which it is easy to jump on the bandwagon.

How do you apply the herd mentality to your daily sales effort? Whether your service is the market leader or a market challenger, first discern if a sales prospect is likely to be an early adaptor or a market follower.

There are abundant signs to suggest where one fits on the early adaptor/market follower continuum. Early adaptors tend to "march to the tune of their own drummer," whether it is their mode of dress, general demeanor, or the type of car they drive. Size up your prospects: Do they appear, act, or dress differently than the norm? What do their offices look like? Do their offices make a statement or fit the norm of office Americana? If the answer is the former, save the herd mentality approach for your next prospect.

Those most amenable to a herd mentality approach are fairly easy to spot. They are painfully cautious, preferring to fit in with their surroundings. Check out their clothes, jewelry, haircuts, or office style. These are the prospects that are more likely to buy out of fear and follow the lead of others.

MARKET LEADER STRATEGIES

If you are the market leader or the only viable market entrant, make the most of your leadership:

1. **Call attention to this leadership** — Tell prospects how your leadership benefits them in case they have not or cannot make this connection themselves.

   "WorkWell provided healthcare services to 81 of the 100 largest employers in Canton during the past year. This strong endorsement from your fellow Canton employers should provide your company with confidence regarding our ability to manage your health and safety and lower your associated costs."

2. **Use testimonial quotes** — Obtain and use quotes from satisfied clients in promotional literature, proposals, and other documents. Seek and use quotes that send a benefit statement to the prospect:

   "After two years, the WorkWell approach has made a demonstrable decrease in our health/safety costs."

   Establish balance between gender, job title (CEO, Human Resources, the company nurse), industry size, and industry type. The more often prospects recognize that the testimonial comes from a company or job title similar to their own, the more likely they will feel comfortable working with you. Nothing seems to trigger the herd mentality quite as well as published testimonials from like-minded employers.

   Gather testimonials through an annual questionnaire. Build a library of testimonial quotes and divide them by categories such as industry type, job title, and message. Correspondence to herd mentality candidate—brochures and proposals—when appropriate, should be peppered with appropriate testimonials.

3. **Create a "knockout" reference list** — Develop a broad base of client references to provide to a prospect at the right time. Typically, a provider of references offers only three or four names. A short list does not inspire confidence or create a sense

of differentiation from other programs: who could not come up with a list of three or four friendly users?

Instead, create a sense of credibility and value. Go beyond the norm by listing as many references as you can. RYAN Associates' consulting services routinely provides a detailed list of twenty-five to thirty references followed by a list of over five hundred clients (some dating back to 1985), listed by state. This lets a prospect know that we have a broad client history, which in turn instills a "five hundred plus programs can't all be wrong" sense of confidence. Develop your list by asking employers individually if you can use their company name as a reference and by soliciting permission as part of an annual client survey.

A client list might have the following format:

CLIENT

Ms. Sonja Ball, CEO
Ball Brakes
Goleta, CA
805-886-0948
WorkWell client since: 2001

OTHER REFERENCES (by industry type)

Aviation

Delta Airlines
Del Mundo Aviation Security
United Airlines

Manufacturing

Acme Steel
Mancuso Iron Works
Montana Engineering

Note: Rotate the order of references so the names at the top are not contacted too often.

The herd mentality kicks in when a defensively minded prospect feels that they cannot afford *not to use* the market leader.

EXHIBIT 6-2. EARLY ADAPTERS VS. MARKET FOLLOWERS

If you are the market leader:

- Script and memorize a market leader statement.
- Use a balanced sample of testimonials often and effectively.
- Create a professional-looking, exhaustive client list.

If you are the market challenger:

- Script and memorize a "market movement" statement.
- Identify industry-specific leadership.
- Emphasize client movement rather than market share.

MARKET CHALLENGERS

For every market leader, there are usually numerous market challengers who offer viable services but do not possess a plurality of market share. Such programs should embrace the herd mentality with a different emphasis. The core strategy for a market leader is to mention being number one at every turn, the core strategy for the market challenger is to emphasize market share growth and industry specific expertise.

The market leader's recurrent message is:

> *"Come with us; we are the leaders, and the bulk of your fellow employers can't be wrong."*

The message from the market challenger should be:

> *"Come with us. Many employers have done so recently, so we must be the best choice."*

Your service line receives bonus points in this instance: not only will the herd mentality prospect view your service favorably because of this momentum, but they are likely to view the market leader less favorably because of presumed attrition.

Market challengers can approach herd mentality prospects by citing the work they have done for employers within their industry. Overall, market leadership is likely to become less important than your insights toward the prospect's unique challenges.

Many prospects buy defensively and are swayed to a safe course of working with the market leader. Market leaders must take full advantage of this mind-set. Market challengers can capitalize on the herd mentality mind-set by selectively citing their successes. Be aggressive in either scenario.

SALES SILOS

Start off your day with a bang: What to do first? The over-riding objective of any day, or even any hour, is to position yourself to generate immediate and ongoing revenue for your program. Consider the four sales silos.

THE FOUR SILOS

You have four sales silos from which to choose: non-clients, former clients, formerly active but dwindling current clients, and solid current clients. Each silo offers revenue potential that varies by service and market.

Allocate your time in a manner that ultimately considers all four silos in a way that is going to optimally leverage gross revenue potential. Let's examine each silo.

SILO 1: Non-clients.

Companies that have never used your services are where most sales efforts are focused. In many markets this silo offers enough untapped and attainable business to make it your highest priority. Companies that do not use your services likely either use a competitor or lack a coherent policy.

In the former instance, the sales professional's job is usually to show that there is a greater value in working with your program than a competitive program. Determine how satisfied the prospect is with your competitor.

Ask prospects:

> *"What is your most significant workplace health and safety challenge?"*
>
> *"What are you doing to address that challenge?"*
>
> *"Is this approach producing satisfactory results? If not, how do you think your challenge might be more effectively addressed?"*

When a concern is expressed, it provides the opening you need to discuss how your service brings real value to the table.

Use a different approach when you meet with non-clients that lack a coordinated approach. Place greater emphasis on educating the prospect about the value of working exclusively with an external service—any service—before extolling the virtues of your particular service. If you can make such companies understand the value of a coordinated approach they will be more likely to use your program.

SILO 2: Former clients.

In a challenging economic climate many companies downsize their workforce. The next step is often to do things more efficiently and cost-effectively with remaining staff. Seek out former clients involved in such practices; they provide an opportunity to be wooed back to your program.

Calling on former clients is another example of a numbers game: Some former clients are dissatisfied with their current situation and will jump at the opportunity to renew their partnership with your program. Others will need to be persuaded to come back to your program, and some will not be willing or ready to change.

Emphasize different factors when you deal with a former client. You should bring up your pre-existing familiarity with their company, your emphasis on economic considerations, and your desire to go the extra mile to get the former client company back in the fold.

SILO 3: Clients with decreasing utilization levels.

This silo includes mid-to-high volume client companies that currently use your services less than before. Such attrition may be the by product of workforce downsizing. In such instances, a sales call may not result in an immediate spike in volume, but it can generate excellent public relations and position you to provide additional services or return to former volumes if and when the company's fortunes change.

SILO 4: Current clients.

This silo involves selling additional services to your current client base.

The relevance of this silo is associated with two variables:

- The breadth of other services in your product portfolio
- The potential value of additional services vis-à-vis the value of acquiring new clients

Geography plays a role in deciding how much emphasis should be placed on cross selling to current clients. If you are based in a large urban market, there is so much untapped business potential with non-clients that cross selling to your current clients can be rendered less important. If you operate in a small market, chances are that you have more to gain by providing additional services to companies that you already serve than by providing new services to smaller companies.

SILOS: RULES FOR THE ROAD

Actively manage your sales prospect silos:

1. **Address every silo** — Do this independently of your market position or geographic base. Winning sales strategy should penetrate all four silos to some degree all of the time.
2. **Evaluate regularly** — Evaluate your relative emphasis on each of the silos annually, quarterly, weekly, and at times, daily.

3. **Learn from experience** — Alter the relative emphasis on each silo by noting the productivity of each silo. For example, you may initially elect to spend 10 percent of your time cross-selling to current clients, find that silo surprisingly fruitful, and adjust your emphasis on that cohort up to 20 percent or more.
4. **Adjust as appropriate** — Recognize that your sales approach is almost certain to vary from silo to silo.
5. **Do not ignore any potential clients** — Times change, and what may seem to have been cast in concrete a year ago may be different this year.

Cold Calls

In sales there are cold calls, cool calls, and hot calls.

A classic cold call: show up at someone's office and hope for the best. This is a blatantly poor idea. Not only is it invariably a waste of precious sales time, it is likely to alienate a prospective buyer before a relationship can be established. Employers who attend our focus groups tell us repeatedly that they find such calls inconvenient—even annoying. So much for cold calls.

A cool call is a traditional way of contacting a prospect: a professional and customized letter and/or phone call serves as an entrée for a face-to-face meeting. Not bad, except the person who writes the letter or makes the phone call is likely to be viewed as just another sales professional and quickly forgotten. Think about it: How often do you contact someone and refer to a letter that you recently sent only to be greeted with silence or a blank look?

That brings us to hot calls, or cool calls with some sizzle. A hot call is one in which the groundwork has been laid via an astute name recognition/marketing campaign or a direct referral, so that the recipient of the call is more likely to be readily aware of who you are and what you represent.

Cold calls can mean different things to different people. I define a cold call as an unannounced visit to a prospect company, whether the intention is to seek an unscheduled meeting with the decision maker or to drop off literature or gifts. I do not consider an initial telephone call to be a cold call, because it should follow an introductory letter and/or email correspondence advising the prospect of the impending call.

Consider several negatives associated with in-person cold calls:

- **Sometimes cold calls do, in fact, work** — Put me in a major league baseball uniform, and I might get a hit or two simply by swinging. The same is true with cold calls: they do work often enough to keep you coming back.
- **Dropping by is a risky way to make a first impression** — Do you have an otherwise well-meaning neighbor or friend who frequently knocks on your door unannounced? It is okay sometimes, but it can be a bit annoying when you are engrossed in another matter. So it is with a cold call; your prospect not only spurns the sales advance, but is left with the impression that you are inconsiderate. Sales is about building relationships, not dooming them from the start.
- **A face-to-face cold call is not necessarily a victory** — Even if you do get in the door for an impromptu face-to-face meeting, that meeting might not occur within the prospect's time-comfort zone. Every in-person meeting should be dictated by the prospect's schedule, not a lucky break.
- **Do not toss preparation to the wind** — Quickly checking out a prospect's website prior to a cold call is not a substitute for appropriate preparation.

When you use a genuine sales cycle (letter ➔ phone call ➔ reminder ➔ appointment ➔ follow-up), you increase the odds of walking in better prepared. A scheduled visit can be preceded twenty-four hours in advance by a call from a provider on your team to set the stage for your visit. You cannot create such an edge during a cold call.

PROTECT YOUR TIME

Your most valuable commodity is your time: an hour saved is an hour earned for more sales activity. The time spent doing one or more in-person cold calls rarely takes into account round-trip auto travel, parking, and waiting time. Two hours of unproductive cold-call time can easily be converted to two hours of active telephone time from the comfort of your office.

REJECT THE "LEAVE 'EM SOME LITERATURE" MYTH

A common justification for doing cold calls is the opportunity to "leave literature behind for the prospect to review." The thinking goes, even if you do not get a face-to-face meeting, you can connect with the prospect by leaving something behind.

Literature or brochures, however, are usually discarded. If someone left behind literature at my office, I would consider it a negative: It would strike me as an impersonal, even desperate, move, and I would be less inclined to welcome overtures in the future.

Speaking of literature, participants have frequently stated at RYAN Associates' employer focus group sessions that they prefer to receive literature from a healthcare organization as a first step. However, this approach is likely to be counterproductive. As the saying goes, "Watch what they do, not what they say." The odds are high that said literature will never be reviewed and that such a request is used as a way to defer the sales professional.

EXCEPTIONS

Are there times or circumstances when a cold call can be justified? Sure. When it comes to healthcare sales, nothing is set in concrete.

There is usually a downside to such exceptions. Think of a recovering alcoholic: He might take a drink at some point, thinking, "What's one drink?" But that drink most assuredly will lead to a "just one more can't hurt" mentality and, in short order, the alcoholic will fall off the wagon. The "just one" scenario applies to cold calling: one exception leads to two, then three, and soon the sales professional has resumed the bad habit of sequential cold calls.

This problem can become acute if a sales professional's compensation is tied to encounters rather than actual sales. In that case, the game is scored in a different manner: number of touches rather than results. The number of meetings (cold or hot) or the number of "new clients" accrued, means little. Performance should be all about bringing in new gross revenue.

Not long ago I met with an otherwise strong sales professional whose sales plan centered around cold calls. When I raised my concern about cold calls, she countered by telling me that she was in a comparatively small market, had worked the market for eleven years with a previous employer (a national for-profit), and knew nearly all of the key contacts in her community. If there were ever an exception to the in-person, no-cold-call rule, this was it. Yet she could have leveraged her name and personal relationships as effectively from her office.

Bottom line: respect your prospect's time above all. Cold calls fall dramatically short in this respect.

COLD CALL ALTERNATIVES

If you remove cold calls from your playbook—whether they are active (seek a meeting) or passive (just to drop off literature)—what should you put in their place?

- **Let marketing lead the way** — Modern marketing (email blasts, voice mail blitzes, clinic tours and open houses, truly dynamic websites) make it easier to get through the door than in days past and are a good substitute for printed matter.
- **Maintain discipline** — Follow a targeted sales strategy by focusing every day on only the highest volume prospects.
- **Use your telephone effectively and send follow-up email messages** — All other things being equal, sales usually comes down to a numbers game—make more phone calls, send more personalized emails, and get out there to make more initial (scheduled) sales calls.

FINDING THE BEST CONTACT PERSON

Have you ever gone to heroic efforts to track down a prospect, finally contact them, and only then learn that they are not the "correct" person? In sales, this is a deflating and relatively common experience.

How about contacting the "right" person only to be unceremoniously dismissed as another sales professional vying for the person's precious time and attention? Upsetting, but an everyday fact in the life of a sales professional.

If you can identify the right contact person more often than not and subsequently enter into communication with a degree of name recognition and credibility, you will be better positioned to make the sale.

IDENTIFYING THE CONTACT

Identifying the right contact person begins with an accurate contact database.

Your contact base must be well conceptualized and updated regularly. The name (or names) of individuals responsible for the health and safety of the workforce should be a central component.

Database confirmation grunt work is best left to someone other than the sales professional, whose time should be spent cultivating prospects and selling.

Manage your contact database with an appropriate contact management system. Such systems include generic products such as ACT! and Goldmine, components of practice management software, or a dedicated product.

Place a preliminary call to a prospect company moments before the actual sales call to confirm that they have the correct information about the contact person. A thirty-second call to a company before a sales call can save considerable time and trouble later ("Could you verify that Luc Richard is still with your company and is responsible for the health and safety of your workforce?"). Indeed, this brief who's-who call can be as important as the sales encounter to follow.

Do not get discouraged if your contact list is never totally accurate. A contact database that is 100 percent accurate is not in the cards. There often is more than one person to contact. The human resources, risk management, and safety professions are somewhat transitory in nature. The gatekeeper may misunderstand your request or make an inadvertent error and provide an inappropriate contact name.

Be nimble-witted and frequently adjust on the fly. A good rule of thumb is to ask who is responsible for workplace health and safety and whether someone else would be more appropriate to deal with whenever the opportunity arises.

CULTIVATING THE RIGHT INDIVIDUAL

Cultivation demands a large dose of discipline and patience.

- **Make your introduction brief and to-the-point** — Articulate who you are, what you do, and the objective of the interchange, whether it is by letter, phone, or in person. Many salespeople do not do this as well as possible. A brief, to-the-point introduction might be something like,

> *"My name is Mike Roll, and it is my responsibility to speak with employer representatives such as yourself to learn more about your challenges and see how our services might help you address those challenges." The old "cut to the chase" proviso is alive and well in the world of healthcare service sales.*

- **Never shut the door when you can leave a crack open** — Always look at defeats during a sales encounter as temporary, not permanent. It is best to pick up your marbles and set the stage to come back and play the game another day.

  In this regard, it is useful to have a "freebie" tucked in your portfolio. It may be a complimentary subscription to your low-cost email newsletter (a perfectly good reason to create such a newsletter), an invitation to a conference or a meeting, or a free password to access password-protected areas of your website. Prospects are often impressed by such tenacity and fair play, even right after they reject your overture.
- **Stay in touch and use multiple modalities to do so** — Strike a balance between being sufficiently visible and being a nuisance. Call the prospect every few months and take the high road. Check in periodically to see how things are going and ask what you (or your program) could do for them.

The axiom "time is money" reigns in virtually every type of sales. Nothing seems to take more time than pursuing dead-end leads. There will, of course, be many dead ends; the secret is to develop and execute a proactive plan to identify, contact, and cultivate the right person.

COMPETITIVE STRENGTHS

Recognize, understand, evaluate, and articulate your program's competitive strengths. Even the most seasoned sales professionals invariably fall short in one or more of these areas. Most services are likely to either neglect its competitive strengths or offer a wooden recital of them.

Programs rarely are proactive in assessing their strengths vis-à-vis their competitors, matching competitive strengths with prospect values as appropriate, or expressing their competitive strengths in a persuasive manner. Your competitive strengths are invariably left in your toolbox.

PRINCIPLE 1: Keep "competitive" in your definition of "competitive strength."

A competitive strength is not necessarily an advantage in the pure sense (e.g., twenty-four-hour service, multiple delivery points, staff certifications). A competitive strength is something you do better than your competition. In one market, a Board-certified physician may not be a competitive strength because the competitors also have Board-certified physicians. In another market, a clinic may have an experienced, but non-certified, medical director and maintain a competitive strength because the competition's medical director is neither certified nor experienced. Consider relative—not absolute—attributes.

PRINCIPLE 2: Let your market define what is important.

Dr. Koehn, a Board-certified Medical Director, has joined your team, and you cannot wait to tell your clients and prospects all about him. Hold on. Evaluate the situation before you rush out to share the good news. If your market is mired in recession, or the majority of encounters seen in your clinic are minor, some prospects may perceive Dr. Koehn as too expensive or over-qualified for their needs. Match your program's distinguishing characteristics with market values before anointing the characteristic as a "competitive strength."

PRINCIPLE 3: A competitive strength is directly correlated with the difference in perceived value of that advantage between you and your competitors.

The value of each of your potential competitive strengths is directly related to the degree of strength of that advantage among your competitors. Assume that research indicates that employers desire twenty-four-hour access and that you have the only clinic or system in town with twenty-four-hour coverage. This is a competitive strength, but not a strong one if a competitor's clinic is open twenty hours a day or the competitor has an arrangement with a local hospital emergency department for after-hours care. It is necessary to subjectively measure the gap between the advantage and the status of the next best option.

Assess how powerful your competitive strength portfolio is by asking yourself:

"Are we the best option based on these criteria?"

"How much better are we than the next best competitor?"

"Just how important is this attribute to our market?"

PRINCIPLE 4: Cite your competitive strengths selectively and only when appropriate.

What is important at the collective market level does not necessarily carry over to the individual prospect level. In a market in which many employers do not find multiple clinic options to be a compelling advantage, many *other* employers are still likely to find that attribute important. Identify how much value prospects place on a variety of potential competitive strengths. You can then refer to the program's strengths without mentioning the "competition."

PRINCIPLE 5: Articulate competitive strengths in simple, concise, and persuasive terms.

The impact of a genuine competitive strength can be so important in sales that it should not be lost in a quagmire of information and verbiage. Competitive strength messages should be simple and easy to understand. Sell on benefits, not features. Analogously, articulate a competitive strength by focusing on the prospect.

PRINCIPLE 6: Summarize relevant competitive strengths at the conclusion of sales calls, phone calls, and written proposals.

The adage that a person says the most important thing they have to say as they are walking out the door is true in a sales call, telephone call, or even in a written proposal. Offer a strong closing statement that goes beyond the obligatory summary of key points and action steps. In closing, one might say:

"It appears that we bring two particular advantages to your company that address the needs you have expressed. First, we have six clinics throughout the area and are well prepared to serve your highly dispersed workforce. Secondly, as the only local program with on-site physical therapy services, we can readily address your company's musculoskeletal problems and reduce lost work time."

PRINCIPLE 7: Develop strengths when none seem to exist.

For every sales professional working for the market leader, several work for market challengers. In many cases, these challengers are new or immature programs, or are hampered by constraints such as poor location, tight financial resources, or a weak reputation. Usually, but not always, such market challengers have fewer competitive strengths than the market leader.

When a service does not carry a genuine competitive strength, it must develop one or more. This process invariably begins by identifying voids that seem to exist among market competitors. Once voids are identified, you can take steps to enhance your service's inherent capabilities in order to fill the gaps.

COMPETITIVE STRENGTH WORKSHEET

Use this worksheet to evaluate your most powerful competitive strengths. Columns 1–4 measure your services against the competition. Columns 5–6 factor in the perceived value placed on the attribute by your market. The net score is the product of the intensity of your strength times the market's value of that strength.

INVOLVING PHYSICIANS IN SALES

When it comes to sales, physicians usually are used sporadically for in-person calls with major clients and prospects. At times this is an effective strategy, but in other cases it can have a minimal impact or even be counterproductive.

Exhibit 6-3. Sample Completed Competitive Strength Worksheet

STRENGTH	YOUR PROGRAM	COMP 1	COMP 2	NET (DIS)ADVANTAGE	MARKET VALUE	NET SCORE
Medical Director	9	5	5	4	3	12
Availability of outcome data	9	3	3	6	1	6
Director	10	8	4	2	2	4
Reports	9	5	2	4	1	4
Locations	9	8	3	1	3	3
Hours of operation	10	6	10	0	2	0
Clinical staff	8	8	8	0	3	0
Link to rehab services	7	7	9	(2)	1	(2)
Reputation	7	8	4	(1)	3	(3)
Fees	7	8	9	(2)	2	(4)

PHYSICIAN CREDIBILITY

Deserved or not, physicians tend to project credibility. A physician is often perceived as having reached the pinnacle of professional achievement. Non-physicians, including the typical employer contact, invariably hold physicians in high esteem and are likely to follow their recommendations.

RYAN Associates conducted a market research project in which a physician received exceptionally high praise from employers. As a result, the organization where he works—despite its limitations—benefits from this halo effect.

Why? Dr. X spends an inordinate amount of time with his patients, communicates with employers frequently and in-depth, and writes thorough, informative reports. Although the physician's productivity is likely to be compromised by this detail-oriented approach to practice, his contribution to his organization's image is off the charts.

PHYSICIAN ROLES

A physician's Midas touch can add a great deal to a program's image and outreach capability. Although what works well for Dr. X may not work as well for Dr. Y, physicians can effectively do most of the following:

1. **Be a website presence** — Create a series of thirty-second video recordings in which your physician offers gems about prevention, sound health practices, and other relevant topics. Place a new video each month on the home page of your website. This will spur interest in revisiting your website and showcase your physician. A side benefit is that it will give most physicians a morale boost.
2. **Send out email blasts** — When you send an email blast to employers to alert them about a service offering or educational opportunity, it is usually sent by the service line director or sales professional. Why not send a number of such blasts under the name of your medical director? Your medical director's name will add substance to your communication and increase the likelihood that the message will be read.

3. **Project a pleasant demeanor** — Most service websites provide a dry and unimaginative overview of their providers. The provider's facial expression often looks like someone who has learned their pet rabbit has died. Take care to personalize the physician's biography and use a confident, congenial head shot. (Remember, a photo is worth a thousand words.)

4. **Set the stage for a sales call** — Imagine how valuable it would be to have your two most important initial sales calls each week preceded by a call from a physician. A physician's time on the phone need not be lengthy; even a voice mail will do. The physician should state something akin to:

   "As the Medical Director for Work Well, I find it useful to learn a little about the challenges a company faces before they meet with our sales professional . . . "

5. **Be available during clinic tours** — Clinic tours should include a brief face-to-face encounter with a physician. Even if the encounter is in the hallway, the physician can show a genuine interest in the prospect or client by asking a few simple questions germane to their workplace:

   "We take pride in communicating effectively with our employer clients. When it comes to communication, what is important to you?"

   "We find that workplace-specific knowledge helps us customize our services. Are there any unique aspects of your workplace that I should know about?"

6. **Script voice mail messages** — Send periodic voice mail blasts from a physician (e.g., "I am calling to advise you we are expanding our clinic hours as of July 1") offers considerable value. It takes little time for the physician to leave such a message.

7. **Write letters** — I advocate using multiple modalities (email, voice mail, regular mail) to "stay in the face" of your prospects and clients. Send a letter to all companies on your mailing list once a quarter. One of those four letters should be sent annually from your medical director.

8. **Be a public health advocate** — If your physician is passionate about the public health aspects of his responsibilities, he or she is likely to want to speak periodically on related topics at community forums and employer gatherings.

   Alternatively, if your physician does not enjoy public speaking, a cogent written advocacy piece can be an effective alternative. Letters to the editor of your local newspaper have a good chance of being published, as do more lengthy pieces for inhouse and local employer publications. The more your market views your providers as *the* authority the more your services ride the credibility wave.

9. **Obtain referrals from internal and external sources** — The credibility factor again. The committed provider can do wonders for their program by proactively reaching out to others for referrals and introductions. Use the same approach with contacts in the community. Physicians may know well-connected people within their neighborhood, country club, or various civic activities. A personal and credible introduction carries as much weight as twenty cold calls.

   Such referrals may be made through other internal staff or from virtually anyone else throughout the community. Many people find it hard to turn down a physician. A physician can query fellow medical staff members, senior administrators, and department heads by stating:

   > *"You can really help our program if you can refer us to a contact of yours that may not be one of our clients. A personal introduction would even be better."*

   Use the same approach with contacts in the community. Physicians may know well-connected people within their neighborhood, country club, or various civic activities. A personal and credible introduction carries as much weight as twenty cold calls.

10. **Participate periodically in high-profile sales calls** — Coming full circle, in most cases your physicians can be helpful participants in targeted sales calls provided they:

- Clearly understand their role going in
- Do not dominate the sales calls
- Exhibit sincere interest in the company and your ability to customize services by taking at least a cursory walk-through of the workplace

A physician's credibility with your client and prospect community cannot be overstated. Service lines are encouraged to showcase their physicians as much as possible.

Managing the Physician's Role

Many sales professionals and service line directors have asked me whether they should bring one of their physicians with them on a sales call and, if so, what role that physician might play. The answer is a clear "it depends." To better manage the role of the physician in sales and marketing, think of their contribution as a continuum in which their value may range from extraordinary to counterproductive.

In order to find their place on this continuum, you should:

- **Know your market** — The degree of physician commitment is related to the nature of your market. More industrialized markets or ones with more unique workplace exposures require a greater on-site physician presence. Likewise, a new service or one that is not the market leader should use its physician more often as a vehicle for winning market share and playing catch-up. Many smaller markets remain high-touch, person-to-person markets. Provider visibility is more critical in a community like Pocatello, Idaho, (where everybody knows everybody) than in a metropolitan market like Chicago.
- **Evaluate sales strengths** — The effectiveness of your sales team is an important variable in the role your physicians will play in sales and marketing. If your service has a strong, experienced sales team or exceptional sales professional, you may find there is less need to use a physician in a sales role.
- **Consider the personality factor** — Physicians, like other professionals, tend to run the gamut of personality types. If a physician is outgoing and an effective communicator,

encourage frequent trips to the workplace. Many physicians are technically gifted but may be shy or otherwise lacking in people skills. In this instance, promote their technical expertise, but keep their sales and marketing activities to a minimum.

- **Define the physician's time commitment** — The degree of the physician's involvement should be spelled out in advance. The physician might be expected to participate in two work site visits every Wednesday afternoon for the first year and one visit per week thereafter. A typical dilemma for many programs with a strong physician is that they want to use him or her more often for sales and marketing activities without simultaneously eroding the physician's finite time availability. Even the most successful programs find it difficult to make the best use of a physician's time.
- **Establish parameters for participation** — Most physicians have little or no training in sales and marketing and are likely to know little about handling objections, discerning between features and benefits, or how to close. Physicians have a tendency to go too far rather than not far enough in these areas, potentially jeopardizing a virtually completed sale.
- **Define degree of involvement** — The breadth of the physician's role in any given type of activity should be clearly defined. The physician visits a workplace to learn about working conditions and to offer preliminary recommendations, not to sell. The physician should be prepared to ask questions about current working conditions and long-term plans and provide ad hoc advice. A physician is a physician, and should be able to recognize his or her own limits on the sales side.
- **Hand pick prospects** — When a physician participates in a sales call, target employers with high-injury incidence rates, hazardous conditions, complex or unusual job functions, and a large workforce. A targeted sales approach is based on market research and part of the program's overall marketing and sales plan.
- **Plan ahead** — The service line director should call or visit a company prior to the physician's visit. The purpose of the call is to obtain a preliminary sketch of special problems, critical

job tasks, and current health and safety practices. The site-visit team should develop a game plan before meeting at the company. Preparing for a visit tends to enhance the physician's value in the eyes of the employer.

- **Match the physician with senior management** — The most effective long-term relationship between providers and employers invariably involves a commitment from the company's senior managers. Physician presence at the work site provides an excellent opportunity to meet senior company management—if only briefly. Such a meeting may go a long way toward establishing a sense of management commitment toward your program.
- **Emphasize planning** — The provider-employer relationship is greatly enhanced if it includes a long-term game plan for ensuring optimal health status. Physician involvement is an excellent opportunity to gauge the quality of the current plan and offer suggestions for developing a more comprehensive one.
- **Offer further contact** — Your physician should conclude the visit with an invitation for the employer prospect to contact the physician as necessary. Although most inquiries are likely to be made through the service line director (or other administrative personnel), the clearly stated availability of physician time is a compelling feature to most employers.
- **Remember to follow up** — A follow-up letter or email from the physician should be sent immediately after a site visit. The letter should summarize key issues and recommendations and project a sense of commitment to the employer.
- **Hire smart** — A service line is often so eager to have a physician with experience at hand that it overlooks or minimizes the personality issue. If a physician's role is to see patients all day, this may work; if you want the physician to assume an active public relations role, this must be factored into your hiring criteria. Place the personality factor near the top of your physician hiring criteria.

ADVICE FOR THE MEDICAL DIRECTOR/ PHYSICIAN

The physician should:

- **Be available** — Sales and marketing should be part of a physician's job description; the physician should be willing to jump in as needed to answer questions and help retain existing clients.
- **Take the lead with internal marketing** — Physician credibility with employers is no less true within your own organization. Gaining the buy-in and understanding of senior management and related departments is an issue that the physician must address.
- **Market at the individual patient level** — The physician's bedside manner is a subtle yet crucial aspect of your service's image.
- **Buy into the plan** — The physician should provide input into, understand, and embrace your service's marketing plan.

EXHIBIT 6-4. PHYSICIAN AS MARKETER: A MINI JOB DESCRIPTION

ACTIVITY	VOLUME	ANNUAL
Workplace walkthrough	2 hours/week	100 hours
Sit in on one sales call	0.5 hours/week	25 hours
Call two clients to check in	0.5 hours/week	25 hours
Call two hot prospects	0.5 hours/week	25 hours
Participate in phone blitz	1 hour/quarter	4 hours
Sign letters to prospects	3 hours/year	3 hours
Total hours	*3.64 hours/week*	*182 hours/year*

CLIENT MAINTENANCE

Sales people should be spending virtually all of their time selling.

"Let Salespeople Sell!" is not a cliché; it is a necessary way of doing business. In healthcare this is rarely the case. Sales professionals spend a disproportionate amount of their time engaged in what is often described as client maintenance or customer service activity.

Client maintenance involves working with a service's existing client base to monitor satisfaction and cross sell additional services. Several principles apply to the client maintenance function:

- **Vertical sales is market specific** — The decision to spend a great deal, a little, or no time on vertical sales (selling new services to existing clients as opposed to horizontal sales, which involves selling core services to non-client prospects) is usually directly related to the market. Place greater emphasis on new prospect sales in larger markets; place more emphasis on selling new products to your existing customer base in smaller markets.

  Other variables play a role. A service with a new product, such as a specific on-site service, will logically spend more time with its existing client base than an initiative mired in product line status quo. There also may be some high-volume clients in your market that require ongoing contact. Review relevant variables, decide where you fit on the client maintenance/new sales continuum, and plan accordingly.

- **Do not try to put out fires that you did not start** — Many sales professionals assume a firefighter role—going back to clients whom they secured to address operational or service problems that have occurred since the sale. The thinking is if sales professional A established the initial relationship with employer client B, then sales professional A is the familiar face who can presumably deal with issues and complaints.

  In most cases, such reasoning is flawed. Manage the handoff in a way that satisfies the client's need for security. Then, if an operational problem arises, an operational person can address it and win the employer's trust. By providing reassurance on the handoff, you are free to sell without jeopardizing an existing relationship whenever a vertical sales opportunity arises.

- **Maintain your relationships in a time-effective manner** — Keep tabs on your clients' satisfaction shortly after the sale and periodically thereafter. Such "maintenance" seldom requires a face-to-face visit. Consider sending an email or leaving an after-hours voice-mail message saying something like:

  "Just checking in to see how things are going with our services to your company. Please give me a call (or respond to my email message) if you have any special needs you would like to address."

The message may take about a minute, while a personal visit could take an hour or more of valuable sales time.

CUSTOMER SERVICE

Everyone seems to talk a lot about customer service, but little is done to manage it. Logic suggests that strong up-front customer service would result in fewer "fires" that consume staff time and energy.

Consider:

- **Hiring appropriately** — Hire the "right" kind of people. Individuals who work in an organization collectively comprise the foundation of excellent customer service. Although experience is an important criteria, there is a tendency to "hire the resume," rather than the person. Rely more frequently on your intuition when evaluating job candidates for positions that involve client and patient service.

  Friendliness should be the most important criteria in your hiring decision. What the candidate would do for you is often more important than what they have done in the past. Ask applicants questions pertinent to their prospective position and to your circumstances.
- **Developing a written plan** — A formal customer service plan is as important as a marketing plan. Most healthcare services rarely have a plan, relying on the assumption that their staff can manage things effectively. To the contrary, a written plan provides an organized approach and instills a sense that your customer service ethic is more than lip service.

- **Involving everyone** — A customer service ethic and mastery of service principles must be instilled in every individual who comes into contact with a patient or employee. This includes physicians, other care providers, receptionists and clerks, clinic or service line directors, and sales and marketing personnel. Optimal customer service should be expected from all members of a team.
- **Setting the bar high** — The term "satisfaction" can be misleading. The absence of documented dissatisfaction may be misinterpreted to mean that your service has a high degree of satisfaction. In healthcare, okay is not okay. Go beyond mere satisfaction and aim for the highest possible degree of effectiveness. Upgrade your service ethic from "standard" to "above reproach."
- **Conducting customer service training** — New members of your team should go through a sixty- to ninety-minute customer service-training period during their first days on the job. All employees should undergo refresher training at least once a year. In both cases, common scenarios should be reviewed and play-acting should be encouraged.
- **Evaluating again and again** — Constant consumer feedback at both the employer and patient level is vital to pre-empt any customer service deficiencies before they become chronic and to obtain positive reinforcement for deeds well done.

  Acquire feedback through a combination of short patient-satisfaction exit surveys and annual employer questionnaires. Try to quantify satisfaction data (e.g., "Were you satisfied with our services?" becomes "On a scale of 1 to 5, with 5 extremely satisfied, how satisfied were you with our services?"). Develop report cards and measure secular trends.
- **Providing rewards** — Make customer service fun. Post a graph with changes in daily patient satisfaction scores in a prominent place in your clinic or office. Provide an award such as the "customer satisfaction deed of the month" for the best above-and-beyond act. Instill the ethic every day in a meaningful manner.

By relieving a savvy sales professional of as many nondirect sales responsibilities as possible, you can increase gross sales by 25–50 percent or more. You cannot afford to do otherwise.

Exhibit 6-5. Customer Service Rules of Engagement

CLIENT MAINTENANCE

- Develop your plan based on market size and other variables.
- Make your operations department responsible for putting out fires.
- Maintain contact with clients in a time-effective manner.

CUSTOMER SERVICE

- Hire personnel who exhibit a customer-friendly style.
- Develop a written, proactive customer service plan.
- Instill a customer service ethic in all team members.
- Set the bar high; strive for an exceptional performance.
- Conduct continuous customer service training.
- Evaluate consumer perceptions of your customer service quality.
- Reward staff for effective customer service.

The Customer Service Plan

Customer service is a trendy theme. However, the gap between "shoulda, coulda, woulda" and reality is invariably significant.

Effective customer service requires five core elements: planning, training, execution, evaluation, and reward/recognition.

PLANNING

Any business dealing with the public needs a well-designed plan that addresses training, execution, evaluation, and recognition. Unlike a sales, marketing, or business plan, a customer service plan need not be an annual event. The plan may be a singular, dynamic document requiring updates only as new ideas or policies come to the fore. Include the following in the customer service plan:

1. **The meaning of customer service** — Exactly what does "customer service" mean to your parent organization?
2. **Customer service responsibilities** — Where does the buck stop?
3. **Customer service training procedures** — Who will conduct the training? How will new employees be trained? How will current employees be refreshed? How will you evaluate the effectiveness of your training procedures?
4. **An index of customer service protocols** — What protocols should staff embrace in their daily work to ensure that your constituencies are wowed by your dedication to their needs?
5. **An index of suggested responses to customer service dilemmas** — How is staff is expected to respond to common displays of customer discontent?
6. **Customer service evaluation methods** — Who will you ask to evaluate your performance? How will you ask them? When and how often will you conduct such evaluations?

TRAINING

Do you systematically train new employees and periodically refresh existing staff on basic customer service? Or do you *assume* that staff will say the correct thing or react in the right way? Typically it is the latter which not surprisingly creates more customer service issues than it solves.

New hires are often asked to absorb their customer service ethic via osmosis by standing around and watching their more experienced coworkers deal with customers. Therein lies the dilemma: a new employee seldom stands around for long since they are needed on the front lines almost immediately. Otherwise they would not have been hired in the first place. An unprepared new employee is forced to deal with patients and clients right off the bat, creating a strong likelihood for a situation to be mishandled.

Set aside significant time during all new hires' first few days so they may study your customer service plan. Study becomes particularly valuable if the new employees know that they will be tested on the back end. Ask new employees to take an oral customer service exam on the last day of their first week.

Typical questions might begin with the phrases:

"How would you respond when . . . ?" or

"What is the standard or benchmark for . . . ?"

When such questions are answered correctly, you can then expose your new hire to your clients.

Remind existing staff about the importance of maintaining a strong customer service ethic. Reinforce your program's standards so they will be constantly and evenly applied.

Schedule quarterly customer service meetings involving all staff. Agenda items might include:

- A review of protocols added since the last quarterly meeting
- A review of customer/patient evaluations received during the last quarter
- Recognition of the customer service "moment" of the quarter
- An in-depth discussion on a pressing customer service issue

EXECUTION

There are several keys to effective execution:

- Hire positive, people-oriented personnel.
- Reinforce the importance of customer service daily. It is easier to design a customer service plan than to continuously maintain the customer service ethic. There should be constant reminders of your program's commitment to the highest standard of customer service.
- Advise receptionists to "think" service whenever they answer the phone (e.g., "Hello. [service line name]. My name is Barbara. How may I serve you today?").

EVALUATION

Assess the expectations and satisfaction of your patients and other customers.

A multi-faceted approach should include:

- Customer input to evaluate your performance and to garner ideas for additional customer service protocols
- Daily patient satisfaction surveys
- An annual survey of all employer clients
- Periodic group discussions
- A quarterly telephone blitz

REWARDS AND RECOGNITION

Add a little fun in the form of rewards and recognition. Rewards are gratifying to those doing a good job and also keep customer service on the front burner. Rewards do not have to be monumental, but should be offered frequently. A "customer service moment of the month" might be rewarded with a gift certificate at a local restaurant. The customer service employee of the year—the employee who wins the most monthly prizes—could be acknowledged with a special reserved parking spot for the following calendar year. A little fun can go a long way in ensuring an effective sales, marketing, or customer service campaign.

SCRIPTS

Develop scripts for common activities such as telephone greetings, placing callers on hold, and giving directions to the clinic. Other patient service situations in which scripts are useful include: patients arriving early or late to an appointment, in-person greetings, closure instructions, and frequently asked questions.

INCENTIVES

"Out of sight; out of mind" comes to mind when addressing the value of incentives. The more staff is reminded to place patient service first and the more tangible the incentives, the more likely your patient service will remain strong and consistent.

EXHIBIT 6-6. SAMPLE PROTOCOL: HANDLING A DISGRUNTLED PATIENT

When a patient is upset about a customer service issue and expresses open concern in the clinic, follow these steps:

1. Do not show anger or contempt, no matter how irrational the behavior.
2. Escort the patient to a quiet, neutral place.
3. Ask the patient to thoroughly express his or her concern.
4. Probe, if necessary, to acquire more details about their concern.
5. Show empathy (e.g., "I can understand your concern, Mr. Dunn").
6. Ask what you can do to make things right. (Caution: Never offer a solution. Let the individual propose one first).
7. Quietly meet their request if possible.
8. Ask, "Now, are you satisfied with this resolution?"
9. Follow-up: confirm via email, voice mail or letter that you are sorry there was a problem and pleased that "we were able to work it out."
10. Remember that critics often become allies when you are willing to take the high road, apologize, and work toward a mutually satisfactory resolution.

Some ideas include:

- Base a minimum of 10 percent of an individual's annual performance evaluation score on patient satisfaction scores and anecdotal information provided by patients.
- Single employees/associates out for recognition by patients and recognize them at staff meetings and other functions.
- Ask staff members to make recommendations regarding appropriate incentives.

BENCHMARKS AND STANDARDS

Include meaningful and measurable patient service performance standards and benchmarks in your patient service plan.

Suggested benchmarks:

- Respond to service requests from client companies within one working day.
- Keep maximum patient time in a clinic to one hour.
- Redirect patients from the reception area to an exam room within fifteen minutes.
- Have personal contact with patients waiting in an exam room every fifteen minutes.
- Answer incoming calls by the fourth ring.
- Establish a maximum time a caller can be on hold to thirty seconds.
- Send no more than 10 percent of incoming calls to voice mail.

Your recorded answering system should be reviewed and updated to make it customer friendly. The system should offer a clear opportunity to opt-out of the recording and speak to a receptionist.

COMMUNICATION PROTOCOLS

Less than optimal communication is an oft-cited concern of both patients and their employers. Do not leave communication to chance:

- Confirm pre-scheduled appointments one day before the appointment.
- Ask providers to introduce themselves to patients and state their role (e.g., "I'm Mary, and I will be checking your blood pressure, height, and weight before Dr. Jones sees you.").
- Train providers to ask, "Are there any questions before we begin?"
- Remind providers to say, "Is there anything you do not understand?" at the end of a patient encounter.

UNDERSTANDING VALUE

I have conducted at least five hundred focus-group sessions with a collective total of more than three thousand employer representatives since 1985. A consistent topic spanning all of these sessions is value: exactly what do employers expect to receive from the typical service provider?

PERCEPTIONS VARY

Perceptions of value are influenced by many factors. Conventional wisdom dictates that the presumed value of a service rests with its ability to reduce costs. This is true, but buyers do not always think in such terms.

You need to sell healthcare services based on their perceived value to the buyer. Learn to assess each buyer's definition of value. Such assessments are traditionally done through the use of astute questioning (e.g., "What specific attributes do you look for when selecting an external provider of wellness services?"). Armed with this information, you can then position your services in the most appropriate manner.

COMMON VALUE MEASURES

Ten frequently cited measures of value are listed below. Some may stand on their own, while others often offer value in combination with other measures:

1. **The core equation** — This is the starting point for many employers and providers: if an intervention lowers the injury/illness incidence rate and/or decreases lost work time, the company will save money.

   This equation is logical, measurable, and often understood by the buyer. Always present this concept to determine whether the prospective buyer will accept it as the value proposition or is only likely to embrace it in combination with other factors.

2. **Incidence prevention** — Many buyers warm to the argument that strong prevention can markedly reduce their company's healthcare cost. Logic reigns: injury and illness prevention, for example, eliminates the need for employees to file workers'

compensation claims or seek medical care. Well-trained, credentialed staff and workplace walkthrough programs are typical selling points to address this perceived value.

3. **Making the buyer look good** — A buyer's parochial interest often wins out. For every buyer with a "company first" concept of value, there is another buyer with a "What's in it for me?" point of view. Emphasize the inherent value of the provider relationship to the company while positioning the release of performance data so the buyer can be recognized for astute decision making.

4. **Convenience** — Never underestimate convenience as a powerful buying motive. Many buyers are happy to be working with a service that is nearby, offers favorable hours, and sees employees in a timely manner.

   Never mind that their clinic of choice may not offer optimal outcomes or systematic management of their workplace health issues—easy is better. Keep convenience cards in your portfolio and play them when you detect the convenience cue.

5. **Communication** — For every buyer who touts convenience, another touts communication. These buyers value the personal touch and are less likely to be swayed by location, technical competency, or outcome data. Emphasize your service's communication skills whenever this attribute comes up.

6. **Price (return on investment)** — Price-conscious buyers are out there in droves. Such buyers tend to view healthcare services as a series of discrete commodities, and they lean heavily toward the lowest price option for most purchases. Often you have little recourse when it comes to price comparisons.

   The recourse can be found in return on investment. In many cases the price-trumps-all buyer who looks at the world in terms of dollars and cents is likely to respond to the return-on-investment argument. Trump the price objection with a strong return-on-investment response.

7. **Depth of resources** — Employer focus group participants often tell me that access to a broad array of professionals offers considerable value. Such breadth is usually a value best offered by a health system, large hospital, or multi-specialty group. Play the depth of resources card as available and appropriate.

8. **Personality** — Have you bought something—trivial or significant—because you liked and trusted the salesperson? Merits of the product be damned—you did not want to disappoint the salesperson. Maintain a keen antenna for those prospects with whom you have chemistry and emphasize the personal connection in negotiations.
9. **Continuity of care** — While the inherent value of a tightly knit service continuum is a given for providers, the value may not be as apparent to prospects. The notion of continuity of care should be explored with the prospect and emphasized when its value is recognized.
10. **Certifications** — Many potential buyers are certification wonks—they are impressed by credentials and uncomfortable with programs that lack such certified personnel. Acquaint yourself with the certifications and training levels of key staff and be able to articulate the value of each certification.

When done with sufficient forethought you should be able to provide a series of sound rationales to differentiate your services from other options.

Rejection

A quarter of a century ago, a former colleague of mine, Jon Kabot-Zinn, told me everyone experiences stress and that what matters is how one manages it. At the time, Jon was the calmest and happiest person I had ever met, so I took his words to the bank. Jon went on to become an author and national authority on stress management.

Analogous advice applies to sales: "Every sales professional experiences rejection, but what matters is how they manage that rejection." The following is a plan for learning how to live with rejection and turning it to your advantage.

THE ACTION PLAN

With due respect to the country music classic "What Part of No (Don't You Understand)," "no" does not always mean no. In sales we are dealing with transactions, not romance.

You usually have wiggle room, even after a prospect seemingly closes their door. A prospect's negativity may be short lived; unanticipated events may occur (e.g., newfound dissatisfaction with the prospect's current providers), or they may hear something positive about your services that change their mind.

You can do several things to ease the pain of rejection and better position you for a future sales encounter:

1. **Employ the classic objection-response cycle** — Immediately after a failed sales effort, respond with objective-handling techniques, including pause, empathize, probe, and reposition:

    - **Pause:** Following most rejections, you are tempted to pick up your attaché case and gloomily move on. In most cases this is counterproductive. Follow a conclusive "no go" with a simple pause. These precious seconds cut the tension that tends to envelop either or both parties at the point of "no" and allows you time to mentally regroup.
    - **Empathize:** The last thing a prospect expects to hear from you is acknowledgement that the prospect made a reasonable choice in using another option. Yet, such a pronouncement tends to endear you to the prospect and provides you with greater leverage to renew your sales effort at a later date. A statement such as "Work Health (your competitor) offers good services. I'm sure you will be happy with them," enhances your credibility and solidifies your relationship with the prospect.
    - **Probe:** If the rationale for the prospect's rejection has not been made clear, ask why they chose not to work with your services. A straightforward, "Please tell me why you prefer not to work with us at this time. Your opinion will help me in future dealings," is a fair request. Tally the reasons for every rejection in order to document the most common reasons. This information provides you with a foundation to refine your sales technique or call attention to recurring deficits.
    - **Reposition:** Following a no, the astute sales professional is often well positioned to seek an opening to re-initiate

contact with the prospect at a later date. Depending on the circumstances, you can do several things:

- **Set a check-in date:** Tell the prospect that you would like to stay in touch and ask if they would mind if you called six months later "just to see how things are going." Most prospects are unlikely to be averse to making such a commitment six month's out, and you have now established both a purpose and a time line for maintaining contact. Schedule such planned contacts.
- **Offer a "freebie":** As previously noted, maintain a bag of "freebies" that can be offered at various stages of the sales cycle, including immediately post-rejection. Freebies might include a subscription to a periodical, a complimentary service, or registration to an upcoming seminar.
- **Add the individual to your email list:** If you send out periodic email transmissions to client and prospects, you can use the moment of rejection to ensure that you have the prospect's email address as well as those of other significant players at the company. You want to be first in line if and when the prospect feels it is time for a change.
- **Strive for agreement:** Whatever your approach (a follow-up call, a freebie, a commitment to being on an email distribution list), try to leave the sales encounter on a positive note. Always find a way to end the most unsuccessful of sales encounters on an emotional uptick.

2. **Companies remain, but the faces change** — A typical company experiences 15–20 percent employee turnover every year. Chances are that one out of every five or six decision makers will have left their company within a year of rejecting your proposal. Those odds increase even more favorably when you factor in those who remain with the company but shift to another position.

   Maintain a list and call that list periodically (e.g., quarterly) to determine who may have moved on. With a new decision maker in place, you have an opportunity to re-initiate the sales process.

3. **Focus on ratios, not wins and losses** — Track your hit ratio rather than dwell on defeats. If you typically close one out of ten prospects and you meet or exceed that ratio, then the rejections are easier to handle. A no is a better result than being strung along only to experience rejection down the line. It is best to get it over with quickly and move on.
4. **Change your mind-set** — Re-orient your mind-set regarding rejection. The more readily you view sales call rejections as opportunities, the more likely you are to ultimately turn many rejections around.

You may find the fear of rejection and actual rejection so uncomfortable that it affects your overall performance. Analogous to marketing, sales is a numbers game: the more calls you make, the more sales prospects you will close, even with a constant batting average. Learn to persevere and not take rejection personally; whenever possible, find a way to turn rejection into a learning experience and an opportunity for a successful sales effort down the road.

Responding to Requests for Proposals

In terms of numbers of clients, business generated through a formal request for proposal (RFP) process typically comprises a small percentage of your overall client base.

However, proposal-generated business usually represents a significant portion of a service's gross revenue because RFPs tend to be issued by local governmental entities and large self-insured companies that require a bidding process.

You already may have all or part of the requesting party's business. If that is the case, a response is necessary to secure and expand on that existing business. If the company or governmental entity is not a client, the RFP represents a golden opportunity to delineate your capabilities with the goal of establishing a long-term relationship.

Consider the following tips to get ahead of the competition.

TIP 1: Dissect the request.

Often a respondent to an RFP will give it the once over and submit an uninspired response. Be certain that you understand *exactly* what the prospect is looking for and respond in kind.

TIP 2: Stick to the outline.

Follow the suggested proposal response outline to a tee. The format may not seem logical to you, but the likelihood of winning the contract is improved when you adhere to the desired format.

TIP 3: Parrot key words.

Responding to an RFP provides an opportunity to show that you understand the employer's perspective. Use the same words the requester uses to describe their challenges and your proposed solutions.

TIP 4: Ask for clarification.

Call the organization that issued the RFP and ask for clarification on selected issues (e.g., "We are interested in working with your company and wish to clarify some issues before we submit our response to your request."). I have placed such calls scores of times and have never found it to be counterproductive. Ask the prospect to define what they *really* need. Take thorough notes and reflect those needs back in your response.

A pre-submission call can be particularly valuable when attempting to zero in on a prospect's cost expectations. You can be forthright by stating,

> *"We can address your needs in a variety of ways, each with a different cost structure. A limited-but-effective approach would cost approximately $xxx, while a more comprehensive approach would cost an estimated $xxx. It would help us to know more about your budget and expectations."*

TIP 5: Provide price options.

The two most likely reasons for not winning a contract via an RFP process are:

1. The bidder's proposed fees are too high (or at least higher than the lowest bidder).
2. The bidder could not offer everything the prospect wanted or needed (e.g., "Your response was really attractive, but . . . ").

Provided that it does not violate a proposal requirement for a single bid, offer at least two, if not three, fee options. Call them the limited, mid-range, and comprehensive options. This will help diffuse obstacles:

- The limited option is the low-cost option and should help overcome a price objection, if it exists.
- The mid-range option represents a compromise that may help satisfy multiple decision makers.
- The comprehensive option is often more appealing for the prospect with deeper pockets and high expectations.

TIP 6: Make subtle competitor comparisons.

If the proposal is open for bid, assume that your most significant competitors also are likely to submit bids. If you make such an assumption and are correct, you are covered; if you are incorrect, it will be harmless. Without mentioning any competitors' names, point out your primary advantages.

> *"Please note that our clinic is the only one in the local area that is open twenty-four hours a day, thereby providing your company with immediate access and continuity of care no matter what time an incident occurs."*

TIP 7: Meet, not beat, the deadline.

Discount any "bonus points" you may get by submitting a proposal early. Although it is sound advice not to submit your proposal at the last second (do not take a chance of missing a deadline), submitting it too soon makes little sense. Additional enhancements to your proposal may come to light shortly before the submission deadline, and being first to the starting line is immaterial in this horse race.

TIP 8: Submit your response in multiple ways.

Unless restricted by the RFP rules to a single mode of transmission, use multiple methods to deliver your proposal. Hand-deliver a hard copy, send one by overnight delivery, and send another one by email. It may seem like overkill, but multiple submissions draw attention to your proposal, and an electronic version facilitates internal transmission to multiple parties.

TIP 9: Make it readable.

Be succinct. Readers, especially those who must review submissions from multiple applicants, are more likely to absorb and remember short points. For the sake of thoroughness, include citations that refer to relevant attachments and appendices. Even though reviewers may never read the appendices, the material suggests that you have done your homework and offer depth of resources.

TIP 10: Emphasize professionalism.

I recently reviewed proposals from prospective host hotels for our next national conference. Beyond content, I was favorably impressed by those with an attractive appearance. It is well worth the extra effort to give your response a professional look. Proofread the entire document. Use colors and font sizes effectively. Print on high-quality paper, submit bound copies, and ensure that electronic submissions are properly paginated.

OVERCOMING NATIONAL CONTRACT BARRIERS

Has this happened to you? A key prospect company turns out to be a non-starter because the company is committed to a regional or national contract. Dealing with prospects who are theoretically wed to a contract is a relatively common occurrence that may seem virtually impossible to overcome. However, such a contract should not be viewed as an impenetrable wall; you can deal with it in several ways.

ALL CONTRACTS ARE NOT CREATED EQUAL

When an employer cites an obligation to a contract, much may be left unsaid. Contracts come in all sizes and shapes.

A contract can be:

- Local, regional, or national
- Prospect specific (relevant only to that company at that location) or part of a contract that affects an entire national chain (e.g., Home Depot)
- Limited in scope of contractual services or all-inclusive
- Binding or discretionary to the prospect company
- Based on a price discount that can be matched or undersold

Given these contractual variants, you have many ways to approach a prospect that is bound to a national contract. Ferret out the exact nature of a contract (or perceived obligation) by learning as much as possible about the company and its contractual obligations.

RELEVANT QUESTIONS

Typical questions that might be posed during a seemingly ill-fated sales call might include:

> *"Is the contract for a specific time period?"*
>
> *"Do you (or does your local office) have unilateral authority when entering into a contractual relationship?"*
>
> *"If not, who is responsible for a final decision?"*
>
> *"Exactly what services does the contract cover?"*
>
> *"What other type of healthcare services does your company use that are not specifically bound to the contract?"*
>
> *"To what degree is the contract binding to your company?"*
>
> *"In what way, if any, might another provider bid for your company's business?"*
>
> *"Beside price, what other factors does your company take into consideration when valuing your return on investment for health and safety management activities?"*

Do not give up when confronting a prospect who touts a contractual relationship. Probe for facts, look for openings, and learn to separate opportunities from closed doors.

EXHIBIT 6-7. RESPONSES TO CONTRACT SCENARIOS

CONDITION	STRATEGY
Long-term contract	Probe for other service needs
Short-term contract	Position to bid for business at conclusion of contract
Contract with actual company	Stay in touch with decision maker
Contract with national office	Identify contact and correspond with national office
Meeting with decision maker	Learn hot buttons; stay in touch
Decision maker in home office	Identify contact and correspond with national office
Limited scope of services	Tout value of your broad, integrated services
All inclusive	Look for missing pieces
Mandatory compliance	Look for missing pieces
Discretionary compliance	Treat as traditional prospect; emphasize ROI
Price discount	Emphasize ROI issues
Vague obligation	Treat as traditional prospect

HAVE OTHER THINGS TO SELL

Prudent business development strategy usually includes product expansion, not maintenance of a narrow menu of services. Be poised to sell a portfolio of services of value to employers. A portfolio expanding strategy provides you with a series of fallback options to use whenever you are unable to crack the national contract dilemma.

TURNING CRISIS INTO OPPORTUNITY

Assume that a national player uses contracts to make inroads with your clients or an appreciable number of your best prospects also become involved in contracts. Crisis or opportunity? View these scenarios as opportunities. Successful healthcare organizations of the future will meet community and worker healthcare needs in an appropriate fashion by offering multiple integrated services.

YOU DO NOT HAVE TO BAT A THOUSAND

During a recent season, Detroit's Miguel Cabrara had the highest batting average in the major leagues at .344. The accolades aside, Mr. Cabrara's .344 batting average indicates that the batting champion failed to get a hit 65.6 percent of the time. So it is with a sales professional in almost any industry. You have to anticipate a mix of home runs, base hits, walks, and strikeouts.

In many cases a company's national contract obligation will close the door on your organization, for at least the time being. It is inevitable and part of the sales management function. Ask questions and probe to seek opportunities when dealing with such companies. Nowadays outright resignation is the typical response, negating opportunities that may be only a question or two away. National contracts suggest that your services are a commodity, when in fact they should be seen as an ongoing relationship. Armed with such an understanding, the national contract roadblock should be viewed as less onerous than it is viewed in many cases.

Chapter 7:

Sales and Marketing Management

Mastery of the sales and marketing tactics and techniques described in this book are unlikely to produce optimal results unless they are executed within an appropriate organizational framework.

In healthcare, the sales and marketing functions are often poorly supervised and haphazardly executed. In many cases, a great deal needs to be done to get everything right.

BASIC RECOMMENDATIONS

A successful sales and marketing initiative requires tight, astute management. Consider the following:

RECOMMENDATION 1: Make sales and marketing an organizational priority.

You are setting yourself up for failure if you operate within a framework that fails to place sufficient importance on the services themselves. One error is that occupational health programs or wellness services are often viewed as "just another service line." This thinking is largely a product of the silo mentality that seems inherent in so many healthcare organizations.

But these services are unique and should be viewed as a broad employer portal for any services within an organization that can be delivered to employers or their employees.

A wide swath of services can be subsumed under the employer/provider umbrella: physical screenings, wellness services, women's health, sports medicine, travel medicine, and blended urgent care services, to name a few. The bottom line: employer outreach is and must be central to an organization's strategic vision.

> **Action step:** *Ask the most influential members of senior management to articulate (preferably in writing) exactly how they think a broadly defined array of services can help their organization. Pull out key concepts and buzz words and incorporate them in your marketing plan. Stay visible!*

RECOMMENDATION 2: Adopt new marketing tactics.

Old marketing habits die hard. The 1980s seemed to be the golden age of healthcare marketing. Books and conferences abounded, branding actively entered the healthcare vernacular, and considerable resources were devoted to print materials and media.

Although progress has been made in certain areas (e.g., a movement by many healthcare organizations to embrace social media as a marketing tool), those old healthcare marketing dogs have not been learning a lot of new tricks. Different service lines often call for a different set of marketing tactics from other service lines. Employer-based health services is a noteworthy outlier in the galaxy of healthcare services in that a finite number of decision makers, rather than a community at large, can make or break a program.

> **Action step:** *If you are affiliated with a large organization such as a hospital or health system, be certain that you have full autonomy over your service's marketing plan. Employer directed services are a different animal and should not be positioned as a small component of a larger plan.*

RECOMMENDATION 3: Position the sales professional correctly in the hierarchy.

Sales may be a foreign concept for many within the organization; hence, healthcare organizations tend to be slow to figure out exactly where to put a sales professional within the organizational hierarchy. The job description of a healthcare sales professional and the ideal place for the role within the organization can often become murky:

- Sales professionals are too often asked to do things beyond the scope of their core job description: assist us with this program, help us with that initiative, and the big one, take care of various customer service (operational shortcomings) issues for us. The sales professional may have precious little time to do what he or she was hired to do: sell.
- The fish-out-of-water nature of many healthcare sales positions seems to create uncertainty regarding where such a person or function belongs.

It usually makes little sense for a sales and marketing professional to report to an organizational marketing department that is likely to know little about their specific service and is removed from the service line's routine activities.

It also makes little sense for a the sales professional to report directly to someone within their department (occupational medicine, sports medicine, wellness), such as a medical director or service line director, who is likely to know little about sales and marketing. Many sales professionals are left to their own devices, with minimal supervision and scant accountability.

> **Action step:** *Carefully select the individual to whom a sales professional will report within a healthcare organization. Ensure that strict standards are followed and the supervisor is versed in the principles of healthcare-related sales and marketing.*

RECOMMENDATION 4: Involve senior management.

During a down economy many service lines could be on the chopping block if and when their parent institution needs to eliminate programs or personnel. Pure profit/loss fails to reflect potentially considerable downstream and other indirect revenues, but few institutions pause to take that into consideration.

Proactively address prospective cuts. Develop a system to measure downstream and other indirect revenue. A viable way to forestall a superficial and potentially calamitous review is to involve your organization's key decision makers in your service initiative right from the start.

Examples of decision-maker involvement include:

- **Signing a mass distribution letter** — Send a letter once a year to local companies (clients and non-clients) emphasizing the administrator's "commitment to working with area employers in order to ensure the best possible health and safety environment at their workplace." Such a gesture represents excellent marketing in its own right; senior administration is likely to feel a sense of buy-in and is less likely to treat your initiative harshly down the road.
- **Speaking at a function** — Ask a senior administrator to welcome guests or introduce faculty during a webinar, live seminar, or task force meeting. This also is good marketing and gives the senior administrator a sense of ownership.
- **Keeping senior administrators up to speed** — Send out a monthly email message summarizing your successes. Keep it short and simple and be consistent. After a while the administrator will begin to have a genuine appreciation for your program's performance.

> **Action step:** *Identify one event during the coming year in which your organization's primary decision maker can play a role. Ask him or her to participate.*

RECOMMENDATION 5: Increase productivity through time management.

Time is money when it comes to sales. Consider the time you spend on the telephone every week, and then cut each call by one third. You can reduce telephone time by being better prepared for the call, being concise, and selecting the time of day to make your calls.

If you are on the phone three hours a day, such a reduction

translates to one hour a day or five hours a week. Not bad. When you project the time saved over a year, your time savings jumps to 260 hours. That is six and a half extra weeks every year to do more productive things such as live sales calls.

There are many time-eating monsters:

- **Telephone** — Watch the chit-chat, telephone tag, and getting directed to the wrong person. Careful and proactive management of your phone time can be worth weeks of saved time.
- **Meetings** — In the email age, we can save a lot of time by monitoring both the incidence and length of meetings.
- **Paperwork** — Some paperwork is good and necessary, but a great deal of paperwork, although superficially interesting, is ultimately extraneous.
- **Driving** — Think out your auto travel. Cluster visits, substitute telephone calls for in-person visits, and keep in mind time-of-the-day travel patterns.

A mediocre sales professional seems to be perpetually caught in traffic, talking on their cell phone, engaged in internal meetings, and meticulously documenting everything they do while the successful sales professional is making the sale. Be proactive and value every minute of your time.

> **Action step:** *Create a time sheet that summarizes your activities throughout a week in fifteen-minute blocks. At week's end, review the time sheet and identify areas of less than optimal time usage. Eliminate time eaters. Complete another time sheet a month later for a comparison.*

Internal Marketing

If external marketing is an entity's ability to publicize its products and services, internal marketing is a program's ability to maintain a strong, appropriate profile within its parent organization. Never has skill in internal marketing been more important.

When a parent organization is forced to make cuts in services, service lines are frequently prone to severe cuts—or even elimination.

The best hedge against such a reduction is to support a strong and continuous internal marketing effort.

ACTION STEPS

1. **Align your mission statement** — Your service has inherently more value if its contribution is seen as consistent with your parent organization's primary mission. In most instances, it is.

   Healthcare organization mission statements invariably refer to such broad homilies as "meeting the unmet needs of our community," "enhancing the health status of everyone in our jurisdiction," or "providing an integrated, cost-effective approach to healthcare delivery in our community." Such statements provide a foundation for a mission statement at the service line level. An example of a program-level mission statement might be something like this:

   > *"In support of [parent organization's name] central mission to provide an integrated, cost-effective approach to healthcare delivery in Canton, WorkWell will work with employers to tighten the prevention-acute care-rehabilitation continuum for injured workers, achieve a higher health status among worker populations, and provide a net cost savings to employers and the community at large."*

   The service line mission statement is little more than a variant of the larger organization's mission statement.

2. **Establish specific expectations** — Many service lines proceed methodically without having senior management's expectations clearly defined. Ask several questions of senior management at the outset of every budget cycle, including:

   > *"If we meet your expectations over the coming year, exactly what type of financial achievement would you like to see?"*

"The value of a service is partly associated with hard-to-measure variables and downstream revenues such as ancillaries, referrals to specialists and rehabilitation professionals, inpatient follow-up, community visibility, and the development of long-term relationships with key community employers. What is important to you, and how can we best measure our impact in these and other areas?"

"Assume that a year from now that our performance exceeds your greatest expectations. Exactly what would we have to do?" (*Note:* This is a good question for any superior in any situation).

It is imperative to document all such requests in writing, often as an email confirmation (e.g., "To summarize our meeting . . . ").

3. **Involve senior management** — Token involvement by senior management can go a long way toward instilling a sense of ownership, which is likely to have an impact if and when the day comes to potentially reduce your budget or eliminate it entirely.

    - Invite senior management representatives to accompany you on at least one sales call per year. Such participation gives management a greater appreciation of how your service connects with the community (to say nothing of increasing the likelihood that you will close the sale).
    - Conduct a quarterly phone blitz of your fifty most significant clients. ("How are we doing?" "What can we do to enhance our services?") Ask senior management to participate in at least one call per quarter. Such calls typically last only a few minutes and help facilitate senior management buy-in.
    - Ask a senior administrator to briefly serve as the kickoff speaker for a live or audio educational conference. Their participation will most likely add luster to your session and make it more difficult for them to turn their back on you down the line.

- Ask the senior administrator to sign a letter that will be mass-mailed to employer prospects.

  "As President of Herman Farms, it is my pleasure to introduce you to WorkWell, the leading occupational health program in Canton. We recognize the value of working closely with our community's employers and their workforce in order to save employers money and enhance the health status of this critical segment of our community population."

SHARE YOUR SUCCESS

You have heard the truisms: "The squeaky wheel gets the grease" and "Out of sight, out of mind." Individuals vested with responsibility to make "continue/eliminate" or budget-cutting decisions often do so instinctively or without a reasonable understanding of a given program's nature or broader contribution. An individual's instinct can be sharpened by learning more about a program's raison d'etre and potential or actual financial contribution.

Call attention to a series of success stories rather than a creating a single, carefully honed presentation. In our information-intensive world, it is that simple: a carefully crafted message repeated frequently is more likely to have a lasting impact than a more detailed message delivered once.

What message do you wish to share with others in your organization? You want to illustrate the wonderful things you are doing on behalf of the organization in terms of both direct and indirect contributions.

The message can be delivered in a monthly email blast to relevant senior managers (who can make or break your program), various department heads (whose support and cooperation are vital), and to members of your own team (who can always use a boost in morale).

Make your monthly update brief (e.g., about one side of one page), succinct (e.g., laden with bullet points), and positive.

Include:

- Information about new clients ("We're pleased to announce that we have added Canton's Municipal Government and its 12,000 employees to our client base").

- Information about prestigious and/or unusual clients ("Did you realize that Bethlehem Steel and the local Ford plant are WorkWell customers?").
- Employer or worker testimonials ("We couldn't survive without WorkWell!").
- Information about financial accomplishments ("By mid-November we had exceeded the projected revenue goal for the year").
- Information about new or expanded service offerings ("Beginning January 1, WorkWell will begin to offer background checks as part of our pre-placement screening package").
- Information about how the program's protocols have been effectively applied to your organization's employee health functions ("Using WorkWell's protocols our parent hospital experienced a 10 percent reduction in healthcare costs").

The design of an internal marketing plan is really not terribly complex. Every organization should design and execute such a plan.

Hiring Sales Professionals

The adage, "You can't make a silk purse out of a sow's ear" is applicable in hiring. Ask any coach, manager, or supervisor, and they will tell you that mediocre personnel beget mediocre results.

This principle illustrates the importance of retaining the best sales professionals for your organization—a necessity heightened in situations when incremental performance yields direct incremental increases to the bottom line.

FINDING THE BEST

The tastes-great/less-filling question typically asked when hiring a health sales professional is: Should we hire a sales professional to train in the service lines, or should we hire/appoint a professional from the service line to train in sales? The former brings sales savvy and the need to learn the product; the latter brings product knowledge and the need to learn fundamental sales skills.

Given these two options, I suggest the former. It is easier to train an experienced sales professional in product knowledge than vice versa. There are numerous exceptions to the rule. An insider with product knowledge may be a natural who easily adapts to the sales role. Further, given cutbacks and contraction in a buyer's market, many programs may be able to attract an experienced sales professional.

Presuming that an experienced sales professional is an optimal candidate, consider what you have to gain by hiring someone who has done this before *in your market.* Such an individual is likely to bring clients, market knowledge, and potentially valuable competitive intelligence to your program.

WHEN OPENINGS OCCUR

Errors frequently occur early in the hiring process when sales positions become available. Often a department does not move quickly enough to fill the position or does not conduct a broad enough search.

Firstly, an open sales position has a direct effect on profitability. Each day the position remains open means less sales calls and less revenue for the service. By comparison, when an operational position is left open for an extended period, operational efficiencies may suffer and there may be an added burden on remaining staff, but at least you are *saving* money for this period. Hence, you must move quickly to initiate the recruiting/interviewing/hiring process.

Secondly, recruiting efforts tend to be too narrow, often featuring a single strategy (e.g., "Let's put an ad in the *Daily Bugle*"). Use multiple modalities to build an extensive candidate pool as quickly as possible. The wider your net, the more likely you will catch the big fish.

Include the following in a multiple modality approach:

National recruiting firm: Consider utilizing one or more national firms specializing in recruitment for the specialty in question. This provides you with the best chance to find a candidate who has been-there, done-that. An experienced sales professional is more likely to hit the ground running and bring in more immediate incremental revenue. A contingency fee and/or relocation costs may well be offset by the new hire's ability to bring in more dollars more quickly.

Local recruiting firm: A local firm that specializes in sales and marketing is likely to bring non-specialty specific sales professionals to your attention. Most search firms routinely provide pure contingency-based fees; hence, you only incur a small financial obligation when you hire a candidate.

Advertising: Depending on the size and nature of your market, newspaper advertising, or advertising on such electronic options as Craig's List may be valuable.

Internet recruiting: Internet recruiting tools such as www.monster.com are increasingly viable methods for enlarging your prospect base.

Internal posting: Post the position internally, out of fairness; give promising employees a chance to cultivate their talent.

NARROW THE FIELD

The good news is that you may now have a candidate pool the size of Jupiter. The bad news is, now what? Programs often intentionally narrow their outreach out of fear that their candidate pool will become too large and unwieldy. The greater danger is missing out on the best candidates in the name of candidate pool management. You do need to intelligently narrow down the pool.

Require that both objective and subjective criteria be included in a candidate's first response. By asking each candidate for a letter of interest that includes the reason for considering the position, the candidate's compensation requirements, current responsibilities, and job title, you can eliminate many candidates after a brief glance.

Send the remaining candidates a packet of materials describing the sales/marketing position, your service line, and your parent organization. Dissemination of information at this juncture serves multiple purposes:

1. It eliminates many candidates that for one reason or another may not be interested in the position, saving you time up front and down the line.
2. It reduces the time you need to describe your services during the interview, providing more time to get to know the applicant.

3. It provides a measure of the job seeker's diligence. You can easily ascertain during the interview how well prepared the candidate is, a key attribute.

Ask candidates to call your office during a specific time period to schedule a telephone interview. Many would-be candidates do not get around to it, or cannot seem to find the time to call during the specified time period; ferret them out now and save time later.

Conduct the telephone interview. A warm, gracious, and self-confident telephone presence is important in sales and can be readily judged. Ask the candidate if they have questions about your services and the position after reading your materials. Minimal comments are typically a negative indicator.

Invite final candidates in for a personal interview. Send them (via email or regular mail, if necessary) a hypothetical sales scenario and ask that they come to the interview prepared to discuss the scenario.

> *"We have been trying to reach Michael Mushlin, Human Resources Director at Ben Rory Rubber, for several weeks without success. Ben Rory Rubber is a former client of ours who left last year to work with our competitor, and we want this client back. How are you going to reach Mr. Mushlin, and what are you going to say when you do?"*

This process will winnow down your field (a surprising number of candidates will be intimidated by this process and back down; these are not the type of candidates you want to hire anyway). Those that you do interview will provide you with a tangible series of comparable skills such as preparedness, articulateness, problem-solving capabilities, and sales instincts.

THE INTERVIEW: WHAT TO LOOK FOR

In many instances the job interview process is misguided in that the interviewer talks too much about the position, which should be covered in writing well before the personal interview. Questions and follow-up probes are often either shallow or nonexistent.

Place special emphasis on the following criteria:

The glow: I base hiring decisions overwhelmingly on persona rather than objective qualifications. You can usually tell in the first few seconds if a person has that "glow" (genuinely warm, sincere, happy, caring); the glow is especially vital for sales professionals who are continually making first impressions. Be willing to sacrifice some technical qualifications if you can bring in such a winner.

Reflect your marketplace: The candidate that I would hire in midtown Manhattan is not the same one I would hire in Tuscaloosa. Look for the candidate who best fits your market and is most likely to feel at home with the prototype decision-makers at local companies.

A sense of commitment: Effective sales professionals develop momentum over the years; you want to ensure as little turnover as possible. Scrutinize the candidate's work history: Have they moved around a lot and, if so, why? What is the likelihood they are going to stay in your city/town for a long time? Is your sales position something they really want to do, or do they feel it is "just another job?"

Exhibit 7-1. Sample Interview Questions

"If I asked ten people who know you well to identify your best trait, what would they say? Why do you think they feel this way?"

"If you were me and you were hiring a person for this position what four traits would you look for in a candidate? Why?"

"You have had the chance to review our materials. If an employer asked you why they should use our program, what would you say?"

"What do you think is the most important thing that you can contribute to any organization?"

"What three things do you like most (and least) about your current position?"

TRAINING SALES PROFESSIONALS

A newly hired sales professional—regardless of inherent potential or sales experience—is often doomed to failure in the absence of a strong training program. Insightful and proactive training programs are rarely done well, if they are done at all.

COMMON ERRORS

Many healthcare organizations are guilty of committing one or more of the following errors in training a new sales professional:

Lack of a training plan: Does your organization have a specific training plan for a new sales professional? I suspect that most readers will say no, which begs the question of how the new professional will hit the street with the requisite skills to succeed. Trial and error seems to be the preferred "training method," with weeks or months of potentially productive sales efforts significantly compromised.

Minimal, haphazard training: Minimal training is a small step forward, if a step forward at all. Yes, some training was done, although probably not in a timely and logical manner. On a scale of 1 to 10, you have catapulted from a 0 to a 2.

Deferred training: All right, a little better. There is training and it may be reasonably good, but there is no urgency associated with the training. You might send the new hire to a sales training program, but that may not occur until four months post-hire. Frequently the new sales professional is left to his or her own devices during these four months, and in the meantime, your sales effort suffers from inertia.

One-dimensional training: Even the better on-site training programs tend to suffer from a single-mindedness that uses one—and only one—mode of training. You could have the sales trainee go on a number of sales calls with your service line director before going out independently. Not a bad idea, but only a small part of a well-rounded sales training program.

SALES TRAINING PRINCIPLES

Apply the following principles in a comprehensive sales training program:

1. **Develop a durable training plan** — Your sales training plan is as important as your sales/marketing plan. A training plan is relatively easy to construct, yet it is seldom done in a systematic fashion. Develop a proactive training plan, modify it as necessary, and deploy the plan immediately upon hiring a sales professional.
2. **Be flexible** — One size does not fit all. Your sales training plan should embody a number of integrated concepts. Take into consideration the nature of the trainee. The new sales professional may have a rich service-specific background but little or no sales experience, or exactly the opposite. The plan should have plenty of wiggle room.
3. **Manage time** — Sharpen the new salesperson's ability to be battlefield ready as quickly as possible. Note the tangible difference if you have a sales professional operating at 95 percent of their potential after four weeks on the job compared to one who takes six months to get fully up to speed. Start training from the get-go; the axiom that time is money certainly applies in this instance.
4. **Use multiple modalities** — The best way to train anyone in just about anything is to use multiple training modalities. Sales training should employ a vigorous mix of one-on-one training, review of written materials, play acting, observation, and detailed critiques of actual and prototype sales calls by fellow staff. Changing the pace and coming from multiple angles enriches the learning experience.
5. **Make trainees trainers** — Once up and running, a newly trained sales professional instantly becomes invaluable as a trainer. Within a month or two of their initial training, it is useful to have the sales professional provide some training to select non-sales staff. This exercise allows the recently trained professional to solidify their understanding of the principles they learned and provides a valuable sales foundation to others who may have cause to draw upon these new sales skills.

6. **Give quizzes** — The new sales professional needs to develop a strong command of service line issues and nuances, policies, responses to common prospect objections, viable closing methods, and employer cost-benefit issues. Typically, little urgency is placed on mastering this information quickly. Scheduled written/oral mini-quizzes are an effective way to "force" the trainee into student mode so they may more quickly master essential information. Do not allow the new sales professional to enter the field until they have passed a battery of essential quizzes.
7. **Expand the scope of training** — Do not limit sales training strictly to dedicated sales professionals. Other staff, such as your service line and medical directors, should also participate in your in-house sales training program.

   Over the years I have spoken on sales and marketing to scores of physicians and have marveled about how little they seemed to know about sales and marketing and how much they valued the information. Physicians, administrators, and support staff all sell your services in some respect. They can be much more effective in this role if they receive some training.
8. **Acquire professional training** — I know you have been expecting this one! As a supplement to any in-house program, sales training programs that attract registrants from programs around the country is invaluable. RYAN Associates' sales training programs are offered a few times a year at venues throughout the country. We have trained more than 1,500 healthcare sales professionals since 1988, many of whom are still achieving success on a daily basis.

Sound, appropriate, and rapid training can markedly affect a program's ability to generate greater revenues in the short term. To the detriment of our field, employer focused sales efforts are often characterized by spotty or nonexistent training. A proactive sales training plan gets a sales professional up to speed more quickly and produces bottom-line results that easily compensate for any training expenses.

EXHIBIT 7-2. A PROTOTYPE WEEK ONE SALES TRAINING PROGRAM

MONDAY	8:00	Facility tours / individual meetings with key stakeholders
	1:00	Privately review written materials
	3:00	Observe clinic registration
TUESDAY	8:00	One-on-one meetings with key department heads
	10:00	One-on-one training: product line
	1:00	Review selected sales principles
	3:00	Quiet time / review
	4:00	Level I quiz
WEDNESDAY	8:00	One-on-one meetings with key department heads
	10:00	One-on-one training: staffing relationships
	1:00	Observe registration in Emergency Department
	3:00	Study time: sales principles
THURSDAY	8:00	One-on-one training: sales / marketing plan
	10:00	Observe actual sales calls with service line director
	3:00	Quiet time / review
	4:00	Level II quiz: sales principles
FRIDAY	8:00	Observe sales call with service line and medical director
	10:00	Play act prototype sales calls with staff
	1:00	Sample sales call with current (supportive) client
	3:00	Quiet time / review
	4:00	Level III quiz: Responding to objections / closing

WIN–WIN COMPENSATION PLANS

Compensation is frequently misunderstood and its importance underestimated. Indeed, the entire sales function is too often devalued. Programs bemoaning a barely break-even profit margin are invariably the ones with sales professionals who perform non-sales responsibilities, are woefully under-compensated, or both. Logic dictates that the more incentive a sales professional has, the greater their likely contribution to the bottom line.

The majority of the country's working population is motivated by financial gain. Unlike some sales professionals, occupational health sales professionals' performance can be measured. A win-win alignment of incentives can be created to optimize a program's revenue potential while simultaneously providing sales professionals with attractive compensation. The question is: What type of incentive structure is most likely to create the optimal win-win scenario?

Despite the logic in a win-win incentive plan, many common errors seem to permeate the industry:

Straight compensation: Many sales professionals have non-incentive laden compensation packages, though this is less common now than a decade ago. Where do you think such a person is going to be this Friday at 4:00 p.m.?

Multi-task job descriptions: I noted at a recent sales training seminar that numerous students were vested with many responsibilities beside direct sales. Sales professionals cannot be particularly effective if they wear many hats.

Flat targets: Many incentive programs provide a reward for hitting a target. In other words, if the sales professional barely misses the target, he or she gets nothing. If the sales professional vastly surpasses the target, he or she gets the same as barely hitting the target. Illogical? Yes. Common? Again, the answer is yes.

Non-revenue quotas: Many incentive compensation plans include non-revenue quotas such as number of sales calls or number of companies signed up. A hundred unproductive sales calls a week, or signing up twenty small companies with little or no volume potential, is not my idea of effective employer-directed sales.

Endless per-client revenue trails: This is my favorite faux pas. Several years ago an ashen-faced hospital vice president called me into her office to ask what she could do about the sales professional who received over $100,000 a year in compensation incentives for companies that he had signed up years before.

His plan entitled him to perhaps 5 percent of gross revenue generated by any company that he signed up. He sat in his office fat and happy while these residuals, like Elvis record royalties, poured in year after year. A sales professional is most valuable to the organization when he or she brings in new business.

Once a customer begins receiving services, the salesperson's value for that customer begins to diminish. Compensation plans should reflect these typical circumstances.

Retain the right to alter the incentive package: A package should be for one year and subject to annual reconfiguration. This would have helped the vice president mentioned above.

BASIC PLAN PRINCIPLES

When designing a compensation plan, keep these two basic principles in mind:

1. **Always offer incentives regardless of industry** — *Always* provide a sales professional with performance-based incentives. It should go without saying that sales professionals are going to be more focused and work harder if they know that their annual compensation is driven in considerable part by their ability to bring in business.
2. **Tie incentive compensation to performance expectations** — Physicians could arguably be judged by and compensated in part for their ability to achieve appropriate outcomes, receive high patient satisfaction scores, and be productive (patients seen per day, adjusted for case mix).

   Likewise a sales professional's raison d'être is to bring in as much incremental business as possible. They should be judged on this aspect alone; multiple other factors might be interesting, but in the end not meaningful.

3. **Follow the 80/20 rule for compensation** — It is an accepted industry norm that sales professionals' base pay should be approximately 80 percent of their total compensation with the remaining 20 percent being incentive-based. A sales professional with a base of $40,000 should receive a projected $10,000 a year ($2,500 in quarterly incentive compensation) if they achieve set goals for a total of $50,000, or one with a base of $80,000 should receive about $20,000 in projected incentive compensation.
4. **Plan for quarterly incentive payouts** — Once a month tends to be too frequent and makes everyone's head swirl. Longer than once a quarter takes the edge out of incentive payouts.
5. **Do not cap possible incentive pay** — Never cap the amount of incentive compensation one can receive. If you do, then all incentive ends when the sales professional hits their goal, whether it is one week or one month before the end of the incentive computation period. If there is a cap, a savvy sales professional may well try to defer sales into the next pay period in order to get that period's incentive pool off to a running start.
6. **Offer higher compensation percentages for higher levels of performance** — As sales professionals glide through their incentive compensation period, their incentive should be to push down harder on the accelerator, not ease up. If a sales professional receives 10 percent of all gross revenue above $500,000 for a given quarter, he or she could receive 15 percent, for revenues generated above a certain plateau and 20 percent for sales beyond an even higher plateau.
7. **Make gross revenue your primary payment metric** — Forget interesting but toothless parameters such as "number of new clients," "number of encounters," or "number of sales calls." Pay incentives on performance; the sales professional's core responsibility is to "bring in the greatest gross revenue in the shortest period of time."

   Why not pay out on net revenue? If you do, you are computing incentive pay in part for something the sales professional has little or no control over, such as discounts and less than optimal collections. Gross revenue is the name of the incentive pay game.

8. **Use previous year's gross revenue as your starting point** — If you want to grow the business 10 percent in a given year, compare each quarter's performance to the same quarter in the previous year. Such a system adjusts for seasonality.
9. **Parse gross revenue by service type and each service's marginal revenue** — If you rely strictly on gross revenue, you run the risk of paying a sales professional handsomely for bringing in low marginal revenue visits (e.g., drug tests) rather than a larger amount of high-end marginal revenue visits (pre-hire screening exams or physical therapy). Determine the profit margin per encounter type and base your incentive pay on a blend of those parameters.
10. **Remember the three revenue silos** — As previously described, a sales professional needs to focus as appropriate on three revenue generating or revenue maintenance silos: new business from new clients, incremental business from existing clients, and a focus on major clients that have been using less services in recent quarters. Do not reward a sales professional solely on the revenue brought in from new clients; you want them to exceed baseline by as much as possible regardless of the source.
11. **Create a common pool for multiple sales professional** — If you employ more than one sales professional, create a common pool to share among each sales professional. Assume that your organization has three sales professionals and each receive 10 percent of incremental revenue above baseline. Pay each at 8 percent of incremental revenue in their territory and place the remaining 2 percent in a common pool to be split evenly three ways. Such a pool provides incentives for inter-territory cross referrals, creates a spirit of teamwork, and generates a degree of competition.
12. **Use non-financial rewards where appropriate** — Non-financial rewards (e.g., special recognition, gift certificates, or trips) are more effective in comparatively large sales organizations where intra-program competition may exist. Recognition is a key motivator for any good salesperson, but it is much more meaningful when there are multiple people on the sales team competing for the same prize.

Many relationships (personal and professional) are built on the alignment of incentives, so both parties' goals are met to the greatest degree possible. For a particular service, the goal of sales is to attract as much business as possible; for the typical sales professional, the goal is attractive compensation.

The design of any sales professional's compensation package should be predicated on the answer to a single question: "How can the plan provide our sales professional or sales force with the greatest degree of incentive to produce the most revenue for our service line in the shortest period of time?"

Exhibit 7-3. A Prototype Compensation Package

Diane Closer: Sales Professional	
Year 1 Quarter 1 gross revenue =	$250,000
Year 2 Quarter 1 gross revenue =	$310,000
Year 2 growth =	$60,000 above Year 2
Base salary:	$48,000
8% gross revenue $250,000–$300,000:	$4,000
10% gross revenue above $300,000:	$1,000
1% pooled new revenue from all clinics:	$1,200
Total quarter 1 incentive compensation:	$6,200

Incentives on their own do "motivate" people to perform. Motivation is an internal characteristic that people bring with them to the job. People are either motivated or they are not. Effective hiring practices are the key. Hire self-motivated individuals. Financial incentives are used to encourage already motivated salespeople to make good decisions, such as selling to the right companies, promoting the services you want to sell, fighting to maintain rates, and moving proposals quickly toward closure.

One size does not fit all in compensation plans. The size of the sales force, the nature of the product, the size of the market, and the nature of the competition may all be confounding variables.

EXAMPLE:

Desired current year growth: 10 percent.

Assume one sales professional and gross revenue of $500,000 in each quarter of the year.

Assume base salary of $50,000 with projection of $12,500 in incentive compensation if the sales professional meets the 10 percent growth expectation; 10 percent growth per quarter is $50,000 in new revenue growth; 25 percent of $50,000 is $12,500; the sales professional should receive 25 percent of any growth above a baseline of $50,000 for that quarter.

MOTIVATING SALES PROFESSIONALS

I recently asked a respected director of a large healthcare service how good she is at a performing certain essential tasks. She answered, "Either extremely good or extremely bad; it depends on how motivated I am."

Ah, motivation! Sales professionals can master every sales and marketing principle in the book and still fall flat if they lack the fire in the belly.

IT STARTS WITH THE JOB INTERVIEW

I try to do three things when I conduct a job interview:

- Learn about the applicant
- Discuss the day-to-day detail of the job
- Offer my thoughts on the inherent value of the position to the applicant

The first two objectives are likely to generate an excellent job match; the third objective is intended to instill a sense of motivation from the outset.

For example, I invariably tell applicants for support roles at

RYAN Associates that (a) because of the relatively small size of our company they will get to do many things, affording them a greater portfolio of skills down the line, and (b) I personally benefited greatly from mentoring that I received years ago and now see myself in the role of mentor.

The applicant who finds genuine value in these purported opportunities is more likely to get the job and will likely see the position for what it is: something that has the potential to go beyond the job description.

Similarly, a bigger picture should be spelled out for budding sales professionals. Advise applicants and new hires about the underlying potential of the service.

Advise candidates that mastery and practice of exemplary sales/marketing skills goes beyond daily professional responsibilities to affect their dealings with all parties, including family, friends, neighbors, and casual acquaintances.

Sales professionals who recognize that the value of what they do goes beyond the confines of their job description are more likely to be highly motivated and do a better job.

OTHER FACTORS

There are other motivating factors. Compensation as a motivator is a given, particularly if the sales professional's compensation is appropriately leveraged to the goal of bringing in the maximum amount of gross revenue in the shortest possible period of time. The problem with financial compensation is not so much that it is undervalued or a non-factor, it is often that financial compensation is left hanging alone as the *only* motivating factor.

There are numerous other factors:

1. **An effective feedback system** — Many sales professionals do not work in an organization in which goals are properly defined and feedback regarding the degree of their achievement of these goals adequately acknowledged. Sales professionals should work in an environment in which expectations are spelled out (with input from the sales professional) and both quantitative and subjective feedback is continuously channeled back to the sales professional.

2. **Thorough training** — As previously discussed, sales professionals are frequently hired and then sent out to face the wolves with little or no formal training, less than optimal supervision, and the absence of an infrastructure within which to manage their daily activities. It is little wonder that many of these same individuals begin to drift, become disillusioned, and quickly lose much of the enthusiasm they brought to the position in the first place.
3. **An inspiring work environment** — Often promised, rarely delivered. Healthcare sales professionals often feel isolated from the rest of the team and feel little or no ownership in the service line they represent. For example, they may work in a stale environment in which praise is rarely, if ever, offered and positive accomplishments are glossed over or ignored.

   If you want highly motivated sales professionals, bring them into the fold, laud their accomplishments, and maintain a happy and supportive work environment. Define ways that provide sales professionals with a *reason* to do well on the job.

TIME MANAGEMENT

Many are familiar with the skills necessary for success in sales: listening ability, product knowledge, perseverance, and attention to detail. Conspicuously missing from most lists is **effective time management,** which may be the most critical attribute of all.

Regardless of whether you are in sales and marketing, think about your own productivity for a moment. In a typical forty-hour week, assume that only thirty hours are truly productive. Imagine that you are able to cut your unproductive time in half—say, to five rather than ten unproductive hours a week. Such a savings would result in about a 17 percent increase in your productivity (and probably more given the power of momentum), an increase that could be applied directly to your performance and your program's bottom line.

Registrants at our sales training seminars report significant discrepancies in the number of sales calls they make, ranging from up to thirty to as few as three calls per week. Assuming comparable quality and effort per call, who do you think generates superior results?

AS TIME GOES BY

Do you often wonder, "Where does my time go?" Begin by maintaining a two-week time allocation chart to see exactly what you are doing with your time. Nothing fancy here, but be honest and impeccable with your entries.

Account for your time in fifteen-minute increments and use meaningful codes to minimize your paperwork.

The results of this ad hoc self-assessment may surprise you. Your objective is to allocate as much of your time as possible to face-to-face sales with the understanding that other events are likely to get in your way.

Experience suggests that the leading time-suckers are:

1. **Customer service** — Whether you put out fires, engage in public relations with established clients, babysit accounts, or follow up on a myriad of operational issues, you are not out there selling. Do what you theoretically do best: bring in new business while minimizing involvement in various clean-up campaigns. The exception tends to be in small organizations where the "salesperson" necessarily wears many hats.
2. **Paperwork** — There is productive paperwork and there is busy work. If completing paperwork will ultimately result in a sale or save you or someone else's time, then it is most likely time well spent. If you engage in a clerical activity that could be easily handled by a non-sales professional, it should be delegated.
3. **Database management** — This is paperwork's electronic cousin. Many sales professionals spend too much time surfing the net and playing with their database. Database management should be about learning how to pick and choose applications that really make a difference, such as tracking sales call results and keeping company contact information and protocols current.
4. **Telephone calls** — I ask registrants at our sales training programs how many phone calls they place or receive daily: Usually it is in the range of twenty-five to thirty-five calls per day. If the average length per call is four minutes, that is 120 minutes, or two hours of telephone time a day. If you decrease your telephone time by 50 percent, you save one hour a day, the equivalent of about 240 hours every year that could be re-directed to

face-to-face sales and other revenue-generating activities.

Phone calls are fertile territory for effective time management. The goal is to minimize unproductive and "unable to contact" calls, reduce the average length of time per call, and ensure that pre-call objectives have been addressed.

Consider some basic techniques:

- Prepare for every call—before dialing—by reviewing notes and crystallizing your primary and secondary objectives.
- Work toward a maximum phone time of five minutes per call.
- State your objectives at the outset.
- Minimize or avoid small talk unless initiated by the other party.
- Develop a Plan B for leaving a voice-mail message or a message with an assistant.

(The charts that follow offer valuable information to assist sales professionals with time management. **Exhibit** 7-**6**, provides a guide for minimizing telephone tag.)

EXHIBIT 7-4. ANATOMY OF A SALES INTERACTION (BY PHONE OR IN PERSON)

- **Purpose/Objectives:** *"The purpose of this meeting (call) is to learn more about your company's health and safety practices and to determine if our services might assist you in addressing any concerns you may have. The meeting (call) should take no more than ten minutes."*
- **Issues/Solutions:** A discussion about their issues/ concerns and your program's potential solutions to these issues.
- **Summary/Action Steps:** *"It is my understanding that your company feels it needs a truly comprehensive provider with a bottom-line focus, and that it will consider a new relationship. As agreed, I will send you a written proposal and a list of references within twenty-four hours and call you next Monday at 4:00 p.m."*

5. **Travel** — Depending on the market, the amount of time that a sales professional is on the road can be substantial. Car trips should be consolidated as much as possible by scheduling consecutive meetings with employers within close proximity of each other.

Given these essential points, a simple, clear message emerges: when sales professionals eliminate the five least productive hours in their typical week, they gain approximately 250 hours of time a year, or about 150 *additional* in-person sales calls.

WHAT IS THE TIME MANAGEMENT PLAN?

A formal, actively deployed time management plan is as important to you as your sales or marketing plan. Note several possible elements of a time management plan:

1. **Commit to a quarterly time-management audit** — Complete a two-week time management audit once a quarter and review and adjust to the findings of each audit. Look for the least productive five hours of your weekly routine and find a way to eliminate those activities.
2. **Cluster your activities** — Conduct most of your outgoing phone calls during a set time period (e.g., first thing in the morning) and make your live sales calls during a set period, for example, between 11:00 a.m. and 4:00 p.m. Put these clusters on your weekly schedule and stick with it.
3. **Select which information you collect and maintain** — Use software applications that will help you maximize the return on the time you invest in routinely maintaining information.
4. **Make meetings meaningful, crisp, and regular** — Meetings are important vehicles to address problems and facilitate communication; they should be held on a regular basis (e.g., weekly). Several basic rules can render meetings more effective and less time consuming:

    - Start precisely on schedule, no matter who is absent.
    - Clearly state the meeting objectives at the outset and focus exclusively on the objectives.

- Send background information out ahead of time via email memo; use the meeting to discuss and resolve issues rather than recite information.
- Ensure that someone is responsible for monitoring time and expeditiously moving each issue along.

5. **Lay out your agenda** — How many times have you wondered where a conversation, phone call, letter, or email is headed? Communication, whether it be in person, on the phone, by email, or by letter, should *always* include the following components:
   - A statement of purpose and objectives
   - A review of the issues
   - A summary, including action steps as necessary

   By laying out an agenda, the average transaction time will be markedly reduced, providing the opportunity for many more transactions. (**Exhibit 7-5** provides an example of such an agenda.)

6. **Develop responses and perfect your delivery** — Sales professionals seem to be saying the same things over and over again *and* re-inventing their verse every time they say it. Examples include responses to the four basic objections (price, location, satisfied with current client, dissatisfied with your program), information about your services, a description of your competitive advantages, or the general economic relationship between employer cost savings and effective services.

   Develop an optimal description for each of these issues, commit them to memory, and focus on delivery rather than content.

7. **Balance your time** — Now that you have a whiff of military discipline, it is time to provide the rule to break the rules: do not be overly obsessive about time management. There will be some small talk, wasted time, and re-inventing of the wheel. The goal is to minimize, not eliminate, these demons. Better to be at 95 percent capacity and relaxed than to be at 100 percent capacity and uptight.

   We all know someone about whom we wonder: How do

they do it? How do they get everything done professionally, find plenty of time for their family, and enjoy their many avocations? The answer is almost certainly effective time management, which is more a learned than an inherent trait. Start working on your time management skills today!

At the end of each day, develop an **action plan** for the following day. Set priorities for each specific task on your to-do list.

Exhibit 7-5. A Day in the Life of a Sales Professional

7:45	Calls to hard-to-reach individuals
8:00	Other outgoing telephone calls
9:00	Internal meetings as necessary
9:30	Email review and communication
10:00	Prepare for today's sales calls
10:30	Auto travel to sales call
10:45	Daily sales call 1
11:30	Daily sales call 2
Noon	Lunch (with or without prospect)
1:15	Daily sales call 3
2:00	Daily sales call 4
3:00	Clinic tour with key prospect
4:00	Return phone messages
4:30	Paperwork, database management
5:00	Calls to hard-to-reach individuals

Exhibit 7-6. Rx for Phone Tag-itis: Minimizing Unproductive Phone Time

- Place most calls during hours that your target prospects are likely to be in the office, unencumbered by meetings or other calls, and unprotected by their assistants. Before 8:00 a.m., during lunch, and after 5:00 p.m. all work well.
- Assume you will be channeled to voice mail and have a scripted voice-mail message ready to go.
- Include both an action step and an objective in your voice-mail message. That is, advise the recipient of the voice mail exactly why you are calling, and provide specifics regarding the next step (e.g., "I will call you at 7:30 tomorrow morning," or "I have set aside from 4:00 to 5:30 this afternoon to receive phone calls.").
- Work your way back. Having trouble reaching David Webb? Call the company's main number and ask for David Webb's assistant, gain the assistant's confidence, and then ask how you best might reach Mr. Webb.
- Get email addresses whenever possible and supplement phone attempts with down-to-earth email messages. Since most companies share the same domain name and use the same style in the email prefix, it may be easy to deduce the email address (e.g., david.webb@alliedsteel.com).

More on Managing Your Telephone Time

If you do not make the call, you will not waste the time. Many calls are unnecessary. Here are some tips to eliminate calls:

1. **Email** — Before placing any call, ask yourself if an email might work equally as well. If so, substitute the email for the telephone call. Email allows you to hone in on the issue at hand without the small talk, leaves a paper trail, is instantaneous, and is free.

Nowadays, my email-to-phone-time ratio is probably 100:1; ten years ago it was the opposite.

2. **Just say no** — Before placing a call, ask yourself if the call is really necessary. If it is not, jettison it. One jettisoned call means little, but over a period of time many eliminated calls add up.

MINIMIZE TELEPHONE TAG

My fellow alumni from Phone Tag U surely recognize the adverse effects of receiving repeated voice-mail messages.

Address these no answer calls by:

1. **Hedging your bets** — Call people when they are most likely available. Many individuals are more likely to be available first thing in the morning, even shortly before 8:00, since they are unlikely to be in meetings or away from the office. The more important the call, the more useful it is to call during non-peak work hours.
2. **Being up front and asking** — Ask prospects exactly what is the best time to reach them. They are likely to provide something specific ("I am almost always at my desk Friday afternoons from 3:00 to 5:00"), or better yet, they might offer their cell number as I often do: "Try me Tuesday afternoon. If you get my voice mail, you are welcome to call me on my cell phone at (number)."
3. **Structure your message** — Although most consider voice-mail messages a nuisance, voice mail certainly beats the days when a phone rang and rang and rang. When you leave a voice-mail message you provide yourself with the option of resetting the dialogue to your liking. Part of that reset is to suggest the next contact mode, time and date, and to shape the issue. The more specific and realistic you are, the more likely the phone-tag cycle will come to an end.

OPERATE MORE EFFICIENTLY

Reducing the time you are on the telephone is only half the battle; making best use of your actual time on the telephone is the other half.

Principles governing telephone time efficiency include:

1. **Prepare** — It is easy and common to dial away and think later. Pause for thirty to sixty seconds before every business call to prepare for the call. Your preparation checklist should include your:

    - **Objective** — What is the objective of your call? Write it down, and in most cases, explain it to the person when they answer.
    - **Fallback** — If you fail to achieve your stated objective, what is your fallback plan? It is folly to be restricted to the whole enchilada vs. the empty plate, when a half enchilada might satisfy.
    - **Voice-mail message** — Do you want to leave a message if you are routed to voice mail? If so, what do you want to say? You are likely to come out ahead if you have developed an appropriate and coherent message *a priori* so you can deliver that message with confidence and clarity.
    - **Facts and numbers** — Is it likely that specific numbers or facts will be discussed during the call? If so, have those numbers or facts directly in front of you.
    - **Notes** — Review your notes from previous calls or meetings with the prospect, client, or associate: you are less likely to err and will sound a whole lot smarter.

2. **Structure** — Orchestrate the call in a logical, methodical manner. Structure will help you achieve your objectives and minimize time on the call. A typical structure might include:

    - An overview of the call's purpose, the amount of time you need, and the topics you would like to discuss
    - A review of events leading up to the call
    - A discussion of the objectives
    - A summary of the call and specific action steps

3. **Document** — Whether you use a laptop, PC, or paper forms, document every meaningful call:
   - You are more likely to remain focused on your initial objectives if you record all key points.
   - Notes provide an electronic and/or paper trail.
   - Note-taking helps you remember what transpired.
   - Documentation provides useful information for anyone who may need it in your absence.

Exhibit 7-7. Telephone Call Time Ledger

Date	Time called	Subject	Resolution	Time spent on call (in minutes)

RESOLUTION CODES:

N/A = No answer/did not leave voice mail
VM = Left voice-mail message
R = Spoke with another individual (referred)
C = Contacted desired individual

KEY DATA SUMMARIES:

Number of calls per day
Percent of unproductive calls per day
Average number of minutes on the telephone per day
Average number of unproductive minutes per day
Notable trends (e.g., most and least hours)

THE SALESPERSON'S TOOLKIT

Not long ago I played a round of golf in Florida using borrowed clubs that would have been too short for a Smurf. Needless to say, my performance was one for the books (and not in a good way). Moral of the story: if you want to do something well, equip yourself accordingly.

Sales professionals often enter the fray with one arm tied behind their back. By not supplying the right tools, their superiors often set them up for mediocrity, if not outright failure.

What are the sales professional's version of a golfer's Titleist clubs?—tangible and intangible support.

TANGIBLES

Tradition-laden healthcare organizations find it difficult to understand and commit to sales and marketing. Lack of sensitivity often means that a position is created without the requisite commitment to providing the sales professional with the tools necessary to succeed. Even a modest commitment to the tangible and intangible support enumerated here is likely to quickly recoup any associated expenditures and result in a quantum leap in sales effectiveness.

Since sales professionals spend much of their time in the field, they need a virtual office. Essential tools include:

Cell phone: Although most sales professionals likely possess a cell phone, it is less likely that their organization pays the bill for the cell phone. A cell phone is an essential tool for shoring up communication processes, saving valuable time, and supporting the availability of program staff, supervisors, prospects, and clients. If a cell phone is critically important to a sales professional (and it is!), the parent organization should support its cost, much like the land phone in the sales professional's office.

Laptop computer: It is unthinkable that a sales professional can be productive without a laptop computer equipped with contact management software (next on this list). The laptop may be used during site visits for PowerPoint presentations, after each meeting to document findings and thoughts, for working on written proposals and presentations while on the road and in the office, when checking relevant websites, and for corresponding by email.

Contact management software: Sales professionals invariably have a sea of prospect and client information to manage. There is no reason to be overwhelmed by the need to enter and keep this information up to date: there are tools that make this relatively painless. The sales professional's laptop should be loaded with sales contact software that can be used to manage activities on a daily basis.

There are two viable routes to pursue for a system: (1) off-the-shelf sales management software such as ACT! and Goldmine, or (2) the sales management modules available in leading service line information management systems. In sales, time is money, and contact management software saves time.

PDAs: Many people swear by the versatility of their personal digital assistant (iPhone, iPad, BlackBerry, and similar devices). PDAs have multiple useful functions including phone, email, web browser, word processor, calculator, spreadsheet, address book, organizer, global positioning system (GPS), music, and video. Many PDAs employ touch-screen technology, and they are exceptionally portable. For those willing to make the investment, the PDA can be an extremely useful sales support tool.

OTHER TANGIBLES

Other tangible incentives include a transportation allowance and a meaningful compensation practice.

Transportation allowance: Sales professionals spend a great deal of time in their car. This is an incremental expense that should not be their responsibility. The government reimbursement rate is a fair barometer; sales professionals should receive appropriate reimbursement. To support efficiency, the allowance may be increased to cover the cost of a GPS unit.

Meaningful incentives: As discussed, a well-crafted incentive compensation plan should be crafted into a healthcare sales benefit package.

INTANGIBLES

On the surface, intangible incentives may seem to pale next to more tangible ones, but in practice they can be very powerful.

Wholehearted support: Most readers can probably think of some parents who provide their children with a vast array of material gifts, but never seem to be there to offer hands-on love, moral support, and guidance. More often than not, the children emerge with stilted values.

The same principle applies in business: provide sales professionals with the tangible support as outlined above, and you are only half way home. Management needs to offer unmitigated and genuine support. Such support includes a willingness to listen to sales professionals and take their ideas seriously, and being available to jump in when it appears management insight is needed.

A well-executed marketing campaign: If your sales and marketing campaign is up to par, it should be attracting as much business from general marketing (name identification, etc.) as from direct sales. Sales professionals benefit in two ways: they will find it easier to get in the door, and they will add gross dollars to their commission base. Conversely, a minimal or poorly executed marketing campaign will run counter to the sales professional's goals.

Value and differentiation: Even the best sales professionals are going to encounter a rocky road if their portfolios are filled with products that lack intrinsic value or do not offer compelling differentiation from other options. Once again a sales professional is being sent into the field with one arm behind the back. Establish a foundation that builds on high-value services and offers a meaningful differentiation in the marketplace.

TEAMWORK

A thinly veiled secret in many healthcare organizations is the marginal role that sales and marketing play in the mores of these organizations. Indeed, a healthcare sales professional tends to be treated like your Uncle Fred: it is always nice to see him, but he is not really woven into the inner fabric of your family.

Why is this so? Healthcare organizations have a difficult time merging the medical side with the business side of their business. Nothing embodies the business side of healthcare more vividly than the sales and marketing function, which even in many traditional businesses is often perceived as fluff.

An organization must come to grips with what sales and marketing really is . . . and what it is not. Get away from the let's-make-a-deal image so often associated with sales, and instead position the critical sales function as the vehicle that educates prospective consumers on the rationale for making various choices.

1. **Keep things in perspective** — I am not talking about most of the service line team being actively involved in day-to-day sales and marketing. Dedicated sales and marketing staff should be responsible for 95–98 percent of all sales and marketing activity. It is the remaining 2–5 percent involving team members that can be used to catapult your service initiative from so-so to one that is operating on all cylinders.
2. **Define responsibilities** — Cheerleading in a staff meeting ("Okay, let's all get involved in sales and marketing this year, rah! rah!, rah!") will not get the job done. Provide each team member with specific responsibilities, and define those responsibilities within the context of each individual's skills, their personality, and the particular needs of the team as a whole.
3. **Be a talent scout** — If somebody asked me to give a ballroom dancing exhibition for the good of the team I wouldn't, couldn't, shouldn't. Not only would I be mad as hell for having to do it, I would embarrass both my team and myself. The same is true here. Do not ask others to do something they neither want to do nor are unlikely to do well.

I often hear the phrase, "I need to get our physician to the workplace more often." In concept, this makes sense, especially for major prospective clients and existing clients where the physicians' presence during sales calls can really have an impact. Physician A may have a persona that wins employers' trust, Physician B may be less convincing, and Physician C may exhibit interpersonal skills that are downright counterproductive.

What can you do to ensure that physicians make the most of their time as members of the sales team?

1. Provide a carefully crafted plan in which the physician is coached to ask certain questions and show genuine interest in an employer's workplace.

2. Know what employers really want to hear and be certain to get these points across during any encounter or call with an employer representative.

Carefully crafted questions indicate that the physician has a genuine interest in the specifics of the employer's workplace. On a sales call (or any other personal or telephone encounter), the physician is encouraged to ask questions such as:

> *"What seem to be your biggest health and safety challenges?"*
>
> *"How have you addressed these challenges?"*
>
> *"In a perfect world, what kind of relationship would your company like to have with an organization such as ours?"*

Physicians should position themselves as true company-oriented physicians (assuming clinical integrity, of course) by learning to look all employer prospects and clients in the eye and saying something such as:

> *"I practice occupational medicine because I genuinely enjoy working with others to address the big picture: getting workers back to work quickly and safely, addressing environmental concerns as they may exist, and working closely with a company to develop a plan for optimal workplace health and safety. I like to speak frequently to a company representative such as yourself to ensure that we are on the same page regarding what is best for your company and your employees, both individually and collectively."*

SALES AS A TEAM SPORT

A program's marketing staff and providers are only part of the larger team. Ensure that all team members—from senior management to receptionists—understand that they have vital contributions to make. Incorporate everyone's input in your marketing plan.

EXHIBIT 7-8. TEAM WORK: SALES AND MARKETING RESPONSIBILITIES

1. SENIOR EXECUTIVE/OWNER

   - Articulate the true value and purpose of the program.
   - Make at least one phone call per quarter on behalf of the program.

2. MEDICAL DIRECTOR

   - Participate in one sales call per week.
   - Learn to articulate personal philosophy.
   - Learn to succinctly articulate the value of the program's interventions.
   - Participate in clinic tours by asking the right questions when meeting visiting employers.

3. PROGRAM DIRECTOR/CLINIC COORDINATOR

   - Participate in periodic sales calls as advisable.
   - Learn to succinctly articulate the value of the program's interventions.
   - Develop/execute an orchestrated clinic tour.

4. RECEPTIONISTS

   - Learn to ask the right questions.
   - Take clinic tour visitors through a prototype registration process.
   - Routinely point out patient flow attributes.

5. ALL STAFF

   - Learn to succinctly articulate the value of your program's interventions.
   - Memorize your program's most compelling advantage.

WHAT ABOUT COMPENSATION?

A potentially vexing issue involves lack of incentive compensation for non-sales professionals who may often be involved in or primarily drive certain sales. A client recently asked why a service line director does not receive extra compensation when the program's incentive-based sales professional reaps the benefit of their effort. In a perfect world, an entire team benefits from an enhanced bottom line (and may, indirectly, through salary increases), but such a concept is presently a reach in most institutions. In such cases, team members may need to be satisfied with the intrinsic rewards associated with a team effort.

A memo to all of you overworked, undervalued sales professionals: help is closer than you may think. Many, if not all, of your coworkers have something to offer if only you would ask. Ensure that employer-directed sales and marketing is a team sport in your organization.

Sales Professionals: Your Eyes and Ears

Many organizations make less than optimal use of their sales team. High on the omissions list is an organization's ability to make full use of a sales team's ability to act as the eyes and ears of their organization's services.

HEAR NO EVIL / SEE NO EVIL

I have noticed that there is typically a disparity between a healthcare organization's perceptions of their community image and the community's actual image. Time and again, organizations tell me about their excellent reputation. But when I review market research findings, I often see a significant disconnect between a community's appraisal of the program or organization and the organization's assumptions.

Why the disconnect?

- Given limited financial resources and staff time, less market research assessing community perceptions often takes place now than it did twenty years ago.

- A no-news-is-good-news dynamic may be at work. By failing to formally gather information about community perceptions and needs, little, if any, critical feedback exists. It is tempting to translate the absence of negative feedback into a feeling of, "they like us; they really, really like us."
- Most services and organizations fail to make an adequate effort to systematically gather market insights, and they routinely fail to communicate anecdotal information internally.

I am a strong proponent of using formal market research (focus groups, telephone surveys) to learn more about the perceptions of one's marketplace. However, the easiest and most expedient way to stay in touch with your market involves little incremental cost and scarcely more than a fraction of personnel time: deploying your sales professionals as the eyes and ears of your program and parent organization.

Three things are necessary to do this well:

1. **Discern** — Determine whether a comment is merely gossip or valuable anecdotal information. If you are doing your job right, you will spend more than 50 percent of your time speaking with prospects or clients, either in person or by telephone. There are innumerable opportunities to hear random comments about your service or organization that could be of considerable value back on the workfront.

   Feedback on almost anything could be valuable: positive experiences or impressions, negative ones, unmet needs, rumors, misconceptions, or competitor activities.

   Separate the vital from the irrelevant. Does a particular complaint come from a person with a litany of grievances, or does the complaint appear to have merit? Does this new insight have relevance to your parent organization, or is it minor in the greater scheme of things?

   If and when your ears perk up, you should probe to learn more about the issue at hand. Trust in the adage, "Where there's smoke, there's fire." Go beyond the rumor and seek the source of the fire.

   Develop techniques to immediately document vital anecdotal information. Always have a pad, recorder, or laptop computer nearby to take notes about fresh market intelligence. You can jot down a few key words about the anecdotal information and denote it with a code (e.g., a plus, minus, or question mark if the comment is positive, negative, or raises a question that needs to be answered). Using the reminder code, you can easily transfer information to a report template. Do not rely totally on memory to capture and later report a relevant anecdotal thought.

2. **Investigate** — Know when, how, and what to ask external contacts in a more formal manner.

   Lost opportunities? Everyone experiences them, whether it is related to our professional career, love life, financial investments, or healthcare sales. When you have a client or prospect at your disposal, why not ask one (or more) casual questions that could unleash a torrent of insight?

   Anecdotal insight is useful, but is also relatively random in that there is little you can do to manage the frequency of such tidbits. A proactive approach using effective questioning is a way to create something out of nothing.

   Try to be more casual than formal. A relaxed, "Oh, by the way" question following the conclusion of a formal sales call is more likely to elicit a relaxed off-the-cuff response.

   Open-ended questions might include:

   "So what do you really think about our service (organization)?"

   "What seems to be the word on the street? What do people really think of our service and our organization?"

   "If you had unilateral authority to run our service (organization), what would be the first thing you would do?"

   "In your opinion, what is the best thing about our service (organization)?"

   Use subjective judgment in deciding when to ask such questions and how many questions to ask. If you are dealing with Mr. Grumpy or Ms. Know Nothing, you may as well pick up your marbles and leave. On the other hand, if the other party does not seem to be in a hurry, appears well-connected in the employer community, and seems to have some useful insights, engage this person with some probing questions after the formal sales call.

3. **Report** — Develop a systematic routine to document and share market insights with relevant internal personnel. A body of insight is of little value unless you routinely share it with others.

   Suggestions include:

   - Create a monthly report ("Word from the Streets"); have a template on your laptop and enter daily insights.
   - Keep the report short and to the point (short bullet points or quotes, no prose); one or two pages will do.
   - Balance the positive with the negative. For example, include four sections:
     - Positive remarks: service line specific
     - Positive remarks: overall organization
     - Concerns/recommendations: service line specific
     - Concerns/recommendations: overall organization

Distribute the report via email to staff, relevant departments, and senior management in your organization. The value of having a monthly report cannot be overstated. If you know that others expect such a report every month, you are more likely to capture relevant insights. The process also benefits you: instead of being isolated and largely forgotten by many in your organization, such reports elevate your visibility and highlight your contributions.

Hardly a day goes by that our nation's political parties do not conduct national market research to ensure that subtle changes are recognized early on. While a healthcare organization cannot formally monitor its market with such vigor, it can systematically collect and share market intelligence that is readily available on the sales front. Being the eyes and ears of an organization is a cost-effective way to acquire information and a natural extension of the sales process.

SALES METRICS

It is common for someone from salesville to ask our office for some type of sales norm or metric. The answer is usually, "It depends . . . "

Metrics may be defined as the measurement of an activity or result to which an organization attaches strategic value.

Using metrics is by no means applicable strictly to the sales function. Metrics can be important and useful regardless of the specific job. Metrics can also be developed and applied to other positions, such as physicians or nurses.

Associate the question of which metrics to gather and analyze with your program's strategic plan. What are your sales goals? How are you going to measure success? Exactly what are the expectations for your sales professionals? What incremental measurements are going to support the tactics that you plan to use in order to achieve this success?

Make sales metrics consistent with the substance of your marketing plan. A metric must be measurable, traceable, and consistent with the goals inherent in the plan.

TYPES OF METRICS

There are many types of metrics to consider:

Results metrics are bottom-line oriented. They can be used to measure total gross or net revenue, segmented revenue by product line, or revenue by company type or sales area (e.g., a specific clinic or delivery point).

Activity metrics (e.g., phone calls, letters, meetings) measure the core activities required to generate the desired results.

Different types of sales metrics can be used for different purposes. Productivity metrics help you identify the need for, and the appropriate deployment of, sales and marketing staff. Sales metrics can be used to establish productivity standards in order to measure and monitor the performance of sales professionals.

Other sales metrics may appear useful but have little value. The number of sales calls per week or the number of companies closed offers little value in the absence of generated total revenue. Your number of sales calls per week means little if you are speaking with the wrong company (e.g., a company with comparatively little volume potential) or with the wrong individual (e.g., a non-decision-maker). Viewed purely as an activity metric, your number of calls per week provides little insight. Combined with the results of a performance metric, calls per week can serve as a useful activity barometer, but little more.

Likewise, your "companies closed" sales metric can be deceptive and counterproductive. Unless a contractual arrangement is involved (e.g., a nurse placement wellness services contract or on-site service), closing can be highly subjective in healthcare sales. Do a smile, a handshake, and a promise to use your services really qualify as a close? Secondly, you should prefer to close three large, high-volume prospects than ten minimal-volume prospects. In the absence of a corresponding metric, a sales professional driven to generate as many closes as possible may actually be harming the cause.

VARIABLES

This is where the "it depends" comes in. Defining, tracking, and analyzing metrics would be simple if every sales and marketing model and every market were the same. However, every market and service line is unique; every metric plan has its own mosaic.

Variables include:

- **Single vs. multiple staff** — Services with more than one sales professional must take a different approach to metrics than those with a single salesperson. Take into account multi-clinic cross referrals and team incentives.
- **Dollar value per relationship** — The total sales value per relationship may be computed either prospectively (e.g., the anticipated book of business given historical standards and projected injury rates) or retrospectively. In either case it adds substance to a salesperson's number of closes.
- **New revenue per sales professional** — Numerous variables impact the level of desired new revenue per sales professional. The larger your market, the greater your opportunity to find new sources of revenue. Fee schedules can have a significant impact on this measurement. Sales professional A and sales

professional B can "sell" exactly the same volume and mix of services in adjoining states yet generate markedly different revenue. The term "new revenue" requires review. It is defined as a combination of new accounts and incremental revenue from existing accounts.

- **New vs. established** — Designing a metrics plan for a new initiative is relatively easy and straightforward. Not so with an established initiative in which you have to sort out established accounts and inherent growth/attrition within accounts that may be as much a product of the local economy as the salesperson's performance.
- **Market leader vs. market challenger** — A market leader places proportionately more emphasis on business retention than a market challenger. Such relative emphasis should be reflected in your metrics.
- **Single market vs. multiple sub-markets** — A single market is easier to measure than services that have to reach out to multiple sub-markets.

EXAMPLES OF SALES METRICS

My colleague Nick Kirby, who oversaw the sales effort for more than forty occupational health sales professionals, cited a variety of metrics that he relies on to monitor the performance of the company's sales force:

1. **Quality telephone calls** — A sales professional might be expected to make, for example, forty telephone calls per week (or eight per day) to a decision maker or influencer. Calls to gatekeepers or to qualify a potential account are not considered quality calls. Never use total calls as a stand-alone measure but rather in conjunction with other metrics such as appointments and generated revenue.
2. **Face-to-face sales appointments** — Face-to-face appointments are another vital sales metric, but only if defined as quality appointments. A quality appointment must involve new sales and likewise involve only a decision maker or influencer. Mr. Kirby feels that fifteen quality appointments per week are reasonable.

3. **Conversion rates** — Rates and ratios constitute a useful application of performance metrics. A salesperson's conversion ratio (e.g., closes divided by face-to-face appointments) provides some measure of the sales professional's performance. Note that the two dilemmas (What constitutes a close? Is the sales professional calling on the best prospects?) are not covered by conversion rates.

A spirited debate exists regarding the relative merit of using gross revenue or net revenue as a program's core new revenue metric. I prefer gross revenue because it maintains a strict focus on one thing: generating optimal sales dollars. Others prefer net revenue, as they believe that the sales professional should be actively engaged in the accounts receivable process.

Mr. Kirby looks for between $35,000 and $55,000 per month in new revenue per sales professional, or a range of $420,000 to $660,000 per year. Further, Mr. Kirby assesses performance versus this metric on a twelve-month rolling average—that is, assessing sales performance based on performance over the past twelve months rather than dwelling on a single month's performance.

Mr. Kirby also studies "opportunities to up-sell" on a sales-professional-by-sales-professional level. Note per-client gross revenue in two discrete areas: injury care and prevention (screening exams, etc.). Usually these two figures offer a fairly predictable ratio. If the ratio for a given client company is notably high or low, it may imply an opportunity to up-sell the other service.

Use metrics when planning and monitoring your sales effort and evaluating and rewarding sales professionals. Metrics can be valuable, but they can also be meaningless or even misleading. As with the sales plan, a metrics plan must be carefully conceptualized and studiously followed.

CUTTING COSTS

The phrase these days seems to be "cut your budget." It is far easier said than done. What can you do when you have such an edict, and you already feel pushed to the budgetary limit?

REVENUE ENHANCEMENT

Righting the financial ship can be accomplished either by increasing revenue or decreasing expenses. Expense reduction tends to receive greater attention than revenue generation. Yet many organizations do little to examine and buff up the revenue side of their equation.

There are four basic ways for a service to prop up revenue:

1. Ensure that you are not missing out on much-needed revenue because of less-than-optimal billing, coding, documentation, and accounts receivable management. Most programs seem to fall short in some, if not all, of these areas.
2. Understand and take credit for the full value of downstream revenues that are generated by your program. Many programs fail to sufficiently quantify less tangible contributions to their parent organization.
3. Develop new or integrate existing fee-for-service products under the service umbrella.
4. Make your sales and marketing effort more focused, aggressive, and accountable.

EXPENSE REDUCTION

Consider the following:

1. **Examine revenue generation before expense reduction** — Expense reduction should be considered only after you have examined the *quality* of the previously listed revenue-generating techniques. If any are sub-par, plans should be made to improve them.

   A dilemma arises when healthcare organizations try to decide whether and to what degree to reduce clinical personnel, management, or sales and marketing personnel. Clinical positions tend to be the most secure. They are usually viewed as the lifeblood of any service, yet staff can become stretched too thin. On the other hand, when we conduct productivity analyses for our consulting clients, we often find that clinics are overstaffed, not understaffed.

2. **Use productivity analysis to determine staffing levels** — Reduce clinical staff only if a strong and valid productivity analyses indicates that a clinic is likely to be overstaffed.

   Several long-standing occupational health programs have recently terminated their non-clinical director and replaced that individual with the program's existing clinic coordinator. Depending on the individuals in question, such a personnel shuffle is likely to diminish the business savvy of the program and may be counterproductive.

3. **Make retain-or-terminate decisions based on revenue enhancement** — This brings us to the wisdom of reducing or eliminating sales and marketing personnel. During difficult economic times, an organization's commitment to sales and marketing should be increased, not curtailed or eliminated. Eliminate sales and marketing staff only after you have explored all revenue enhancement opportunities, non-personnel reductions, and staff reductions in other areas.

   This does not mean that sales and marketing personnel get a free keep-their-job pass. Minimal sales personnel accountability tends to run rampant in healthcare organizations: many professionals are barely supervised, not supervised at all, or supervised with minimal metrics by a staff member with little or no sales and marketing savvy. Do not maintain a sales professional whose performance is not up to speed, but appropriate accountability and associated performance metrics must be in place and reviewed before a fair retain-or-terminate decision can be made.

4. **Look closely at current expense-cutting trends** — Terminate fair to poor performing sales and marketing personnel, but only after you are comfortable that they have been held accountable to an appropriate report and have failed to meet clearly defined metrics.

   Cutting non-staff expenses seems to be endemic these days. Although there is usually less meat in this part of the budget compared to staff costs, there tends to be some reasonable expense-cutting opportunities.

5. **Reduce expenses by relying on electronic communication** — *Arivaderci* to paper. Cut, if not eliminate, paper costs. Are you ready to reorder more copies of your brochure? Don't do it—rely on links to your website and highly customized printouts regarding specific services you wish to promote. Do you want more letterhead and envelopes? Cut, cut, cut, and rely more heavily on electronic communication.
6. **Minimize or curtail advertising** — Unless you represent a new service line or an organization going through a branding campaign, you should view most paid healthcare advertising as a dinosaur from the 1980s. Radio ads, print media, billboard advertising, and yellow page ads seldom provide an adequate ROI for services even during good times, let alone tough times; they are a luxury that few can afford.
7. **Just say no to auto mileage reimbursement** — I believe that auto mileage reimbursement is a counter-intuitive benefit that sends an inappropriate message to sales professionals: drive all over yonder and get paid extra for your time. A sales professional's time is golden: he or she should be selling face to face, prospecting, or doing other things rather than driving for hours a day.

   Now for the good news: I would not eliminate auto mileage reimbursement without offering sales professionals the chance to recoup that income. The fairest approach may be to substitute incentive pay for an auto allowance. A sales professional who received $2,000 in mileage last year should warrant an increase in their incentive pay structure that projects to new incentive pay equal to the old annual auto allowance payout.

   Cutting costs in order to remain competitive is never easy and often involves a choice of the lesser of multiple evils. Yet such costs are often essential and may even be a blessing; in the longer term, you learn to become leaner and meaner. Such expense reduction needs to be made in a careful and longsighted manner, as sales and marketing is invariably the engine that makes a program financially viable.

Sales Professional Accountability

Imagine a business world in which there is no accountability. If no one reported to another person, had her performance evaluated, or was provided with specific quantifiable expectations, your organization would be a haphazardly run, unproductive place.

Unfortunately, the world of healthcare sales and marketing accountability is often such a barren desert. Many sales professionals seem to go it alone with little or no supervision or strict expectations. Such neglect is a formula for mediocrity, if not failure.

COMMON DENOMINATORS

Why is this so? Although reasons vary by organization and individual practices, there seem to be common threads.

1. Many healthcare professionals are not sales and marketing savvy. Sure, they acknowledge the importance of sales and marketing, but there are rarely strong personnel in place with a broad overview of what it takes to succeed.
2. The majority of hospitals and health systems structure their service lines by silo or business unit, which suggests that most healthcare sales professionals report to non-sales personnel who know little or nothing about sales and marketing. Meanwhile, independent urgent care clinics invariably lack senior sales and marketing personnel.
3. When there is an organization-wide sales and marketing initiative, it usually positions the service as "just another product line" rather than a discipline central to the organization's integrated marketing approach. Many service lines do not receive the attention they deserve.
4. Healthcare sales professionals often find themselves betwixt and between: they either report to someone who knows little about sales and marketing, or they report to a marketing department whose personnel know something about promoting their macro-organization but hardly anything about the role of its specific service lines.

ESTABLISHING AN ACCOUNTABILITY PLAN

Chances are that you, too, have less than full accountability. What to do?

The best approach is to deploy one or more of three strategies:

1. **Initiate self-accountability.**

    - **Keep your own timesheet**: As stated earlier, measure your activity in fifteen-minute increments for large categories (e.g., prospecting, face-to-face sales, marketing, paperwork etc.). Contact management software facilitates this process.
    - **Review each week's time allocation:** Compare your previous week's allocation to established goals. Note where changes need to be made; work diligently to effect those changes. Time is money.

2. **Promote time management.**

    - **Tighten your job description**: Avoid or eliminate activities that have little or nothing to do with attracting incremental business. Common culprits in this instance are the time-honored customer maintenance bugaboo, paperwork overload, excessive time spent coordinating health fairs and other mega-events, miscellaneous meetings, and non-clustered travel.
    - **Do not be a utility player**: Healthcare organizations often view their sales professionals as go-to staffers who are available for almost anything that does not have an anointed "doer." Before long, the sales professional is doing little sales and business is suffering. Proactively head this off.

3. **Instill discipline.**

    - **Set aside personal time**: Sales professionals are often "out there," meaning that they are on their own schedule and manage their own time and pace. Temptations arise to sleep in, pack it in early, and squeeze in myriad errands throughout the day. Without really noticing, the sales professional's real professional time commitment can begin to slip.

- **Give yourself a little, but not too much, slack**: You could commit to thirty-eight hours of genuine professional activity a week, no matter what. If you leave early one day, make up the exact amount of time later that week. Give yourself, for example, two hours a week for personal activity (dentist, food shopping, shrink, you name it) but never more.

AN ACCOUNTABILITY SYSTEM

Because your direct report does not understand sales and marketing, this does not mean you need to go it alone. It is far better to take definitive steps to get your supervisor up to speed and working on the same page.

Establish common expectations. Define quantitative expectations and the best use of a salesperson's time. Be certain that the direct report understands that sales professionals are employed to sell, not to perform a myriad of other roles.

EDUCATIONAL OPPORTUNITIES

Those who have oversight for the sales and marketing function must know as much as possible about the topic.

If a sales professional wants a direct report to understand more about what sales and marketing is all about, the sales professional should invite that person to sit in on multiple sales calls. Ask your direct report to join you for at least one sales call per month, ideally on the same day at the same time (e.g., first Thursday of the month, 4:00–5:00 p.m.).

Solicit outside expertise. As a consultant, I am often invited to mentor sales professionals' performance. We review time sheets, skills, strategies, and sales issues, and we take steps to ensure that the marketing plan is being executed in a timely fashion. Sales professionals who have been accountable to me tend to make it happen daily. External oversight by a sales and marketing expert is vastly superior to little or no internal supervision.

RESPECT FOR THE SALES FUNCTION

If the late comedy legend Rodney Dangerfield were alive today, I would suggest he consider a career change to healthcare sales. I can see him now, fiddling with his tie and uttering, "I get no respect!"

In many instances, sales professionals do not get the respect from their superiors that they deserve.

The good news is that there are many things sales professionals can do to minimize or erase negative perceptions about sales and marketing among their superiors and coworkers.

WHY IS SALES UNDERVALUED?

Many healthcare cultures are under-accommodating to sales and marketing efforts. In most business entities, profit is the ultimate goal, and sales and marketing is the lifeblood of that profit. This is not typically the case in healthcare, especially in not-for-profit organizations. Although financial performance is certainly important, the traditional "we are a service organization" mind-set is difficult to change.

Some healthcare organizations paradoxically focus on profit while simultaneously treating sales and marketing as a marginal function. These negative perceptions create a frequent dilemma for the healthcare sales professional. In a common scenario, an experienced sales professional is recruited to perform a crucial function (serve as the liaison between buyers and the organization's impeccable services). Yet, that individual is often denied the tools needed to do the job well.

I have seen it often: an excellent candidate is recruited but is shortchanged with respect to emotional and tangible support. Not surprisingly, sales numbers languish, the sales professional moves on to another opportunity, and the organization repeats the same cycle with a replacement.

REMEDIES

If you are proactive and aggressive there is a lot you can do:

- **Define expectations, preferably in writing** — Years ago when I worked for people other than myself, my first question usually was, "If I do an A+ job, exactly what do I have to do?" I often found that the expected A+ performance was either different or easier than the requirements I would have set for myself. If I had not asked the question, I might have fallen short of expectations out of ignorance. It is wise (and safe) to ask for those expectations in writing.

- **Go to the well early and infrequently** — Develop a plan that lists the tools that are necessary to accomplish the goals set forth in the plan. It is easier to get the green light on a package of tools and incentives than to make each request episodically and often out of context.
- **Stay visible internally** — If you subscribe to the adage, "Out of sight, out of mind," then you will understand its cousin, "Out of sight, then who needs you anyway?" Engage in high-profile internal marketing by sending a monthly update to all relevant parties, including the key stakeholders in your organization. Highlight your major news of the month. Look for the good and emphasize it, whether it is an uptick in volume or revenue, the acquisition of one or more major new clients, a complimentary testimonial from a client or patient, or a positive return on a new service variant.

  Some basic rules apply:

  - Send it once a month—never let a month slip by.
  - Send it to as many individuals as you can; this is an excellent way to show your respect for each recipient and keep everyone on the same page.
  - Keep the email to the equivalent of about half a page and never more than a single page.
- **Stay visible externally** — A former healthcare professional who has since achieved considerable success in another sales niche stopped by one of our recent sales training programs. I asked him, "What is the best lesson you can share with our registrants?" His response: "Spend as little time as possible at your desk. There is a built-in bias that if you are not at your desk you are not really working, and that perception often leads to

paralysis because you are not out there as much as possible. Go out there and sell, and let your results speak for themselves."

- **Understand the marketing philosophy** — If a service line is part of a larger organization, try to learn more about how sales and marketing fit into the organization's broader strategy. The more you know about your organization's sales and marketing philosophy, the easier it will be to align your activities at the service line level with the broader plan and gain internal support for your efforts.
- **Involve key stakeholders** — Your organization's sales and marketing culture is likely to improve the more the people driving that culture are actually involved in sales and marketing. Opportunities for senior management to become more involved are plentiful.

  They can:

  - Join you in a sales call once a year
  - Make introductory comments during an audio conference
  - Sign a series of letters that are going directly to employer prospects
  - Add a signed statement as part of promotional materials
  - Record a greeting for your website
- **Be a messenger** — Routinely share nuggets—whether good or bad—with appropriate parties within your program or organization. This is a great way to remind multiple parties of your value.
- **Network with your peers** — Graduates of our sales training programs do an excellent job staying in touch with their fellow classmates. Whether by email, phone, or an occasional meeting in person, they discuss challenging issues and offer ideas to one another or catch up. Attaining support (to say nothing of helping to define said support) is a prominent part of the agenda during such contacts. Employer-directed sales targets compose a relatively small universe; do all you can to stay in touch with one another.

Sales as the Route to Leadership

Sales professionals rarely think of themselves as leaders. They may be leaders off the clock, leaders of the future, or even a leader among one or two other individuals. But more often than not, such professionals feel isolated from their teams and characterize their roles as little more than "sell, sell, sell."

Nothing could be further from the truth. If your job is people-oriented, then leadership opportunities abound. Cultivating your leadership skills and becoming a true leader is an opportunity inherent in your job.

Two leadership principles stand out:

1. **Seek balance** — A true leader is like a symphony conductor. A leader dictates pace by identifying appropriate limits in either direction on a plethora of issues, has a sense of when to move to either extreme, and knows when to seek equilibrium between the extremes. A leader will constantly seek middle ground in order to keep others interested, motivated, and balanced.

   Examples of such balance are numerous:

   - Serving as a patient advocate vs. serving as a company advocate
   - Enhancing profit vs. exacting thoroughness of care
   - Managing acute injuries/illnesses vs. emphasizing injury/illness prevention
   - Planning for the future vs. acting in the present
   - Building relationships vs. executing a discrete sale
   - Expressing concern vs. accepting reality
   - Emphasizing return-on-investment vs. emphasizing short-term process variables

2. **Develop leadership in others** — My first mentor in occupational health, back in 1981, was Dr. Barry Levy. In those days, Barry spoke often about how "one person can make a difference," and then proceeded to do exactly that. At first I was skeptical, but I bought into the concept and modeled my career on that premise.

One person can make a profound difference, but only if one is willing to cultivate others for leadership roles. Barry has made his own profound difference, and the difference he has made is even more profound when you factor in the difference that his numerous protégées have also made since 1981.

Cultivating leadership in others can be done in many different ways:

- **Be a role model** — Practice balance, openness, integrity, and a positive attitude. Others will admire you, and it is infectious.
- **Talk openly and often** — Share your enthusiasm for what you do and why you do it to anyone who is willing to listen. Share your vision of what your service can be. Compliment others (whether they are professionally above you, your peers, or your protégées) and encourage everyone to seek a higher level.
- **Educate those around you** — Teach others what you know. Involve those you are educating by exhibiting patience and enthusiasm.
- **Practice equanimity** — Most of us cherish a particular trait in each of our parents. My late father always looked out for the little guy by showing the same degree of respect for everyone regardless of a person's station in life, connection to him, or outward appearance. A leader who empowers others gains credibility by showing interest in one and all.

LEADERSHIP AND THE SALES PROFESSIONAL

Leadership concepts may appear to be all well and good, but what does this have to do with you, the little ol' sales professional? The short answer is: a great deal.

You are in a unique position to apply marketplace realities to day-to-day operations. You have a special opportunity to mold opinion, clarify issues, educate, motivate, and in general, influence others.

If they have chosen the right avocation, most sales professionals are ideally suited for this role. Who on a team has better

EXHIBIT 7-9. A LEADERSHIP PLAN FOR THE HEALTHCARE SALES PROFESSIONAL

1. Develop and share a vision of what employer-directed healthcare can really be some day. Refine it in writing. Describe it well and often.
2. Look for positive feedback and results and share them with all relevant constituencies. If a client or prospect says something positive about your staff, share the comments with all personnel. Motivate and stimulate.
3. Share any lessons you learn or wisdom you accrue with anyone who is not as well along in their career path as you. Great leaders are the product of great mentors; be a great mentor.
4. Separate real problems from those that are superficial, passing, or irrelevant. Act quickly on real problems by encouraging consensus and striving to see the larger picture; minimize wasted energy by keeping problems in perspective.
5. Bring people together. There are employer representatives who want to meet your physician or your director of rehabilitation services. Be a matchmaker.
6. Be an idea machine. Chances are that you (and fellow sales professionals, if appropriate) possess a lot of creative energy. Marketing is, after all, about innovation, differentiation, and fun. If you do not churn out new and innovative marketing ideas, who will?
7. Look for the best in everybody, including your team members, clients, and prospective clients. Each of us has our shining moments and admirable traits. Look carefully for them and acknowledge them.
8. Minimize negative thoughts and keep negative feelings largely to yourself. Adopt Ralph Waldo Emerson's classic credo, "The true test of a man is his ability to be the same in good times as in bad."

communication tools and a more people-oriented style than a salesperson? And who, other than sales professionals, have daily contact and insight on both the internal and external side of a healthcare organization/employer relationship?

Take pride in what you do, whom you work for, and the extraordinary relevance of the services you represent.

Success is usually a self-fulfilling prophecy based on enthusiasm, commitment, and a genuine interest in leading others.

GETTING MANAGEMENT UP TO SPEED

If you are a service line director, medical director, or senior administrator and you supervise a sales professional, it is your responsibility to learn as much as you can about occupational health sales and marketing. An increasing number of supervisors have begun to attend our training programs with the rationale that they need to know how to supervise their sales professionals.

Those responsible for managing sales professionals should:

1. **Establish accountability standards** — Sales professionals need to be held accountable for their time and activity. Ask your sales professionals to send you two forms every Friday afternoon: (1) a weekly time sheet accounting for the past week of activity, in fifteen-minute increments, and (2) a basic weekly summary report. Being responsible for their time and metrics makes sales professionals more focused and provides you, the supervisor, with ongoing learning opportunities.
2. **Meet weekly** — Meet with your sales professional weekly. Monday mornings are normally a down time for sales calls and a good time to place the new week in perspective.

   Take time to understand what your salespeople are encountering out in the field. Ask them about their biggest challenges ("Can't get the first appointment," "Can't close," "Too many objections") and brainstorm solutions to those challenges. Always ask the sales professional if there is anything you can do to help.
3. **Get out there** — You will never really understand the job your direct reports do unless you spend some time with them on sales calls. Participation in one sales call a month is sufficient,

provided you stay on schedule and participate in at least twelve calls a year. Be a fly on the wall during some calls, a co-presenter on others, and occasionally take the lead role. There is nothing like walking in someone else's shoes to appreciate what another faces every day.

4. **Write your marketing plan** — Play an active role in writing your next marketing plan. Ideally, a marketing plan is a collaborative effort involving multiple staff members. Close collaboration with your sales professionals on your marketing plan will provide you with enhanced insight and a greater sense of buy-in.

Exhibit 7-10. Prototype Weekly Summary Report

Name:

Week of:

Introductory letters sent:

First-time calls arranged:

First-time calls conducted:

Follow-up visits arranged:

Follow-up visits conducted:

Clinic visits conducted:

Marketing activities, if any:

Most significant accomplishments of week:

Most significant frustrations of week:

Your bottom line: do not let a sales professional operate with little or no accountability. Despite the best of intentions, it is too easy for them to succumb to bad habits, which can quickly undermine an entire initiative. Develop and follow an active plan in which you, the supervisor, can better understand the job, offer meaningful counsel as appropriate, and address all-important sales and marketing issues as a team.

Professional Reflection

It is never a bad time to reflect on who we are, what we do, and why we do it. Howard Anderson, my favorite graduate school professor, once proclaimed to our class, "If you ever wake up in the morning and do not want go to work, walk away. Leave. It is not worth it."

When people prosper at their jobs, the odds are that they genuinely love their jobs. If they work in healthcare there is much to love, such as helping others and working with like-minded peers in a respected and constantly evolving profession.

There is also a lot to love about a job that involves sales and marketing. It is the ultimate people profession, and one that emphasizes creativity and ingenuity far more than execution and repetition. If you blend healthcare with sales, you have the best of both worlds.

During any period of reflection, be mindful of what really matters: family, other loved ones, our health and happiness, and the privilege of life itself. Do not overlook the meaning of our work, which consumes about 36 percent of our waking hours.

Virtually all of us involved in healthcare, in one manner or other, are working to ensure the well-being of our fellow man. At the end of the day we are all blessed.

Appendix A:

Measuring Proficiency

Sales / Marketing Proficiency

I often refer to my good friend Joe Grata's three As: attitude, action, and attention to detail. Each A embodies a trait central to the daily routine of every sales professional. Action may be the most undervalued of the three and the one least often applied in daily practice. It is one thing to graduate from our sales training program; it is quite another to actively adopt and practice all of the recommended actions.

TAKE THE TEST

Take the following three-part test, grade yourself, and note the areas in which you are in synch with the best healthcare sales and marketing practices. Each question features a 5-to-1 scale, whereby 5 = extremely well or extremely often and 1 = poorly or virtually never.

As you complete each section, enter your score in the assessment scoreboard matrix. Note how much you deviate from the best practice in each category. Focus on upgrading potentially deficient areas. If you act to move to an "extremely well" rating on every question, you will soon be at the top of your sales and marketing class.

EXHIBIT A-1. ADMINISTRATIVE ASSESSMENT

1. We use gross revenue as the base for our incentive plan.
   5 4 3 2 1
2. Our sales professionals spend almost all of their time on sales.
   5 4 3 2 1
3. Our sales professionals organize their time well.
   5 4 3 2 1
4. We are spending more time using email than telephone.
   5 4 3 2 1
5. Our sales professional's package includes electronic tools.
   5 4 3 2 1
6. We maintain a proactive internal marketing campaign.
   5 4 3 2 1
7. We make optimal use of contact management software.
   5 4 3 2 1
8. We utilize progressive and innovative techniques in process.
   5 4 3 2 1
9. We periodically complete a time allocation matrix.
   5 4 3 2 1
10. We routinely cluster phone calls and travel.
    5 4 3 2 1
11. Our service line maintains and reviews sales metrics.
    5 4 3 2 1
12. We use a mystery shopper to see our services objective.
    5 4 3 2 1
13. We keep current through an annual questionnaire.
    5 4 3 2 1
14. We continually look for cross- or up-selling opportunities.
    5 4 3 2 1
15. We stay in touch with our highest volume clients.
    5 4 3 2 1

EXHIBIT A-2. MARKETING ASSESSMENT

1. We have a well-designed marketing plan.
   5 4 3 2 1
2. Our marketing plan is dynamic—we update it often.
   5 4 3 2 1
3. We follow an "action agenda" in our marketing plan.
   5 4 3 2 1
4. We maintain a large client and prospect email base.
   5 4 3 2 1
5. We send frequent email tips or to our email database.
   5 4 3 2 1
6. Our website is modern, innovative, and better than most.
   5 4 3 2 1
7. We use photos and/or video clips on our website.
   5 4 3 2 1
8. Our clinic tours are routinely planned and well orchestrated.
   5 4 3 2 1
9. We maintain an active employer advisory council.
   5 4 3 2 1
10. We carefully target whom we ask to be on our council.
    5 4 3 2 1
11. We curtail labor-intensive activities such as newsletters.
    5 4 3 2 1
12. We strive to develop new and innovative marketing tactics.
    5 4 3 2 1
13. We make "fun" central to most of our marketing tactics.
    5 4 3 2 1
14. We replace most of our live education with audio education.
    5 4 3 2 1
15. We maintain a formal patient and customer service plan.
    5 4 3 2 1

EXHIBIT A-3. SALES SKILLS ASSESSMENT

1. We include all possible employer prospects in our database.
5 4 3 2 1

2. We target our sales calls to high potential volume prospects.
5 4 3 2 1

3. Our sales professionals have received formal training.
5 4 3 2 1

4. Our sales professionals have strong public speaking skills.
5 4 3 2 1

6. During sales calls we do 20% or less of the talking.
5 4 3 2 1

7. During sales calls we pose questions more than offer features.
5 4 3 2 1

8. We state objectives and offer a roadmap at the outset.
5 4 3 2 1

9. We script and memorize our prime competitive advantage.
5 4 3 2 1

10. We script and memorize responses to common objectives.
5 4 3 2 1

11. We use personality profiling to size up our sales prospects.
5 4 3 2 1

12. Our sales calls include a well-honed first thirty seconds.
5 4 3 2 1

13. Our sales calls include a well-honed last thirty seconds.
5 4 3 2 1

14. We tend to identify the appropriate contact at a company.
5 4 3 2 1

15. We work to strengthen our listening and probing skills.
5 4 3 2 1

GRADE YOUR PROGRAM

Now, add up and enter your total points in each of the three areas and calculate the difference between your score and the maximum score.

Make note of:

1. Any question that received an unsatisfactory score (1 or 2)
2. The area with the greatest variance (**Exhibit A-4**)

This information provides you with an indication of where to place your focus in the coming months.

Exhibit A-4. Self-Assessment Scorecard

AREA	MAXIMUM	YOUR SCORE	VARIANCE
Marketing	75		
Sales Skills	75		
Sales Administration	75		
Total	225		

Complete this assessment again in six months and then again in a year. Note the areas in which you have improved, remained static, or slipped; re-orient your focus accordingly. It is all about introspection and continuous improvement.

GRADE YOUR SALES PERFORMANCE

The sets of questions on the following three pages are designed to grade your program's performance in three major categories:

1. Sales skills
2. Marketing
3. Sales professional management

Grade your performance in each area on a scale of 5 to 1 (5 = definitely, 1 = not at all).

Use the grades to identify your program's strengths and weaknesses in each area, and target areas for improvement.

Take the self-assessment again at the same time next year in order to assess the progress you have made during the year.

Exhibit A-5. Personal Performance Assessment

AREA 1: SALES SKILLS	NOW					NEXT YEAR				
We have developed written scripts for important issues.	5	4	3	2	1	5	4	3	2	1
We have developed a sense of urgency in closing a sale.	5	4	3	2	1	5	4	3	2	1
We have a routine for executing the first 30 seconds and last 30 seconds of a sales call.	5	4	3	2	1	5	4	3	2	1
We effectively identify and get to the key decision makers within a prospect company.	5	4	3	2	1	5	4	3	2	1
Our sales professionals have a strong understanding of our program's products and services.	5	4	3	2	1	5	4	3	2	1
We effectively ask questions, listen carefully, and probe during sales calls.	5	4	3	2	1	5	4	3	2	1

EXHIBIT A-6. PERSONAL PERFORMANCE ASSESSMENT

AREA 2: PROGRAM MARKETING	NOW					NEXT YEAR				
We have developed an innovative, action-oriented marketing plan.	5	4	3	2	1	5	4	3	2	1
We use email as a core communications tool.	5	4	3	2	1	5	4	3	2	1
Our program's website is educational and fun for visitors.	5	4	3	2	1	5	4	3	2	1
We are replacing live educational programs with webinars.	5	4	3	2	1	5	4	3	2	1
We routinely involve physicians and upper management in our marketing efforts.	5	4	3	2	1	5	4	3	2	1
Clinic tours are highly routine and carefully orchestrated.	5	4	3	2	1	5	4	3	2	1

Exhibit A-7. Personal Performance Assessment

AREA 3: SALES PROFESSIONAL MANAGEMENT	NOW					NEXT YEAR				
Our sales professionals have a compensation plan that includes incentive compensation based on gross revenue.	5	4	3	2	1	5	4	3	2	1
Time sheets are used periodically to enhance time-management skills.	5	4	3	2	1	5	4	3	2	1
Our sales professionals routinely attend and participate in staff meetings.	5	4	3	2	1	5	4	3	2	1
Our sales professionals are provided with appropriate support tools such as a laptop, a cell phone, and a PDA.	5	4	3	2	1	5	4	3	2	1
Our sales professionals have received sufficient high-quality training in service-specific sales.	5	4	3	2	1	5	4	3	2	1
We utilize a computer program to support sales management.	5	4	3	2	1	5	4	3	2	1

Appendix B:

52-week Sales and Marketing Action Plan

Week 1

- Meet with senior management to identify specific service line goals
- Meet with key colleagues to brainstorm possible marketing tactics
- Carefully define your service's (or organization's) competitive advantage
- Establish a formal mission statement
- Consider possible market segments and appropriate strategies for each segment
- Complete the self-assessment surveys included in this book as a baseline

Week 2

- Draft your marketing plan, including your internal assessment, marketing tactics, and action calendar
- Develop an email tip library for use in subsequent email blasts
- Develop a strategy to develop or refine your master employer email lists
- Initiate prospect universe expansion and clean-up campaign
- Meet with physician or medical director to participate in priority sales calls

Week 3

- Distribute your marketing plan draft to key colleagues for their input
- Develop or refine a patient satisfaction survey instrument
- Prepare clinic staff for their role in orchestrated clinic tours
- Schedule physician or medical director to participate in priority sales calls

Week 4

- Incorporate various input to create a consensus marketing plan
- Email blast to complete employer email list
- Send monthly service update to key stakeholders
- Schedule service line director to participate in a priority sales calls
- Develop a plan for the Golden Minute of a sales calls

Week 5

- Formally field refined patient satisfaction instrument
- Gather essentials for reinvigorated website: staff photos and bios, other photos, employer testimonials
- Cull through prospect list to identify A, B, and C prospects
- Complete and analyze a weekly time sheet in 15-minute allocations

Week 6

- Announce/market first quarterly open house
- Develop and memorize scripts for objection responses and value statements
- Identify in-house staff to serve as participants on employer-service line task force
- Invite high-target employer to serve on employer-service line task force

Week 7

- Identify three core topics for onsite education
- Develop and memorize a script for your sales call "knockout punch"
- Identify speaker/back up speaker for each topic
- Schedule physician or medical director to participate in priority sales calls

Week 8

- Email blast to complete employer email list
- Begin building social media contact lists (e.g., add employer contacts to LinkedIn links)
- Send monthly service update to key stakeholders
- Schedule service line director to participate in a priority sales calls

WEEK 9

- Inaugurate reinvigorated website
- Quarterly sales/marketing update meeting with program staff
- Quarterly sales/marketing meeting with senior management
- Complete and analyze weekly time sheet in 15-minute allocations
- Begin to develop a comprehensive patient satisfaction plan

WEEK 10

- Quarterly "just checking in" call to top 40 employer clients
- Complete prospect universe expansion and clean-up campaign
- Monthly personalized mailing to 10–25 new prospects, suggesting a meeting
- Begin to develop an electronic library of service line information

WEEK 11

- Conduct first quarterly open house
- Schedule physician or medical director to participate in priority sales calls
- First quarterly employer-service line task force meeting

WEEK 12

- Email blast to complete employer email list
- Complete design on onsite education curriculum development; begin to market
- Send monthly service update to key stakeholders
- Schedule service line director to participate in a priority sales calls

Week 13

- Quarterly annual questionnaire to 25% of your employer client base
- Complete and then analyze weekly time sheet in 15-minute allocations
- Review and help amend your service line's customer service plan
- First quarterly employer-service line task force meeting

Week 14

- Identify topic and begin arrangements for semiannual webinar
- Monthly personalized mailing to 10–25 new prospects, suggesting a meeting
- Provide first of weekly onsite education programs

Week 15

- Identify and schedule social media marketing tactics (e.g., Facebook page)
- Schedule physician or medical director to participate in priority sales calls

Week 16

- Email blast to complete employer email list
- Schedule service line director to participate in a priority sales calls

Week 17

- Complete and then analyze weekly time sheet in 15-minute allocations
- Send monthly service update to key stakeholders

Week 18

- Monthly personalized mailing to 10–25 new prospects, suggesting a meeting
- Deadline for implementing social media plan

Week 19

- Announce/market first quarterly open house
- Schedule physician or medical director to participate in priority sales calls
- Develop strategy for offering free product or service as necessary

Week 20

- Email blast to complete employer email list
- Conduct semiannual webinar
- Send monthly service update to key stakeholders
- Schedule service line director to participate in a priority sales calls

Week 21

- Quarterly sales/marketing update meeting with program staff
- Quarterly sales/marketing meeting with senior management
- Identify a potential partner for a cause related marketing initiative

Week 22

- Monthly personalized mailing to 10–25 new prospects, suggesting a meeting
- Complete and then analyze weekly time sheet in 15-minute allocations

Week 23

- Quarterly "just checking in" call to top 40 employer clients
- Schedule physician or medical director to participate in priority sales calls

Week 24

- Email blast to complete employer email list
- Conduct first quarterly open house
- Send monthly service update to key stakeholders
- Schedule service line director to participate in a priority sales calls

Week 25

- Complete and then analyze weekly time sheet in 15-minutes allocations
- Second quarterly employer-service line task force meeting
- Complete arrangements with cause-related marketing partner

Week 26

- Quarterly annual questionnaire to 25% of your employer client base
- Monthly personalized mailing to 10–25 new prospects, suggesting a meeting
- Second quarterly employer-service line task force meeting
- Complete the self-assessment surveys included in this book and compare to week one results

Week 27

- Schedule senior management representative to participate in priority sales calls
- Schedule physician or medical director to participate in priority sales calls

Week 28

- Email blast to complete employer email list
- Send monthly service update to key stakeholders

Week 29

- Complete and then analyze weekly time sheet in 15-minute allocations
- Schedule service line director to participate in a priority sales calls

Week 30

- Monthly personalized mailing to 10–25 new prospects, suggesting a meeting

Week 31

- Announce/market third quarterly open house
- Schedule physician or medical director to participate in priority sales calls

Week 32

- Email blast to complete employer email list
- Send monthly service update to key stakeholders
- Schedule service line director to participate in a priority sales calls

Week 33

- Monthly personalized mailing to 10–25 new prospects, suggesting a meeting
- Complete and then analyze weekly time sheet in 15-minute allocations

Week 34

- Quarterly sales/marketing update meeting with program staff
- Quarterly sales/marketing meeting with senior management

Week 35

- Schedule physician or medical director to participate in priority sales calls
- Quarterly "just checking in" call to top 40 employer clients

Week 36

- Email blast to complete employer email list
- Send monthly service update to key stakeholders
- Schedule service line director to participate in a priority sales calls

Week 37

- Conduct third quarterly open house
- Complete and then analyze weekly time sheet in 15-minute allocations

Week 38

- Third quarterly employer-service line task force meeting
- Monthly personalized mailing to 10–25 new prospects, suggesting a meeting

Week 39

- Quarterly annual questionnaire to 25% of your employer client base
- Schedule physician or medical director to participate in a priority sales calls

Week 40

- Email blast to complete employer email list
- Send monthly service update to key stakeholders
- Schedule service line director to participate in a priority sales calls

Week 41

- Complete and then analyze weekly time sheet in 15-minutes allocations
- Identify topic and begin arrangements for semiannual webinar

Week 42

- Monthly personalized mailing to 10–25 new prospects, suggesting a meeting

Week 43

- Announce/market fourth quarterly open house
- Schedule physician or medical director to participate in a priority sales calls

Week 44

- Email blast to complete employer email list
- Send monthly service update to key stakeholders
- Schedule service line director to participate in a priority sales calls

Week 45

- Begin design process for next year's marketing plan
- Complete and then analyze weekly time sheet in 15-minute allocations

Week 46

- Quarterly sales/marketing update meeting with program staff
- Quarterly sales/marketing meeting with senior management
- Monthly personalized mailing to 10–25 new prospects, suggesting a meeting

Week 47

- Conduct fourth quarterly open house
- Schedule physician or medical director to participate in a priority sales call

Week 48

- Schedule service line director to participate in a priority sales call
- Email blast to complete employer email list
- Send monthly service update to key stakeholders

Week 49

- Quarterly "just checking in" call to top 40 employer clients
- Complete and then analyze weekly time sheet in 15-minute allocations

Week 50

- Conduct second semi-annual webinar
- Reach out to a non-profit (e.g., American Heart Association) for joint venture
- Fourth quarterly employer-service line task force meeting

Week 51

- Monthly personalized mailing to 10–25 new prospects, suggesting a meeting
- Third quarterly employer-service line task force meeting
- Send quarterly annual questionnaire to 25% of your employer client base

Week 52

- Email blast to complete employer email list
- Send monthly service update to key stakeholders
- Schedule service line director to participate in a priority sales calls
- Complete next year's marketing plan
- Complete the self-assessment surveys included in this book and compare to week one results

Appendix C:

40 Final Action Tips

1. Keep your message simple and benefit-oriented.

2. Wow prospects and clients with your timeliness.

3. Brand your program name with your core message; make the two indistinguishable.

4. Include an action calendar in your marketing plan and follow it weekly.

5. Stay on message.

6. Send your message at a time when it is not competing with other messages.

7. Use the education card as your prime marketing tactic.

8. Expand your employer universe and keep it current.

9. Shorten all of your written and oral communications.

10. Create a task force, not an advisory council, recruit employers and community leaders to serve on it, and make it educational for all parties.

11. Give everyone in your clinic a role during a client tour; orchestrate every visit.

12. Cap attendance and include an educational talk at open houses.

13. Frequently ask your physician/medical director to place a call on the salesperson's behalf the day before a sales appointment.

14. Use physicians and administrators to help with sales and marketing, being certain to agree on their role and desired frequency of assistance.

15. Be market driven. Formally assess your employer base once a year.

16. Develop a dynamic program-level website.

17. Eliminate advertising, bulk mail, and cold calls.

18. Develop an informational e-library and send links to constituents as appropriate.

19. Develop new innovative marketing tactics every year. Marketing is all about being different.

20. Be flexible and prepared to change direction as reality dictates.

21. Instill accountability in sales professionals; do not leave them to their own devices.

22. Measure and address client utilization slippage.

23. Facilitate introductions to prospects through social networking vehicles such as LinkedIn and Facebook.

24. Use strong, descriptive, positive words; avoid weak, ambiguous, and negative words.

25. Get to the point. State your purpose, course of inquiry, and recommendations in a concise, logical manner.

26. Be sensitive to people's time constraints. Thank them for their time, define your anticipated time commitment, and move matters along.

27. Speak ROI: the message does not have to be complex but should quantify the value of your services.

28. Never accept a rejection as final; leave gracefully and establish a date to get back in touch.

29. Adjust to different personality styles and company cultures; take stock of the situation and adjust your approach accordingly.

30. Maintain a fallback option; be ready to move to plan B (e.g., a lesser relationship) if plan A (e.g., a full sale) falls short.

31. Sell on value and economic impact, not features or intangibles.

32. Learn how to talk "employer-speak." Think and talk as a buyer, not as a provider.

33. Leverage the negative. Many people buy out of fear; ask prospects to describe their greatest concern.

34. Act like a market leader if you are one. Emphasize your track record and market share; people gravitate to winners.

35. Script. Write out and memorize the ten most important things you seem to say all of the time.

36. Always associate a feature or attribute with its inherent value.

37. Keep time sheets and minimize activities that are not related to your core responsibilities.

38. Eliminate interesting but non-essential sales metrics.

39. Avoid using platitudes—always.

40. Stay loose and have fun. Be yourself and put others at ease.

Exhibit Index

CHAPTER 2: STRATEGIES FOR MARKETING TO EMPLOYERS

CHAPTER 3: MARKETING TACTICS

CHAPTER 4: MARKETING AND SELLING RELATED SERVICES

CHAPTER 5: SELLING HEALTHCARE SERVICES TO EMPLOYERS

CHAPTER 6: SALES TACTICS

CHAPTER 7: SALES AND MARKETING MANAGEMENT

APPENDIXES